Vedibarta Bam

And You Shall Speak of Them

A compilation of selected Torah insights,
thought-provoking ideas, homilies and
explanations of Torah passages

Volume II — Shemot

by

Rabbi Moshe Bogomilsky

5756 . 1996

VEDIBARTA BAM—AND YOU SHALL SPEAK OF THEM
VOLUME II — SHEMOT

Published and Copyrighted © by
Rabbi Moshe Bogomilsky
1382 President Street
Brooklyn, New York 11213

5756 • 1996

ISBN 1-8808-8015-6

Table of Contents

ב״ה

Foreword

With much thanks to Hashem, I present to you dear readers, the second volume of *Vedibarta Bam*. This volume discusses *Chumash Shemot,* and follows the same format as the one on *Chumash Bereishit.*

I must admit that I never realized the difficulties of publishing a *sefer.* To gather stimulating material and present it in an accessible language is quite a challenge. Fortunately, the encouraging comments and compliments the first volume received facilitated the bringing of this second volume to fruition.

Purim takes place during the weeks when *Chumash Shemot* is read, therefore, I included a separate section on *Purim* and *Megillat Esther.* As already mentioned, the purpose of the *Sefer* is *Vedibarta Bam* — and you shall speak of them — that it be a source of Torah discussion at the *Shabbat* table. Hopefully, the section on *Purim* will add to the *freilichkeit* of *Purim* day and the *seudah.* Moreover, in keeping with the traditional spirit of *Purim,* also included is a section containing some light-hearted *Purim* Torah.

It is gratifying that, thank G-d, the *sefer* became a guest at the *Shabbat* table in many homes. However, my greatest surprise was that it reached all the corners of the globe through Judaism on the Internet. For this I thank most profusely Yosef Yitzchok Kazen, director of Chabad-Lubavitch in Cyberspace. May his efforts to propagate Torah universally be crowned with immense success.

My nephew, Shneur Zalman Sudak, should be commended for his meticulous proof-reading of this volume and for his valuable comments.

Rabbi Moshe Bogomilsky

16 Tevet, 5756
Yartzeit, Harav Eliyahu Moshe ben Aharon Eliezer ע״ה Liss

Note on Transliteration and Format

Transliteration generally employs the Sephardi accent, with the following usages:

1. Words with a final *hei* are spelled with a final "h."
2. "Ei" (the vowel-sound in "freight") is used for a *tzere*.
3. "Ai" is used for the vowel-sound in the word "tide."
4. An apostrophe is used between distinct consecutive vowels, as in *"Ba'al."*
5. An "e" is used for a vocalized *sheva,* i.e. *"bemeizid,"* not *"b'meizid."*
6. "F" is preferred to "ph."
7. "O" is used for *cholem.*
8. Doubling of consonants is generally avoided.

Use of Italics:

Transliterated Hebrew words are generally given in italics without capitalization, except for proper nouns, which are capitalized and, in the case of names, not italicized. Some exceptions are made for very familiar Hebrew words, such as "Torah."

English and Hebrew:

Names of Biblical persons and names of the books of the Pentateuch are given in Hebrew, but other books of *Tanach* are given in English; thus "Moshe" is preferred to "Moses," *"Bereishit"* to "Genesis," and "Proverbs" to *"Mishlei."* Generally English words are preferred to Hebrew ones, but often the content requires the use of the Hebrew.

Exceptions:

Exceptions to these rules most often involve forms already familiar to the English reader, forms that would otherwise be awkward, and ones likely to be mispronounced.

SHEMOT • שמות

"ואלה שמות בני ישראל הבאים מצרימה"

"And these are the names of the children of Israel who were coming to Egypt." (1:1)

QUESTION: It should have said *"asher bo'u"* (אשר באו) — in the past tense instead of *"haba'im"* (הבאים) — in the present tense, which suggests that they were arriving just now?

ANSWER: When an immigrant comes to a new country, in the early period following his arrival he usually maintains his old customs. Upon becoming acclimated in the new country, he assumes resident status and adapts to the ways of the land.

Throughout the years the Jews lived in Egypt, they always considered themselves as newly arrived immigrants who had "just come." Not assuming resident status facilitated their endeavors to maintain their unique identity.

In the merit of not changing their names, their language, and style of clothing, our forefathers were redeemed from Egypt. (See *Midrash Rabbah Vayikra* 32:5 and *Pesikta Zuta* 6:6.)

* * *

Alternatively: the last letters of the words ואלה שמות בני ישראל הבאים can be arranged to spell the word *"Tehillim"* (תהלים) — the Book of Psalms, compiled by King David. In Egypt, the Jewish people served as slaves and they experienced one of the most difficult times of their history. Throughout the time the Jews were in Egypt, they prayed to Hashem from the *Tehillim*.

"Mitzraim" also comes from the word *"meitzar,"* which means a difficult and tight situation. Whenever one is confronted

with a difficulty, the best thing to do is to use the book of *Tehillim* as a medium of prayer to Hashem.

According to the *Midrash Shochar Tov* (124), during Yaakov's 20 years in the unpleasant environment of Lavan's estate, he did not sleep, occupying himself instead with saying *Tehillim.*

(אור דוד)

"ואלה שמות בני ישראל הבאים מצרימה את יעקב איש וביתו באו"
"And these are the names of the Children of Israel, who were coming to Egypt with Yaakov; each man and his household came." (1:1)

QUESTION: After the initial statement "these are the names of the Children of Israel, who were coming to Egypt" the balance of the *pasuk,* beginning "with Yaakov," seems superfluous.

ANSWER: When a person marries and raises a family, he is considered the head of the household. The entire family looks up to him for advice and guidance. Often, as he ages and the children mature, they take over the father's position and begin to run all the family affairs. If a major move has to be made, they make the decisions and *take* their aged parents along with them.

The Torah is attesting that the children of Yaakov had the highest respect and greatest admiration for their father. Though he was already 130 years old and they were in their forties, full of zest and vigor, it was Yaakov who led the way with the rest of the household following.

* * *

Alternatively: Yaakov was the *tzaddik* of his generation. His entire family looked to him for leadership and guidance. The final letters of the words "את יעקב איש" spell the word *"Shabbat"* (שבת). Each *Shabbat* the family would gather around the *"tish"* (table) of Yaakov *Avinu.* Being in the presence of a *tzaddik* was a source of inspiration, helping them endure the difficulty of the Exile of Egypt.

The first letters of the words "שמות בני ישראל הבאים" spell the word "שביה" — "captivity." Thus we are cautioned that when exiled and in foreign captivity, we should gather around the *tzaddikim* of the generation.

(בעל הטורים, ספר נפש יהונתן מר' יהונתן בנימין הכהן ז"ל מסעליש)

"ובני ישראל פרו וישרצו"

"And the children of Israel were fruitful, and increased abundantly." (1:7)

QUESTION: They bore six children at each birth. (Rashi) Why did Hashem cause such an unusual phenomenon?

ANSWER: According to the *Yalkut,* the Jews were enslaved in Egypt for a total of *one hour.* This enigmatic statement is explained as follows:

In Psalms (90:4) it is stated, "A thousand years in your eyes are like the day that has passed and a watch of the night." According to an opinion in the *Gemara (Berachot* 3a), the night is divided into four watches. Thus, one day and one watch — which equals fifteen hours — are one thousand years in Hashem's eyes. Consequently, to Hashem, 66 years and 8 months are one hour. Hence, the *Midrash* is saying that the entire Egyptian bondage was for a period of sixty six years and eight months (1000 years ÷ 15 = 66 years and 8 months).

Hashem had told Avraham that his descendants would be slaves in Egypt for a total of four hundred years. In order to lessen the years of slavery, He increased the birthrate by six fold. Thus six times the normal population working for sixty six years and eight months is exactly equal to four hundred years of slavery (66 years and 8 months × 6 = 400 years).

(פרדס יוסף בשם ר' מאיר יחיאל הלוי מאסטראוונצא זצ"ל)

"ובני ישראל פרו וישרצו...ותמלא הארץ אתם"

"The children of Israel were fruitful and increased abundantly...and the land became filled with them." (1:7)

QUESTION: The *Midrash (Shir Hashirim* 1.15:3) relates that Rebbi, Rabbi Yehudah *HaNasi,* once while delivering a lecture, noticed that the congregation had become drowsy. In order to rouse them he said: "One woman in Egypt brought forth six hundred thousand children in one birth." A disciple named Rabbi Yishmael son of Rabbi Jose said to him: "Who can that have been?" He replied: "This was Yocheved, who bore Moshe, who was counted as equal to six hundred thousand of Israel."

1) Is it not audacious for the students to drowse off during their Rabbi's lecture? 2) Why did he use this particular unbelievable story to awaken them?

ANSWER: The episode related in the *Midrash* may be a metaphor for a period of Jewish history. The destruction of the second *Beit Hamikdash* took place in the year 3828, and Rebbi was born approximately 50 years afterwards. He was the leader of the fourth generation after the destruction. The Roman government oppressed the Jews bitterly, and unfortunately the Jews were losing hope of the coming of *Mashiach* and the ultimate redemption. Rebbi noticed that while he was propagating Torah, the community was "falling asleep," thinking that there will never, G-d forbid, be a *Geulah* — redemption — and that the *galut* is eternal.

In an effort to distract them from such a train of thought, he told them that in Egypt a woman gave birth to 600,000 children. The message to his generation was "Do not despair! Our forefathers in Egypt thought that they were doomed to be slaves forever and there was no hope to be redeemed. Suddenly, Yocheved gave birth to Moshe, who ultimately took out all the 600,000 enslaved Jews from Egypt and brought them to Sinai for the giving of the Torah — the greatest event in Jewish history. Likewise, never give up hope. The salvation of G-d is like the wink of an eye — which can come immediately and unexpectedly."

(מצאתי בכתבי אבי הרב שמואל פסח ז"ל באגאמילסקי)

"וימררו את חייהם"
"And they made bitter their lives." (1:14)

QUESTION: Why do the words *"vayemararu et chayeihem"* have a cantillation *("trope")* of a *kadma ve'azla*?

ANSWER: When Hashem spoke to Avraham, He told him that the Jewish people would be in Egypt for a period of 400 years. Actually, they lived in Egypt only 210 years. One reason for the Jews' departure 190 years early is that the Egyptians made them work extremely hard. Therefore, in 210 years they had endured the equivalent of 400 years of normal suffering.

The *"trope"* of *kadma ve'azla* expresses this thought: The word *kadma* means to rise early, and the word *"azla"* means to leave. The Torah is telling us that they rose and left Egypt earlier than the appointed 400 years because *"vayemararu et chayeihem"* — "they made their lives extremely bitter" to the extent that 210 years were the equivalent of 400 years.

It is interesting to note that the numerical value of the words *"kadma ve'azla"* (קדמא ואזלא) is 190, the number of years deducted from the original 400.

(קול אליהו - זכרון ישראל)

"ותיראן המילדת את האלקים ולא עשו כאשר דבר אליהן מלך מצרים ותחיין את הילדים"
"The midwives feared G-d and they did not do as the King of Egypt spoke, and they caused the children to live." (1:17)

QUESTION: The words *"vatechayena et hayeladim"* — "and they caused the children to live" — seem extra. If they did not listen to Pharaoh, is it not obvious that the children lived?

ANSWER: In every hospital with a maternity ward, a small number of children die naturally at birth.

The Jewish midwives feared that during the time of Pharaoh's decree a child would die, and the mother would accuse them of obeying Pharaoh. Being righteous women, they prayed to Hashem, and through their prayers they "made live" even those children who would have died naturally at birth.

(מדרש רבה שמות א, ט״ז)

"ויצו פרעה לכל עמו לאמר כל הבן הילוד היאָרה תשליכהו"

"Pharaoh commanded all his people saying, 'Every son that is born cast him into the river.'" (1:22)

QUESTION: The word *"leimor"* usually means "to say to others." Since Pharaoh spoke to *all* his people, for whom was the message intended?

ANSWER: Pharaoh looked for ways to kill the redeemer of the Jewish people. Originally, he called the Jewish midwives and commanded them to kill the Jewish children. When this attempt failed, he called upon his entire nation to assist him.

Pharaoh feared that he would be accused of gross anti-semitism for singling out the Jewish children. Therefore, he called together his people and told them, "The Jews are a threat to us, and we must unite to destroy them. To avoid being accused of anti-semitism, I advise you to *'say'* that the decree is not only for the Jews, but that *every* newborn male is to be cast into the river. However, spare your children while making sure that the Jewish children are drowned." (Onkelos in his commentary writes clearly that Pharaoh's decree applied only to the newly born children of the Jews.)

(הגש״פ טוב דבריך מר׳ שאול בראך ז״ל אב״ד קאשאוי)

"ויצו פרעה לכל עמו לאמר כל הבן הילוד היאָרה תשליכהו"

"Pharaoh commanded all his people saying, 'Every son that is born cast him into the river.'" (1:22)

QUESTION: Why did Pharaoh add *this* to his original decree that the Jewish boys be drowned?

ANSWER: Shifra and Puah did not obey Pharaoh's original order to kill the Jewish children. Pharaoh summoned them and asked, "The Jews have a rule — *'dinah demalchuta dinah'* — 'the law of the government is binding' — why are you not obeying my order?" The midwives told Pharaoh that this principle applies only to a law for *all* the residents of the land. However, since "לא כנשים המצרית העבריית" — "the women of Egypt do not have the same law as the Jewish women" (1:19) — they were not obligated to observe it (see *Choshen Mishpat* 369).

Pharaoh, who was eager for the death of the Jewish children, then issued a decree that the Egyptian newborn also be killed.

(פנינים יקרים)

"ויצו פרעה לכל עמו לאמר כל הבן הילוד היארה תשליכהו וכל הבת תחיון"

"Pharaoh commanded all his people saying, 'Every son that is born cast him into the river, and every daughter you shall sustain [keep alive].'" (1:22)

QUESTION: Pharaoh's sole concern was for all the boys to be cast into the river, while the fate of the girls did not seem to interest him. Why did he add, "Every daughter you shall sustain"?

ANSWER: The word *"techayun"* means *"you* shall be the actual source of their life." Pharaoh ordered the Egyptians to cast Jewish children into the river in order to cause their physical death. The same Egyptians were also told by Pharaoh that those children who would remain physically alive (i.e., the girls) were to be *sustained* by them, that is, assimilated and totally raised in the Egyptian way of life — in order to exterminate their Jewish souls.

This explains the difference in the command to the Jewish midwives and the Egyptians respectively: The Jewish midwives were simply told to leave the girls alone, "If it be a girl *vechaya* — let her live" (1:16). Pharaoh hoped that by telling them to let the girls live, it would be easier for him to persuade them to carry out his order to kill the boys. However, he told the Egyptians *"techayun,"* not just to let the Jewish girls live, but to make sure to assimilate them into Egyptian culture.

The Torah cites both decrees together in the same *pasuk* to indicate that "Every daughter you shall sustain" is a decree equivalent in its harshness and even surpassing the decree regarding the boys, "Every son that is born you shall cast into the river." To destroy the soul is equal to the killing the body, and indeed even worse — for spiritual death far surpasses physical death.

(לקוטי שיחות ח"א)

"ותרא אותו כי טוב הוא"

"And she saw him that he was goodly." (2:2)

QUESTION: According to Rabbi Meir *(Sotah* 12a) the good thing about him was that he was born circumcised. How did Rabbi Meir derive that the word *"tov"* — "good" — alludes to this?

ANSWER: In the description of Hashem's creation of the world, we are told for each day that He "saw that it was good," except for the second day. The reason is that the creation of the second day was incomplete. Therefore, when the creation of the waters is completed on the third day, the word *"tov"* appears twice.

Man is created incomplete, and he needs to be circumcised on the eighth day. Thus, the word *"tov"* cannot apply until then. Since Yocheved said that he was *"tov"* — "good," obviously he was circumcised, and thus fully complete.

(ילקוט האורים)

* * *

Alternatively, when Hashem instructed Avraham concerning circumcision, He said "והי' לאות ברית ביני וביניכם" — "It shall be a *sign* of the covenant between me and you" *(Bereishit* 17:11), so the *brit* is referred to as a sign *(ot).* The *pasuk* is telling us that Yocheved saw that *"oto"* — *"his sign"* — was *"tov"* — "totally complete."

(נחל קדומים)

"ותשלח את אמתה ותקחה"
"She stretched out her hand and took it." (2:5)

QUESTION: The word *"amatah"* is used for her hand because she was standing far away and Hashem miraculously extended her hand many *amot* — cubits (Rashi). What sense did it make to stretch out her hand?

ANSWER: From this we can learn a very important lesson: When a child has to be saved, a person should not stop to calculate whether he can succeed or not, and give up if the situation seems hopeless. If, when a child is in danger, we will sincerely do all that is in our power, Hashem will provide a miracle and the seemingly impossible will be accomplished very easily.

The same also applies to any challenge with which one is confronted: Never succumb or give up! Do the utmost and Hashem will help.

(ר׳ בונים מפשיסחא זצ״ל)

"ותפתח ותראהו את הילד והנה נער בכה ותחמל עליו ותאמר מילדי העברים זה"
"She opened it and saw the child and behold a lad wept...She said, 'This is from the Hebrew's children.'" (2:6)

QUESTION: Instead of saying "this is from the Hebrew's children," why did she not say "this is a Jewish child?"

ANSWER: The King of Austria once issued an evil decree against the Jewish community. After intervention, the King agreed to receive a delegation of Rabbis. During the meeting, one of the Rabbis began to yell. The King looked at him sternly and said, "Don't you know that in the presence of a King one should talk softly and not yell?" The Rabbi apologetically responded, "Your Majesty, it is not I who is yelling. The loud voice you hear is the voice of the thousands of Jews who are in great jeopardy because of your evil decree."

When Pharaoh's daughter opened the basket, she was startled to see a little baby whose voice was strong and loud like a lad's.

Cognizant of her father's decree to kill the Jewish children, she realized that the strong voice she heard was not only that of Moshe, but also the voices of all the Jewish children crying out through him.

(פרדס יוסף)

"ותקרא שמו משה"

"She called him Moshe." (2:10)

QUESTION: Why is he called *"Moshe Rabbeinu,"* while the Rambam is known as *"Rabbeinu Moshe"?*

ANSWER: Though Moshe had many names, (see *Midrash Rabbah Vayikra* 1:3) the name his parents gave him at birth, was not "Moshe." If so, why throughout the 120 years of his life did he keep as his official name the name "Moshe," which he first received three months after his birth?

Indeed, he was well aware that his original name was not "Moshe." However, he retained the name to never forget one who had acted toward him with great kindness. Whenever he was addressed as "Moshe," it would remind him of his being drawn from the water by Batya, the daughter of Pharaoh, and he would thank her in his heart. Thus, the term *"Rabbeinu"* follows the word "Moshe" to *teach* a lesson to humanity on *hakarat hatov* — recognizing kindness and feeling gratitude.

On the other hand, the Rambam is renowned for his scholarly works, through which he has educated generations of Jews. Therefore, he is affectionately known as *"Rabbeinu* Moshe" — "Our teacher, Moshe Ben Maimon."

* * *

Incidentally, it is most appropriate that the words "Moshe *Rabbeinu"* (משה רבינו) have the numerical value of 613, since he gave us the Torah which consists of 613 *mitzvot.* Also *"Rabbeinu Moshe"* adds up to 613 because he expounded on the *mitzvot* in his monumental work known as *Mishne Torah,* the repetition, review and explanation of the Torah.

(ילקוט ראובני)

״ותקרא שמו משה ותאמר כי מן המים משיתהו״

"She called him Moshe saying, 'Because I drew him out of the water.'" (2:10)

QUESTION: What is the connection between the name "Moshe" (משה) and *"Mayim"* (מים) — "water"?

ANSWER: There is a system in *gematriya* (numerical value of letters) according to which each letter equals its value plus the cumulative total of all previous letters. i.e., א = 1, ב (2+1) = 3, ג (3+3) = 6, ד (4+6) = 10, ה (5+10) = 15, ו (6+15) = 21, ז (7+21) = 28, ח (8+28) = 36, ט (9+36) = 45, י (10+45) = 55, כ (20+55) = 75, ל (30+75) = 105, מ (40+105) = 145, etc.

Thus, Batya said, "I obtained the name "Moshe" (משה), which equals 345, out of *"mayim"* (מים), which (according to the above method) also equals 345."

(פרדס יוסף בשם ספר ארץ החיים על תהלים)

״וירא איש מצרי מכה איש עברי מאחיו ויפן כה וכה וירא כי אין איש״

"And he saw an Egyptian striking a Jew, one of his brothers. He turned here and there and saw no one." (2:11-12)

QUESTION: The Jews were slaves and constantly oppressed and beaten by their Egyptian supervisors. Why did Moshe kill *this* slave-driver?

ANSWER: When Moshe went out to visit his brethren, he observed their tedious labor and oppression at the hands of the Egyptians. With flagrant cruelty they were beaten to increase their output. Their oppressors sadistically derived immense joy in beating the unfortunate Jewish slaves.

Moshe perceived that *this* supervisor, before hitting the Jew, "turned here and there" — looked to all sides, and only after he was sure that no one was watching did he begin to beat the Jew. From this Moshe deduced that the Egyptian obviously had a personal vendetta against the Jew and was somewhat guiltily hitting him for reasons unconnected to the slavery. Otherwise, he would have beaten him in the presence of everyone, as the other supervisors were constantly doing. Therefore, he came to the aid of the Jew and killed the Egyptian.

(שו״ת תירוש ויצהר סי׳ קס״ב)

"ויפן כה וכה וירא כי אין איש"
"He turned here and there and saw no one." (2:12)

QUESTION: Why did Moshe not see the person who on the second day said to him, "Do you think you will kill me like you killed the Egyptian?" (2:14)

ANSWER: When Moshe saw a Jew being beaten, he was startled and dumbfounded. He could not believe his eyes. Why was an innocent Jew being beaten with nobody raising a protest? Immediately, Moshe "turned here and there": He ran to the police, to Government agencies, and to "humanitarians," screaming at the top of his voice, "Do something! An innocent Jew is being beaten for no reason!"

After turning to all sides and getting no response, *"vayar ki ein ish"* — "He came to the realization [that the world] does not consider [Jewish blood] human." Therefore, he had no other choice but to take the law in his own hands and kill the Egyptian.

(שמעתי מהרב מנחם מענדל שי׳ אלפערין)

"ויצא ביום השני והנה שני אנשים עברים נצים...הלהרגני אתה אמר כאשר הרגת את המצרי...וישמע פרעה את הדבר הזה"
"And he went on the second day and behold, two Hebrew men were fighting... 'Do you propose to kill me as you killed the Egyptian?'...And Pharaoh heard this thing." (2:13-15)

QUESTION: From the remark "As you killed the Egyptian" it is obvious that the man witnessed Moshe killing the Egyptian the day before. Why did he wait till the second day to inform Pharaoh?

ANSWER: Moshe did not do a *ma'aseh* (physical act) to kill the Egyptian. He did it through *dibur* (speech) — by uttering the *Sheim Hameforash* — Hashem's Holy name. Datan and Aviram thought that Moshe did not consider speech to be equivalent to action. Therefore, he was not guilty of murder.

On the second day, Moshe called one of them a *rasha* (wicked person) for only lifting his hand to hit another. Since what he did was only *machashavah* (intent), he said, "If you consider intent like action, then speaking is surely like action. Consequently, your killing through speaking is equivalent to a physical act, and you are guilty of murder."

(פרדס יוסף בשם ר׳ אברהם מרדכי זצ״ל מגור)

"וַיִּירָא מֹשֶׁה וַיֹּאמַר אָכֵן נוֹדַע הַדָּבָר"

"Moshe feared and said 'surely the thing is known.'" (2:14)

QUESTION: Rashi explains that with this Moshe meant "I was wondering what sin the Jews committed to be punished with hard labor, but now I see that they deserve it."

What did Moshe see that made him understand why the Jewish people deserved the Exile of Egypt?

ANSWER: On the first day, when Moshe went out to the fields, he saw a group of Jews chatting among themselves. Suddenly, an Egyptian grabbed one of the Jews, separated him from his Jewish brothers, and began beating him. This is alluded to in the word *"mei'echav"* — "from among his brethren" (2:11). Moshe wondered to himself why none of the other Jews came to the rescue of the poor Jew who was being beaten? He thought that perhaps the Jewish people were very gentle or timid and unable to fight. Seeing no other alternative, Moshe killed the Egyptian.

When he visited the fields on the second day and noticed two Jews fighting among themselves, he realized that the Jews indeed knew how to fight, but that they lacked interest in helping a fellow Jew. Moshe now became aware that unfortunately there is much hatred *(sinat chinam)* among the Jewish people. Therefore, after witnessing both incidents and recognizing the lack of *Ahavat Yisrael* among the Jewish people, he said, "Surely the thing is known" and "Now I understand why the Jewish people are in exile."

(בינה לעתים - אברבנאל)

"וישמע פרעה את הדבר הזה ויבקש להרג את משה"
"Pharaoh heard this thing and he wanted to kill Moshe." (2:15)

QUESTION: Why was Pharaoh so enraged against Moshe?

ANSWER: When Moshe was a young boy, once, while Pharaoh embraced him, he took off Pharaoh's crown and put it on his head. Pharaoh feared that Moshe was the redeemer of the Jewish people, who was recently born according to his astrologers. His advisor Bilam urged him to kill Moshe. However, another advisor, Yitro, said that perhaps Moshe's interest in the crown was mere childish curiosity and that he should be tested. They placed before him a plate with valuable gems and a plate with red glowing coals. Moshe was very clever, and was about to take the gems, but the angel Gavriel pushed his hand, and instead, he grabbed a burning coal. He put his hand with the hot coal to his mouth and burned his tongue, thus causing himself a speech problem. This relieved Pharaoh and he changed his mind about killing Moshe (Midrash Rabbah 1:26).

Years later, a report was brought to Pharaoh that, as soon as Moshe grew up and matured, he went out to inquire after the welfare of the Jewish people and killed an Egyptian who was hitting a Jew. This convinced him that Moshe was indeed the redeemer of the Jewish people and he immediately wanted to eliminate him.

(מלא העומר)

"ותאמרן איש מצרי הצילנו מיד הרעים...ויאמר אל בנתיו ואיו...קראן
לו ויאכל לחם"
"And they said, 'An Egyptian man saved us from the shepherds.' He said to his daughters, 'And where is he...call him that he may eat bread.'" (2:19-20)

QUESTION: Why did Moshe disguise himself as an Egyptian man?

ANSWER: Yitro was the High Priest of Midian. When he gave up idol worship the angry of the city excommunicated him and his family. His daughters were shepherdesses and all the shepherds harassed them when they would come to draw water for their cattle. When Moshe noticed their troubles and came to their rescue, they were very grateful.

Moshe, being very humble, felt that he did not deserve any appreciation or credit. He told Yitro's daughters, "Everything that happens in this world is *behashgacha pratit* (by individual Divine providence). The fact that I am here today is not my doing but because of something that happened in Egypt. He went on to tell them that one day when he was out in the field he noticed an *"ish Mitzri"* — "an Egyptian man" — viciously beating a Jew. Moshe then rescued the Jew by killing the Egyptian oppressor.

He continued, "When Pharaoh found out that I killed an Egyptian man, he sought revenge, and I had to flee. Were it not for the episode with the *'ish Mitzri,'* I would not have left Egypt to come to Midian. Thus, 'I am actually here today thanks to the *'ish Mitzri.'"*

The daughters returned home and told their father Moshe's explanation that thanks to an — *"ish Mitzri"* they had been saved. Yitro concluded that surely it was a very honorable and humble person who did not want any credit for himself. Therefore, he told his daughters, "Such a respectable person should be invited to our home. It will be an honor to have him at our table and perhaps he will marry one of you."

(מדרש רבה א׳, ל״ב)

"וימת מלך מצרים ויאנחו בני ישראל מן העבדה ויזעקו ותעל שועתם אל האלקים מן העבדה"

"And the King of Egypt died, and the Jewish people sighed from their work, and their cry went up to G-d from their work." (2:23)

QUESTION: Instead of *"min ha'avodah"* — "from their work" — it should read, *"al ha'avodah"* — "Because of their work"? Moreover, why didn't the Jews cry before the King died?

ANSWER: The Egyptians knew very well that if the Jews would cry to Hashem, He would indeed answer their prayers and free them from slavery. Therefore, they made the Jews work extremely hard, and whenever a supervisor would notice a Jew crying, he would beat him and yell, "There is no time for crying; get back to your work!"

When Pharaoh died, all of Egypt sadly attended his funeral. The Egyptians, not wanting to lose labor, did not let their slaves attend. During the funeral, *while working,* the Jews cried bitterly about their enslavement. The supervisors were unable to stop them because they claimed they were mourning the wonderful "dearly departed" King.

Hashem heard the cries of the "pretend-mourners," which came to Him *from* their work, and knew that they were lamenting, not the King's death, but their slavery.

(שער השמים)

"ומשה היה רעה את צאן...וינהג את הצאן אחר המדבר"

"Moshe was shepherding the sheep...he led the sheep far into the wilderness" (3:1)

QUESTION: Why is it necessary to tell us where he shepherded the sheep?

ANSWER: The Torah is now introducing Moshe as the shepherd and liberator of the Jewish people. The words *"vayinhag et hatzon"* — "he led the sheep" — can be a reference to the Jewish people (see Jeremiah 50:17: *"seh pezurah Yisrael"* — "Israel is a scattered sheep"). The word *"achar"* literally means "after," and *"achar hamidbar"* can mean "to the letters that are after the word מדבר," i.e., נ, which is after מ, ה after ד, ג after ב, and ש after ר.

The letters נ,ה,ג,ש have the numerical value of 358, which is also the numerical value of משיח (Mashiach). At the very outset of his leadership he set it as his goal to lead the Jewish people to the revelation of *Mashiach.*

(קול שמחה)

"ויאמר משה אסרה נא ואראה את המראה הגדל הזה מדוע לא יבער הסנה"

"And Moshe said, 'I will now turn aside and see this great sight, why will the bush not be burnt.'" (3:3)

QUESTION: In lieu of saying *"yivar hasneh,"* in the future tense, it would have been more appropriate to say *"nivar hasneh,"* in present tense?

ANSWER: The unconsumed thorn bush represented the indestructibility of the Jewish people. This amazed him greatly, and he wanted to understand the spiritual secret that assured their survival. Hashem told him, "The place on which you are standing is a holy land. In this place the Jews will receive the Torah, which will give them the strength to survive all attempts to annihilate them physically or spiritually."

(שמעתי מהרב מנחם מענדל שי׳ אלפערין)

* * *

Rabbi Chananya Ben Tradyon was one of the ten martyrs who were killed by the government. His body was wrapped in a *Sefer Torah* and consumed by fire. While he was experiencing excruciating pain, his students asked him, "Our teacher, what do you see?" He responded, "I see the parchment being burnt and the letters flying into the sky" *(Avodah Zarah* 18a).

He meant that all attempts of the Gentile world to destroy the Jewish community and the Torah would be of no avail. Even at a time of damage to the "parchment" (the Jewish community), the "letters" of Torah would ascend and be transferred to another part of the world, where another Jewish community would be built anew.

(מצאתי בכתבי אבי הרב שמואל פסח ז״ל באגאמילסקי)

"של נעליך מעל רגליך"

"Remove your shoes from your feet." (3:5)

QUESTION: Why did Hashem order Moshe to remove his shoes?

ANSWER: Unlike one who wears shoes, one who walks barefoot feels even the smallest piece of debris. In preparing Moshe to be the leader and teacher of *Klal Yisrael,* Hashem told him the utmost importance of "sensitivity." A leader must be sensitive to even the most minute detail concerning his people.

(עוללות אפרים)

"ויאמר משה אל האלקים מי אנכי כי אלך אל פרעה"
"And Moshe said to G-d, 'Who am I that I should go to Pharaoh?'" (3:11)

QUESTION: If Hashem had selected Moshe, why did Moshe doubt his suitability?

ANSWER: When Hashem notified Avraham that his descendants would be enslaved in Egypt, he also promised that **אנכי** דן יעבדו אשר הגוי **"וגם** — "And also that nation whom they shall serve I will judge" *(Bereishit* 15:14).

Yaakov feared going to Egypt till Hashem assured him **אנכי**" עלה"" גם אעלך **ואנכי** מצרימה עמך ארד — "I will go down with you into Egypt, and I will also surely bring you up from there" *(Bereishit* 46:4).

When Hashem approached Moshe to go to Egypt, in amazement he asked, "Whenever you spoke about Egypt, You used the term *'Anochi'* — 'I personally will be involved.' Suddenly, You are asking me to go. I do not understand it — *mi anochi* — Who is *'anochi'* — is it You or me? Obviously it is You, so why are You sending me to deal with the Egyptians?"

(מדרש רבה ג':ד, ט"ו:ד')

* * *

Hashem responded שלחתיך **אנכי** כי האות לך וזה עמך אהיה "כי — "Certainly I will be with you and this shall be the proof that I sent you" (3:12). What is the reason for the apparently superfluous words *"vezeh lecha"*? It would have been sufficient to say *"veha'ot"* — "and the sign." Moreover, it could have said *"ki shelachticha"* — the word *"anochi"* is redundant.

All prophets conveyed messages from Hashem saying *"Ko amar Hashem"* — "Thus says Hashem." Moshe, however, was an exception, and he would use the term *"zeh"* — "this is" *(Sifri, Bamidbar* 30:2). The reason for this distinction is that Moshe was the only prophet to whom Hashem revealed himself face to face, and when Moshe would speak to *Klal Yisrael,* it was actually Hashem speaking through him (שכינה מדברת מתוך גרונו).

Hashem told Moshe, "I am not retracting my promise. Be assured that I will be there with you. The term *'zeh,'* which only you are permitted to use, is the proof that through you *'Anochi'* — *'I'* — will be there."

"ויאמר משה אל האלקים הנה אנכי בא אל בני ישראל ואמרתי להם אלקי אבותיכם שלחני אליכם ואמרו לי מה שמו מה אמר אליהם ויאמר אלקים אל משה אהי׳ה אשר אהי׳ה ויאמר כה תאמר לבני ישראל אהי׳ה שלחני אליכם"

"Moshe said to G-d: "Behold, when I come to the Israelites and say 'Your fathers' G-d send me to you,' and they will tell me 'What is His name?' what shall I say to them?" And G-d said to Moshe, "I Shall Be As I Shall Be;" and He said: "So shall you say to the Children of Israel: 'I Shall Be has sent me to you.'" (3:13-14)

QUESTION: 1) Instead of *"ve'amru li"* — "they will tell me what is His name," Moshe should have said *"veyishalu mimeni"* — "they will ask me?" 2) Why did Hashem tell him to use the name "אהייה" and not one of the more familiar names?

ANSWER: To sell a product, one must show the potential buyer all its good qualities. If the buyer knows more than the seller about the product, the sale is very difficult for the salesman.

Moshe said to Hashem, "The people of Egypt are very great, and I am afraid that when I come and tell them that You — Hashem — have sent me, *ve'amru li mah shemo* — They will *tell* me, 'We already know everything about Hashem, and we even know Him by His personal name.' When I hear that they know so much about you, *mah omar aleihem* — What should I tell them?"

Hashem told Moshe, "One of my names is 'אהי״ה — 'I will be' — The word 'אהי״ה has the numerical value of 21, and 'אהי״ה אשר אהיה' is 21 times 21 which totals 441. The word 'אמת' (truth) also adds up to 441." Thus, Hashem assured Moshe, "You have nothing to fear. Just tell them the truth and they will listen. Truth is extremely powerful and will have the desired effect."

(דגל מחנה אפרים - ר' ישראל מרדכין זצ״ל)

"ויאמר משה...לא איש דברים אנכי...כי כבד פה וכבד לשון אנכי"

"Moshe said...'I am not eloquent...my speech is impaired and my tongue is slow.'" (4:10)

QUESTION: Logically, Moshe was right. Why did Hashem choose an emissary who was tongue-tied?

ANSWER: Pharaoh was very stubborn about freeing the Jews from Egyptian bondage. Moreover, Hashem hardened his heart and he became even more reluctant. Due to a series of wonders and miracles performed by Hashem, the Jews were enabled to leave Egypt.

If the Jewish leader had been a renowned articulate and eloquent speaker, some people could have erroneously credited Israel's liberation from Egypt to his power of persuasion. Therefore, Hashem selected Moshe who was not eloquent. Thus, his power of speech would never be seen as the cause of the redemption of the Jewish people from Egypt.

(דרשות הר״ן)

"ויאמר בי אד-ני שלח נא ביד תשלח"

"And he [Moshe] said, 'Oh L-rd please send by the hand of whom You will send.'" (4:13)

QUESTION: Whom did Moshe want Hashem to send?

ANSWER: According to *Targum Yonatan ben Uziel*, Moshe asked Hashem to send Pinchas. In later years Pinchas became Eliyahu the prophet. He will be sent before "the great day" to announce the arrival of *Mashiach* (Malachi 3:23).

According to *Midrash Lekach Tov,* Moshe asked Hashem to send *Mashiach.* Moshe was also hinting to Hashem to spare the Jewish people the Egyptian bondage and allow them to immediately experience the ultimate redemption through *Mashiach.* Hashem refused because the Exile of Egypt was a preparatory stage to receiving the Torah, and through these two events the Jews would merit the coming of *Mashiach.*

* * *

The *Midrash Rabbah* (2:4) states that Moshe is the first and final redeemer. This does not mean that Moshe will be *Mashiach* because Moshe was a Levite and *Mashiach* will be a descendant of King David, who is from the tribe of Yehudah. The meaning is that *Mashiach* will redeem the Jewish people from exile in merit of the Torah, which was given to the Jews through Moshe. This is stated clearly by the prophet Malachi (3:22-23) in his prophecy regarding the coming of *Mashiach:* "Remember the Torah of my servant Moshe... [in it's merit] behold I am sending you Eliyahu the prophet before the arrival of the great day (revelation of *Mashiach*)."

A connection between Moshe and *Mashiach* is also alluded to in the Torah: Yaakov blessed his son Yehudah, "The scepter shall not depart from Yehudah...until *'Shiloh'* arrives" *(Bereishit* 49:10). According to *Onkelos* and Rashi, *"Shiloh"* refers to *Mashiach,* and the numerical value of the word "שילה" is 345, the same value as "Moshe" (משה).

(עי' לקוטי שיחות חי"א)

"ותקח צפרה צר ותכרת את ערלת בנה"
"Tzipporah took a stone and circumcised her son." (4:25)

QUESTION: Why is it our custom to do a *brit* with a knife made of steel instead of a stone?

ANSWER: In the days of King Shaul, Goliath of the Philistines challenged the Jewish people to appoint a representative to bout with him. David was a young boy at the time and volunteered to take on Goliath.

Goliath was dressed in steel armor and David approached with a slingshot and a few stones. He aimed at Goliath and the stone sunk into Goliath's forehead and killed him. According to a *Midrash*, Hashem asked the steel to make an exception to the normal order of nature and weaken itself, permitting the store to penetrate it. In return, he gave him a present that the Jewish people would perform a *brit* with a knife of steel instead of a sharp stone.

(פרישה יו"ד סי' רס"ד ס"ק ז')

"ותקח צפרה צר ותכרת את ערלת בנה ותגע לרגליו"

"Tzipporah took a sharp stone and cut off the foreskin of her son and touched it to his [Moshe's] feet." (4:25)

QUESTION: Moshe's life was in danger due to his failure to fulfill his obligation to circumcise his son prior to leaving for Egypt. Instead of performing the circumcision by herself, why didn't she tell Moshe to do it?

ANSWER: A Hebrew name is not merely an arbitrary method of distinguishing one person from another, but is actually related to the person's soul. This elucidates the statement in the *Gemara (Yoma 83b)* that Rabbi Meir carefully studied and analyzed the names of people (see *Sha'ar Hayichud* 1, *Likkutei Sichot*, vol. 7, pg. 308). In retrospect one often sees how the name fits the character of the person, and sometimes the name even indicates an event which may happen in the future.

Observing the dangerous situation confronting her husband, Tzipporah quickly analyzed her name. In it she saw the word, *"tzor"* (צר) — "a sharp stone" — and the number 85 (פי"ה), the numerical value of the world *"milah"* (מילה) — "circumcision." Consequently, she realized her spiritual mission to circumcise her son.

(דגל מחנה אפרים)

൭ ൸

VA'EIRA • ואראּ

<hr>

"וידבר אלקים אל משה ויאמר אליו אני ד'"

"G-d spoke to Moshe and said to him, 'I am G-d.'" (6:2)

QUESTION: This is the second *pasuk* of the sixth chapter and it is a continuation of Hashem's response to Moshe for his sharp criticism. Why does the latter *pasuk* start with the words *"vayomer Hashem"* white this *pasuk* starts *"vayidaber Elokim"?*

ANSWER: Moshe's complaint to Hashem was twofold: 1) "Why have you done evil to this people; why have you sent me?" (5:22). 2) "You created a *chilul Hashem* — a desecration of Your Holy name — because since I came to Pharaoh *'ledaber bishmecha,'* to speak in Your name, he did evil to this people. Hence the world will not respect Your Eminence, because they know that I spoke in Your name and Pharaoh disregarded it and nothing occurred to him."

The word *"amar"* — "said" — implies a mild form of speech, and the word *"daber"* — "spoke" — connotes a stronger form of speech. Hashem's holy four lettered name indicates mercy while the name *Elokim* denotes Hashem in His attribute of justice.

Consequently, the different terms used in the *pesukim* indicate the tone of Hashem's response to *both* of Moshe's complaints. 1) Regarding Moshe's concern that a chilul Hashem had taken place, *"Vayomer Hashem el Moshe"* — "G-d said to Moshe" — in a soft and gentle tone, "I appreciate your concern, however, you need not worry, because very soon "you will see what I shall do to Pharaoh, for through a strong hand will he send them out," (6:1) — and there will then be a tremendous *Kiddush Hashem* — sanctification of My name."

However, regarding Moshe's other complaint, "Why have you done evil to this people, sending me to Pharaoh only made it worse for them," *"Vayedaber Elokim"* — He spoke like a judge — and in a very harsh tone admonished Moshe for doubting His infinite merciful love for the Jewish people and trustworthiness to redeem them.

(שמעתי מהרב מרדכי ע״ה וויינגארטען, מישיבה דקראון הייטס)

"וארא אל אברהם אל יצחק ואל יעקב"
"I appeared to Avraham, to Yitzchak and to Yaakov" (6:3)

QUESTION: Rashi comments, *"el ha'avot"* — "[I appeared] to the forefathers."

It is already known that Avraham, Yitzchak and Yaakov are our *avot*. What does Rashi want to teach us with his comment?

ANSWER: The word *"avot"* stems from the word *"ava"* which means "want," as in *"velo ava"* — "he did not want" (10:27). Rashi is telling us that Hashem said to Moshe, "I appeared to Avraham, Yitzchak and Yaakov because they *wanted* to have contact with me." Every Jew can have Hashem appear to him if he wants.

(חתם סופר)

"והוצאתי...והצלתי...וגאלתי...ולקחתי...והבאתי אתכם אל הארץ...ונתתי אתה לכם מורשה"
"I will take you out...rescue you...redeem you...take you... bring you to the land, and give it to you as a heritage." (6:6-8)

QUESTION: At the *Seder* table we drink four cups of wine in honor of the four expressions of redemption. Why don't we drink a fifth cup for the fifth expression, *"veheiveiti"* — "I will bring you"?

ANSWER: The first four expressions of redemption are addressed to the entire Jewish community. However, the fifth expression, "I will bring you," refers to the giving of *Eretz Yisrael* to the Jewish people and does not apply to the tribe of Levi, because they did not have their own portion of *Eretz Yisrael.* They only had 42 cities plus the 6 cities of refuge which were given to them by the other tribes *(Bamidbar* 35). Since "I will bring you" does not apply to everyone, we do not drink a fifth cup.

Nevertheless a fifth cup is placed on the table and called *"kos shel Eliyahu"* because he is the prophet who will announce the coming of *Mashiach.* When *Mashiach* comes, *Eretz Yisrael* will be divided into 13 portions *(Bava Batra* 122a), and also the tribe of Levi will receive its own portion. The tribes of Ephraim and Menashe will together have the one portion of the tribe of Yosef, and the 13th portion will be for *Mashiach.* Hence, it is most appropriate to associate Eliyahu with the fifth cup, for through him *all* the Jews will be given a heritage in the land.

(הדרש והעיון)

"וידבר משה כן אל בני ישראל ולא שמעו אל משה מקצר רוח ומעבדה קשה"

"And Moshe spoke this to the children of Israel; but they did not listen to Moshe for anguish of spirit and for cruel bondage." (6:9)

QUESTION: Moshe brought them good tidings. Why didn't they heed his words?

ANSWER: Originally, Hashem had told Avraham that his descendants would toil in bondage for a period of 400 years. However, Moshe appeared after they had been in Egypt only 210 years.

When the Jewish people asked him why he was coming early, Moshe answered that Hashem had sent him then for two reasons: 1) They had so declined spiritually that they were now in danger of assimilation and spiritual annihilation. 2) The Egyptians exploited them harshly and cruelly; thus, their intensified period of slavery was equivalent to 400 years of normal servitude.

Knowing that they were destined to be in Egypt for 400 years, they refused to accept Moshe's explanation that his coming now was because of *"kotzer ruach"* — their decline in spiritual status *("ruach"* as in *"ruchniut")* or *"avodah kashah"* — intensively excessive labor imposed upon them.

(פרדס יוסף)

"הן בני ישראל לא שמעו אלי ואיך ישמעני פרעה ואני ערל שפתים"

"Behold, the children of Israel have not listened to me; how then shall Pharaoh hear me when I am of uncircumcised [closed] lips?" (6:12)

QUESTION: Should he not have first said that he was "of uncircumcised lips," and then that if the Jews did not listen, Pharaoh would surely not listen?

ANSWER: Moshe loved the Jewish people and was very concerned about their well-being. Therefore, he said to Hashem, "The Jewish people have not listened to me. Unfortunately, they are not willing to leave the *galut* in Egypt and move to *Eretz Yisrael, ve'eich* — and what would be if — *yishma'eini Paroh* — Pharaoh grants my request — and agrees to let the Jewish people go, then *ve'ani aral sifataim* — my lips will be closed — for I will be unable to plead any longer for my brethren, who do not recognize their plight and who do not want to leave."

(ר' יצחק מווארקא זצ"ל)

"אלה ראשי בית אבתם"

"These are the heads of their father's houses." (6:14)

QUESTION: Because of Moshe and Aharon the Torah provides a genealogy to tell us how they were born and to whom they were related (Rashi). Why is it necessary to trace and record their *yichus* — pedigree?

ANSWER: Contrary to the belief of the Gentile world regarding their own leader, the Torah wants to emphasize that a Jewish leader is not one who is born in a supernatural way. He is a normal person who has a father and mother and who has spiritually elevated himself to be worthy of his rank. Every Jewish boy has the potential to become a Moshe *Rabbeinu* — a leader of the Jewish people in his generation.

(מעינה של תורה)

"ואלה שמות בני לוי לתלדתם גרשון וקהת ומררי"

"These are the names of the children of Levi: Gershon, and Kehat and Merari." (6:16)

QUESTION: Why is the word *"shemot"* — "names" — mentioned only for Levi's children while for all the others it simply says "the children of... are..."?

ANSWER: With the exception of the tribe of Levi, the children of all the tribes were enslaved in Egypt. Levi felt that although his children were not personally enslaved, they should participate in some way and remember the troubles which confronted their brethren. Therefore, he named his children in a way which would remind them of the exile.

The name "Gershon" (גרשון) means that the Jews were גרים בארץ לא להם — strangers in a land that was not theirs. The name "Kehat" (קהת) means that שיניהם קהות — their teeth became dull from difficulties they endured. The name "Merari" (מררי) means וימררו את חייהם — [The Egyptians] embittered their lives.

(של"ה)

"ויאמר משה אל ד' הן אני ערל שפתים"

"Moshe said to G-d, 'Behold, I am of uncircumcised (closed) lips.'" (6:30)

QUESTION: He was referring to the injury which he suffered when he touched his tongue with a burning coal. Why was his tongue injured and not his hand?

ANSWER: When Batya found baby Moshe in the Nile River, she asked a number of Egyptian women to nurse him. Destined to speak with Hashem "mouth to mouth" (see *Bamidbar* 12:8), Moshe refused their milk. However, during the process, some of the milk of the Egyptian nurses fell on his tongue and he spit it out immediately.

When non-kosher food comes in contact with a kosher utensil it needs *"kashering."* This is normally done by purging or glowing. Moshe's tongue was burned in order to purge it of any impurities with which it had come in contact.

(שפתי כהן)

"וַיֹּאמֶר מֹשֶׁה אֶל ד' הֵן אֲנִי עֲרַל שְׂפָתַיִם...רְאֵה נְתַתִּיךָ אֱלֹקִים לְפַרְעֹה
וְאַהֲרֹן אָחִיךָ יִהְיֶה נְבִיאֶךָ"

"Moshe said to G-d, 'Behold I am of uncircumcised (closed) lips'...'See, I have made you master over Pharaoh; and Aharon your brother shall be your spokesman.'" (6:30-7:1)

QUESTION: How did the fact that Hashem had made Moshe a master over Pharaoh and had appointed Aharon his spokesman refute Moshe's argument that his speech difficulty made him an unsuitable messenger?

ANSWER: Every nation has its own language. Usually, when heads of governments meet, each speaks his native tongue with an interpreter between them. An exception to this rule is a meeting between the head of a small country and the head of a major power; then it is customary to speak the language of the larger country.

When Hashem told Moshe to deliver a message to Pharaoh, he assumed that he was to speak in the Egyptian language. He therefore told Hashem that since he had left Egypt at a young age and was now 80 years old, he lacked fluency in the Egyptian language and would have to stutter to find the proper words. (See *Rashbam* 4:10.)

Hashem told him, "I have appointed you a master over Pharaoh. Thus, he is your inferior, and you are the head of a major empire. Consequently, in accordance with proper protocol, you will address him in *Lashon Hakodesh* — Hebrew. Do not be concerned about his inability to understand Hebrew because Aharon will be your interpreter."

(חתם סופר)

"ראה נתתיך אלקים לפרעה"
"See, I have made you a master over Pharaoh." (7:1)

QUESTION: It should have said, "I *will* make you" (in the future tense).

ANSWER: In the famous incident during Moshe's childhood, in which Pharaoh tests the young lad who has taken off his crown (see p. 14), Pharaoh is unable to discover that Moshe is the redeemer of the Jews, but Moshe injures his mouth, affecting his power of speech.

There is nothing in the world that occurs accidentally. Every incident is governed by divine providence. When the episode with Moshe and Pharaoh's crown occurred, Hashem declared him Pharaoh's master and took away from Pharaoh the power to harm him.

Now, eighty years later, Hashem said to Moshe, "I have *already* made you a master over Pharaoh for many years, and just as he was unable to do you any harm then, now too, efforts to harm you will be of no avail."

(של"ה)

"כי ידבר אליכם פרעה לאמר תנו לכם מופת"
"When Pharaoh will speak to you, saying: 'Provide a wonder for yourselves...'" (7:9)

QUESTION: Pharaoh was speaking to Moshe and Aharon. He should have said: *"tenu li mofeit"* — provide *me* a wondrous sign?

ANSWER: Egypt was the headquarters for magicians and magic. When a magician performs a trick, he knows himself, of course, that the trick is only a deception.

Pharaoh told Moshe and Aharon, "Magic tricks are commonplace in Egypt. If you want to impress me, do a thing that will be considered wondrous *even to you.*"

(נועם אלימלך)

"וישלך אהרן את מטהו לפני פרעה ולפני עבדיו ויהי לתנין"

"Aharon threw his staff in front of Pharaoh and his servants, and it became a snake." (7:10)

QUESTION: What message did Moshe and Aharon want to give Pharaoh?

ANSWER: Pharaoh claimed that the Jews had sinned and that they did not deserve to be taken out of Egypt. Moshe and Aharon responded that a person's environment plays a very important role in his development. Even a holy staff can turn to a vicious snake in the company of Pharaoh. On the other hand, a "snake" in the company of Moshe and Aharon can transform itself into a holy staff.

(הרב מאיר ז"ל שאפירא מלובלין)

"כבד לב פרעה"

"Stubborn is the heart of Pharaoh." (7:14)

QUESTION: The word *"kaveid"* means "heavy" — it would be more appropriate to say that his heart was *"kashah"* — "hardened" — or *"ikeish"* — stubborn and unyielding?

ANSWER: In Hebrew *"kaveid"* also means "liver." The longer meat is cooked, the softer it becomes. Liver must be broiled and the more it is broiled, the harder it becomes. Usually, when a stubborn person is beaten and punished, his heart softens and he begins to concede and yield.

The Torah is telling us that the heart of Pharaoh was like liver: the more plagues he received, the more stubborn he became.

(מיוסד על מדרש רבה שמות, ט,ח)

"ויאמר ד' אל משה אמר אל אהרן קח מטך ונטה ידך על מימי מצרים...ויהיו דם"

"G-d told Moshe 'Tell Aharon to take your staff and stretch out your hand over the waters — there shall be blood.'" (7:19)

QUESTION: Rashi explains that since the river offered protection to Moshe when he was cast into it, it was not smitten through him. For the same reason, the plague of frogs, which had to do with water, was performed through Aharon. The third plague of lice was also performed through Aharon: when Moshe killed the Egyptian he buried him in the sand; therefore, he did not strike the dust of the earth to bring lice over Egypt.

Why would these reasons preclude Moshe from delivering the plagues so many years later?

ANSWER: From this we can learn a very important lesson: Often, when someone does a favor, we forget it and fail to show gratitude. Hashem, in His instructions to Moshe, was conveying a lesson that one should remain thankful for a lifetime. Though the favor Moshe received from the waters happened approximately 80 years earlier and Moshe benefited from the earth approximately 70 years earlier, Moshe was told to be appreciative and not hurt them in any way.

If this is true in regard to water and earth, which are inanimate, how much more so must this apply to a human being who does a favor.

"ויהפכו כל המים אשר ביאר לדם והדגה אשר ביאר מתה"
"All the water in the river turned to blood, and the fish in the river died." (7:20-21)

QUESTION: Is it not obvious that the fish would die, because they can only live in water?

ANSWER: The plague of blood might have happened in one of two ways: 1) All the waters might have been blood, turning back into water only when a Jew filled a glass. 2) There could have been no change in the water except that when an Egyptian filled a glass, it would become blood.

In reality it was the latter that occurred. Consequently, the Egyptians received a double punishment: The fresh waters turned into blood when used, and the fish died in fresh water and then stank terribly.

It is necessary to explain it in this way because we are told that the Egyptians were compelled to purchase water from the Jews, who prospered thereby *(Midrash Rabbah* 9:9). If all the water had been transformed to blood, the Jews would have been unable to charge the Egyptians for water, because it is forbidden to derive benefit from a miracle. (See *Ta'anit* 24a.)

(פרדס יוסף)

"ויפן פרעה ויבא אל ביתו ולא שת לבו גם לזאת"

"And Pharaoh turned and went into his house, neither did he set his heart to this also." (7:23)

QUESTION: Rashi explains that the word "also" refers to the wonder in which the staff turned into a snake and then back to a staff, swallowing all the staffs belonging to the Egyptian magicians. Why did Pharaoh now remind himself about that wonder?

ANSWER: Originally, Pharaoh and the magicians were flabbergasted when they noticed how Aharon's staff swallowed their staffs. It is impossible to even imagine an object that lacks life being able to swallow. In all probability, the only way they were able to rationalize it to Pharaoh was that Aharon's staff was a snake originally then magically converted into a staff. It was thus able to swallow the other snakes.

The *Gemara (Sanhedrin* 67b) relates a story concerning Ze'iri, who purchased a camel in Alexandria, Egypt. When he wanted to give it water to drink, it turned into a plank of wood of a bridge. It was later determined that the camel was originally made through magic from a plank of the bridge (and water possesses the power to nullify sorcery.)

Since Aharon initiated the plague of blood by smiting the water, it proved with certainty that his staff had always been a staff, for had it originally been a snake, the water would have nullified the magic, and it would have reverted to being a snake.

Now, by means of the blood plague, Pharaoh was convinced that the wonder with the staff and snakes was not related in any way to sorcery, but truly an act of Hashem. Nevertheless, he stubbornly disregarded it, paying no attention to both the miracle of the water transformed into blood and *also* the wonder of the staff.

(פרדס יוסף)

"וירא פרעה כי היתה הרוחה והכבד את לבו ולא שמע אלהם"

"But when Pharaoh saw that there was relief, he hardened his heart and did not listen to them." (8:11)

QUESTION: When Pharaoh begged Moshe to take away the frogs he said *"va'ashalchah et ha'am"* — "And I will send the people away" (8:4); Why didn't he keep his word?

ANSWER: Pharaoh was uncertain whether Moshe was really Hashem's emissary to redeem the Jews or merely a magician with unusual spiritual powers. Pharaoh was totally evil and had no intention of liberating the Jewish people. He thus decided to put Moshe through a test and determine the source of Moshe's power.

Pharaoh called Moshe and lied, "If you remove the frogs, I will send away the people." Pharaoh thought, "If Moshe is really Hashem's messenger, he will know that I am lying and will not remove the frogs. If he does remove the frogs, then I will know that he is merely a great magician." Pharaoh concluded that Moshe had failed the test and became even more adamant in refusing to free the Jewish people.

(ערבי נחל)

"ויאמרו החרטמים אל פרעה אצבע אלקים הוא"

"And the magicians said unto Pharaoh, 'This is the finger of G-d.'" (8:15)

QUESTION: Why, after the plague of lice, did the magicians finally concede "This is the finger of G-d?"

ANSWER: After the wicked Titus burned the *Beit Hamikdash,* he blasphemed against Hashem. While returning to his city, his boat was threatened by strong waves. Arrogantly he stated, "The power of the Jewish G-d is only within the limits of water. Throughout history He used water as a means of punishment. If He is really all-powerful, let Him meet me on dry land, and we shall see who will conquer." A voice emanating from heaven said, "Wicked one, son of the wicked, I have a small creature in my world called a *'yatush'* (a gnat) — come on dry land, and we will see who is stronger!" Titus presumptuously came on dry land and a *yatush* entered his nose and bore through his brain till he died *(Gittin* 56b).

The first two plagues to hit Egypt were blood and frogs, which originated from the water. The magicians consoled Pharaoh, "Don't worry, it appears that their G-d is not omnipotent: His strength is limited to water." Therefore, Hashem responded with the plague of lice, extremely minute creatures which come from the earth. Upon seeing this, the magicians were forced to concede that "This is the finger of G-d, and if His finger is so powerful, He is indeed omnipotent."

(שער בת רבים-ראשית בכורים)

"ומלאו בתי מצרים את הערב וגם האדמה אשר הם עליה"

"The houses of the Egyptians shall be full of the mixture of animals and also the ground upon which they are." (8:17)

QUESTION: The words "and also the ground upon which they are" seem superfluous?

ANSWER: Among the animals of the world there is an extremely rare one found in the wild jungles of Africa and known as the *"adnei hasadeh."* It has the face of a person, long hands that reach to its knees, and a very unusual relationship to its habitat.

It is always connected to the ground through a string that comes out of its navel. Although it is very dangerous and kills anyone that comes within its reach, there is one way to capture it: by shooting arrows at the string which connects it to the ground. As soon as it becomes detached, it screams bitterly and dies immediately.

Hashem brought upon the Egyptians a mixture of all animals from the entire world, including the strange and vicious *"adnei hasadeh."* In order that they not die before arriving in Egypt, they were brought together with the ground to which they were connected. Therefore, Moshe told Pharaoh, "The homes of the Egyptians shall be filled with the mixture of wild animals and also *'adnei hasadeh'* will come, together with the earth to which they are attached.

(פנים יפות, ועי׳ כלאים פ״ח מ״ה ברע״ב ותפארת ישראל)

״ושמתי פדת בין עמי ובין עמך״

"I will make a distinction between my people and your people." (8:19)

QUESTION: Why concerning the plague of *arov* (harmful creatures) did Hashem specify that there would be a distinction between the Jews and the Egyptians?

ANSWER: The plague consisted of a mixture of all wild animals. Species of completely different natures roamed together throughout Egypt. One might have concluded that since Hashem removed all natural boundaries and distinctions, it was also proper for a Jew to intermarry with a Gentile.

Therefore, Hashem insisted, even in a time when mixture and confusion is prevalent in the world, it is forbidden for Jews to assimilate, and it is imperative to intensify all efforts to maintain the distinction between Jew and Gentile.

(כ״ק אדמו״ר)

״ושמתי פדת בין עמי ובין עמך למחר יהיה האת הזה״

"I will make a distinction between my people and your people: tomorrow this sign will take place." (8:19)

QUESTION: Why is the word *"pedut"* (פדת) spelled without the letter ״ו״?

ANSWER: The letter ״ו״ can be spelled out fully in three ways:

1) "ואו," which has the numerical value of 13, the same numerical value of the word *"echad"* (אחד) — one. Thus, the letter "ו" represents Hashem, who is truly the only One.

2) "ויו," which has the numerical value of 22 and represents the Torah, which is written with the 22 letters of the *alef-beit*.

3) "וו," having the numerical value of 12, and representing the Jewish people, who consist of 12 tribes.

The *Zohar (Vayikra* 73) says, "קודשא בריך הוא אורייתא וישראל מתקשרין דא בדא" — "Hashem, the Torah and the Jewish people are all united as one." While this is true at all times, when *Mashiach* comes the glorious unity of all three will be recognized by the entire world.

The *pasuk* is alluding to this by saying "והשמתי פדת" — "I will make a distinction" — the Jewish people are distinct from the entire world because they are one with Hashem and Torah. However, at present the letter "ו" is missing, because the glory of the Jewish people is not fully recognizable, but *"lemachar"* — tomorrow — when *Mashiach* comes — *"yiyeh ha'ot hazeh"* — the letter "ו," which represents Hashem, Torah, and the Jewish people as one, will be in its fullest glory before the eyes of the entire world. (In Hebrew, *"ot"* means "letter.")

(ר' דוד זצ"ל מלעלוב)

"ויצא משה מעם פרעה ויעתר אל ד'"
"And Moshe went out from Pharaoh and entreated G-d." (8:26)

QUESTION: Why does the Torah say, regarding the plague of a mixture of noxious animals, *"vayetar"* — "and he entreated" — while in connection with the plague of frogs it merely states *"vayitzak Moshe"* — "and Moshe cried out"?

ANSWER: The *Gemara (Sukka* 14a) compares the prayer of *tzaddikim* to a pitchfork. Just as the pitchfork transfers the harvest from one place to another, the prayer of *tzaddikim* converts Hashem's attribute of judgment to mercy.

The word *"vayetar"* is used regarding the mixture of noxious animals, illustrating that just as a pitchfork moves harvest from one place to the other, through Moshe's prayers, the noxious animals were entirely removed from the land of Egypt. After Moshe's earlier prayer, frogs still remained in the water, and those on land were gathered in heaps so that they stank. Thus the word *"vayitzak"* is used, rather than *"vayetar."*

(חתם סופר)

"וימת כל מקנה מצרים וממקנה בני ישראל לא מת אחד"
"All the cattle of Egypt died, but not one of the cattle belonging to the children of Israel died." (9:6)

QUESTION: In the following *pasuk* it is written that Pharaoh inquired and he found out "לא מת ממקנה ישראל עד אחד" — According to the literal translation *"ad echad"* means "except one" (see *Midrash Rabbah* 11:14). Thus *one* of the cattle belonging to the Jews died. How do we explain this discrepancy?

ANSWER: According to *halacha,* when a Jewish woman marries a Gentile, the children are considered Jewish. This law took effect after the giving of the Torah. However, prior to the giving of the Torah, the child's identity followed the father's and he was considered a Gentile (Ramban, *Vayikra* 24:10).

In Egypt, Shlomit the daughter of Divri married an Egyptian and gave birth to a son. Although his mother was Jewish, he was not considered as one of the children of Israel.

During the plague of pestilence, her son's animal, too, was killed. Pharaoh thought that since his mother was Jewish and he grew up among the Jews, he should be considered a Jew as well. Therefore, when he inquired as to the results of the plague and found out that an animal belonging to a Jewish owner died, he was convinced that Moshe's threat of a severe epidemic striking the Egyptians was not realized. Consequently, his heart hardened and he did not send out the Jews.

* * *

The above clarifies another difficulty: The Torah says *none* of the cattle belonging to the *B'nei Yisrael* died. The report to Pharaoh was that "none died" — "ממקנה ישראל" — "of the cattle of the Israelites" — *"ad echad"* — "except one" — and it does not say *"B'nei Yisrael."*

This is because the *one* animal that died belonged to the son of Shlomit. Regardless of the fact that Pharaoh considered him a Jew, he was really not a member of *B'nei Yisrael* — the *children* (the true descendants) of Israel.

(פרדס יוסף-שמן המור ח"ב סי' י"ג)

"כי בפעם הזאת אני משלח את כל מגפתי"
"For at this time I am about to send all my plagues." (9:14)

QUESTION: Rashi says that from the phrase *"kal mageifotai"* — "all my plagues" — we can learn שמכת בכורות שקולה כנגד כל המכות" — "that the plague of the killing of the firstborn was equal in severity to all the other plagues combined."

We are now discussing the plague of hail. Why does Rashi discuss the plague of the firstborn?

ANSWER: Rashi is not referring to מַכַּת בְּכוֹרוֹת, the plague in which the firstborn were killed, but מַכַּת בִּכּוּרוֹת, the plague of the ripened harvest. The Torah relates that the hail destroyed the flax and the barley, which were already fully ripened (Rashi 9:31). This plague was the worst one, because it caused a famine throughout the entire land of Egypt.

(חזקוני)

* * *

Alternatively, Rashi *is* referring to the plague of the firstborn (*Siftei Chachamim*). The reason that Rashi writes about the severity of the plague of the firstborn in connection with the plague of hail is the following:

Hashem told Moshe to warn Pharaoh that if he refused to permit the Jews to leave, "Behold, I will slay your firstborn son" (4:23). Rashi comments, "Though this was the last plague, he warned him about it at the beginning, because it was the most severe."

If the plague of hail was as severe as all of the plagues together, then Hashem should have warned Pharaoh of it in the beginning. Therefore, Rashi concludes that if hail is referred to as "all my plagues" — because it was equal to all the others together — then obviously the plague of the killing of the firstborn, which he was warned of at the outset, was also equal to all other plagues and even *more* severe.

(חנוכת התורה)

* * *

The very early editions of Rashi, using an abbreviation, state, "שמי״ב" was equivalent to all plagues together." The correct interpretation of "שמי״ב" is "שמכת ברד" — "the plague of hail" — is compared to all other plagues. Later, an unlearned typesetter spelled out Rashi's abbreviation incorrectly and wrote "שמכת בכורות" instead of "שמכת ברד."

(חנוכת התורה)

"ויאמר אליו משה כצאתי את העיר אפרש את כפי אל ד'"
"Moshe said to him, 'When I go out of the city, I will spread my hands [in prayer] to G-d.'" (9:29)

QUESTION: Why only during the plague of hail, which was the seventh plague, did Moshe insist on praying outside of the city?

ANSWER: When Moshe warned Pharaoh of the coming plague of hail, he told him that the Egyptians should take in all the cattle from the fields because any man or animal in the fields would die. The Egyptians who took the warning seriously brought their cattle into their houses. Others, who did not regard the words of Hashem, left their servants and cattle out in the fields, where they were killed by the hail (9:19-21).

Egypt worshipped the sheep. Therefore, during all other plagues, Moshe was willing to pray in the city since the sheep were normally out in the fields. However, during the plague of hail the city was filled with the sheep, and Moshe went out of the city to pray because he did not want to pray in a place full of idols.

(ר' יהונתן אייבשיץ ז"ל)

"ואתה ועבדיך ידעתי כי טרם תיראון מפני ד' אלקים"

"As for you and your servants, I know that you are not yet afraid of G-d." (9:30)

QUESTION: Why did Moshe rebuke Pharaoh during the plague of hail that he was not G-d fearing?

ANSWER: The Egyptians worshipped sheep. Pharaoh knew that Moshe would not pray to Hashem in the city because it was full of idols.

When Egypt was struck with hail, Pharaoh confessed, חטאתי הפעם ד' הצדיק ואני ועמי הרשעים" — "I have sinned this time: G-d is righteous; I and my people are the wicked ones" (9:27). Eager to be rid of the hail as quickly as possible, he pleaded with Moshe to make an exception and pray to Hashem while still *in the city*. He argued that according to *halacha,* a Gentile can nullify an idol verbally. Consequently, through his proclamation, the idols were nullified and no longer prevented Moshe from praying within the city.

Moshe's response was *"terem tire'un* (9:30) — You do not yet have true fear for Hashem — the nullification was done under duress. Hence, it is *halachicly* invalid, and I will pray *outside* of the city."

(אמרי שפר)

 C3 80

בא • BO

"ולמען תספר באזני בנך ובן בנך את אשר התעללתי במצרים ואת
אתתי אשר שמתי בם וידעתם כי אני ד'"

**"You will then be able to tell your children and grandchildren
my miraculous signs that I have performed among them, and
you will know that I am G-d." (10:2)**

QUESTION: Since the Torah is telling us to relate to our
children and grandchildren what happened in Egypt, should it *not*
have said *"vayeide'u"* — "and thus *they* will know"?

ANSWER: Parents are obligated to teach their children about
Hashem and enhance and strengthen their faith in Him. Their
efforts carry a two-fold reward: 1) Ultimately, their work will bear
fruit and they will merit to have children who will be attached to
Hashem. 2) Through teaching and talking to the children, the
parents, too, will experience an enhancement and strengthening of
their faith.

Similarly, in the *Gemara (Ta'anit* 7a), Rabbi Chaninah says "I
learned much from my teachers and more than that from my
colleagues, and from my students *more* than from all."

(עיטורי תורה)

"ויבא משה ואהרן אל פרעה ויאמרו אליו כה אמר ד' שלח עמי
ויעבדוני. ויאמרו עבדי פרעה אליו שלח את האנשים...לא כן נא
הגברים. ועבדו את ד'"

**"Moshe and Aharon went to Pharaoh and said, 'So says G-d:
Send out My people so they may serve Me.' Pharaoh's
servants said to him, 'Send out the men'...[Pharaoh replied]
'No, let the adult males go and serve G-d.'"** (10:3,7,11)

QUESTION: What is the reason for the three different
expressions denoting the Jewish people?

ANSWER: The word *"gevarim"* is the plural of *"gever."* The
minimum of a plural is two. Twice the numerical value of the
word *"gever"* (גבר) is 410, which is the same numerical value of
the word *"kadosh"* (קדוש) — "holy." The word *"anashim"* is the
plural for the word *"enosh."* Twice the numerical value of
"enosh" (אנש) is 702, which is also the numerical value of the
word *"Shabbat"* (שבת).

Pharaoh said to Moshe, "Only the *holy* Jews should go to
serve Hashem; all others should stay home in Egypt." His servants
were more lenient, and they said that not only the holy Jews
should go, but also the ones that were at least *Shomer Shabbat*.
Moshe insisted that anyone who is a member of *"ami"* — *"My*
[Hashem's] *people"* — must leave Egypt and serve Hashem.

(עיטורי תורה)

"ויפן ויצא מעם פרעה"

"And he turned his back and left Pharaoh." (10:6)

QUESTION: Why concerning locusts, the eighth plague, does
the Torah tell us that Moshe left immediately after giving the
warning?

ANSWER: Moshe always came to Pharaoh as Hashem's
messenger to inform him of the coming plague. Moshe thought
Pharaoh an extremely stubborn man, and therefore, he always
pleaded with him to relent and listen to Hashem about letting the
people go.

Prior to the plague of locusts, Hashem said to Moshe, "Go to Pharaoh and warn him, for I have hardened his heart" (10:1). Moshe now realized that it was not Pharaoh's stubbornness, but Hashem causing him not to listen. Thus, there was no purpose in his pleading with Pharaoh to let the people go. Therefore, after delivering the message of the coming plague of locusts, he immediately turned his back and left.

(שער בת רבים)

"ויאמר אליהם לכו עבדו את ד' אלקיכם מי ומי ההלכים: ויאמר משה בנערינו ובזקנינו נלך"

"And he said to them, 'Go and serve G-d your Lord; Which ones are going?' Moshe said, 'With our young and with our old shall we go.'" (10:8-9)

QUESTION: Moshe's request to Pharaoh was very explicit: "Let my people go!" Why now, after receiving seven plagues, did Pharaoh ask, "Which ones are going?"

ANSWER: The words *"mi vami haholchim"* (מי ומי ההלכים) have the numerical value of 216, the same as *"Kaleiv uBin Nun"* (כלב ובן נון). Pharaoh was telling Moshe, "I know your ultimate plan is to bring the Jews to *Eretz Yisrael,* but you should know that you are wasting your time, because they will all die in the wilderness and only Kalev and Bin Nun (Yehoshua) will live to reach *Eretz Yisrael."*

Moshe replied, *"Binareinu uvizkeineinu neileich"* — "Do not worry, all those who are now under 20 or over 60 will also survive the wilderness and come to *Eretz Yisrael."*

(בעל הטורים)

* * *

Alternatively, Pharaoh, slowly but surely, began to realize that fighting Moshe was a losing battle. Instead of being stubborn and refusing to let the Jewish people go, he decided to use reverse psychology. Pharaoh said to Moshe, "I am your friend who would not want to see you as an outcast or a failure. Many years have passed since you left Egypt. *I* know the people better than you do.

I do not doubt your sincerity in wanting to take them to serve Hashem, but I urge you stop your campaign, because *mi vami haholchim* — which ones are going?! None of these people are interested in leaving Egypt to go seek a new way of life."

Moshe smiled and replied, "You are greatly mistaken. Just open the doors and give them freedom, and I assure you that young and old, men and women will eagerly run to serve Hashem."

"ויעל הארבה על כל ארץ מצרים וינח בכל גבול מצרים"

"The locusts went up over the entire land of Egypt and rested in all the borders of Egypt." (10:14)

QUESTION: Why does the Torah repeat "all the borders of Egypt" after it already says that the locusts "went up over the *entire* land of Egypt"?

ANSWER: The Jews of Egypt lived in the city of Goshen and were not affected by any of the plagues. The locusts were meant to destroy any vegetation not previously destroyed by the hail. Knowing that very shortly the Jewish people would be leaving Egypt, Hashem sent the locusts. They covered Egypt from border to border — including Goshen — in order to ensure that the Egyptians would have no benefit from the produce of the Jewish fields in Goshen.

(שער בת רבים)

"וימהר פרעה לקרא למשה ולאהרן ויאמר חטאתי לד' אלקיכם ולכם"

"And Pharaoh called for Moshe and Aharon in haste and said, 'I have sinned against G-d and against you.'" (10:16)

QUESTION: Why did Pharaoh then confess that he also sinned against Moshe and Aharon, while after the plague of hail, he only confessed, "I have sinned this time; G-d is righteous" (9:27)?

ANSWER: Moshe told Pharaoh to release the Jews to enable them to worship Hashem. Pharaoh inquired, "Which ones are going?" Moshe responded, "We will go with our young and with our old, with our sons and with our daughters." Pharaoh became enraged and chased them out, saying, "Not so, let the men go now, *ki otah atem mevakshim* — for this you are seeking." Superficially, one may question, why was it necessary for Pharaoh to add the words *"ki otah atem mevakshim"* — "for this you are seeking"?

Pharaoh accused Moshe and Aharon of illogically seeking to take the children on a pilgrimage to serve Hashem: "Undoubtedly, your G-d only wants the adults. However, *otah — this* request for the children to participate — *atem mevakshim* — is something which *you* want, and which Hashem never asked for."

When Pharaoh saw that regardless of his consent to send the males he was plagued with locusts, he realized that Hashem was not satisfied, because *He* wanted the children's participation. Therefore, he quickly called Moshe and Aharon and told them, "Now I have not only sinned against G-d, but *also* against you, because I falsely accused you."

(שו״ת תירוש ויצהר סי׳ קי״ט)

"ויהי חשך אפלה בכל ארץ מצרים שלשת ימים"

"And there was a thick darkness in all of Egypt for three days." (10:22)

QUESTION: Rashi explains that during the first three days of darkness, no one was able to see anyone else. During the succeeding days, the darkness was so thick that if an Egyptian was sitting, he was unable to stand up, and if he was standing, he was unable to sit down.

Every plague lasted seven days (except the plague of the firstborn). Why did the plague of darkness last only six days?

ANSWER: When the Jews left Egypt and traveled in the desert, clouds of glory accompanied them. During the day the clouds would clear a path in the desert, and at night a pillar of fire lit up the camp. When the Egyptians pursued the Jews, the Torah says, "There was a cloud of darkness [for the Egyptians] and the night was illuminated [for the Jews through a pillar of fire]" (14:20). Thus, Hashem reserved the remaining seventh day of darkness to punish the Egyptians when they chased after the Jewish people.

(מדרש רבה שמות י"ד, ג')

"ויהי חשך אפלה בכל ארץ מצרים שלשת ימים לא ראו איש את אחיו"

"There was a thick darkness in all the land of Egypt for three days. One did not see his own brother." (10:22-23)

QUESTION: They were unable to see *anything;* why the emphasis on one's brother?

ANSWER: Many years ago a man emigrated from a small town in Russia to the United States. His business enterprises were blessed with success and he became very wealthy. A few years later, his brother arrived, found his way to the successful brother's house, and presented himself to the doorman as the brother of his master. The doorman directed him to the waiting area and afterwards came back with a message that his master had no brother. He sent back a number of signs hoping that his brother would recognize him. Again the doorman came back: "Sorry, my master says he has no brother and does not know you." Disappointed and hurt, he told the doorman to tell his master, "I advise him to make a will immediately, because he does not have much time left to live."

Petrified, the brother rushed to the door and asked in alarm, "How can you make such a statement? My doctor proclaimed me in excellent health!" The immigrant brother looked his brother in the eyes and said, "The city in which we grew up as brothers was very small and poor. The townspeople were unable to afford a full-time physician. I studied first-aid and administered their medical needs. From my experience I learned that when a patient can no longer 'recognize' his own brother, his situation is extremely serious and he has little time left to live."

Some aspects of the plague of darkness are unfortunately prevalent in contemporary times. Sadly, there may be Jews enveloped in darkness who do not recognize fellow Jews as their brothers who deserve to be helped materially and especially spiritually. Such conduct endangers the continuity of the Jewish community.

Hopefully, like the Jews of Egypt, we too will merit, "For all the children of Israel, there was light in their dwellings." Everyone will see the true light and do the utmost for his brother — his fellow Jew.

(מיוסד על אשכול ענבים - פרדס יוסף)

"וגם מקננו ילך עמנו לא תשאר פרסה כי ממנו נקח לעבד את ד' אלקינו"

"And also our cattle will go with us; not a hoof will be left behind. For from it must we take to serve G-d, our G-d." (10:26)

QUESTION: Why does it say *"mikneinu yeileich"* — "our cattle will go" — instead of *"nikach"* — "we will take"?

ANSWER: When the prophet Eliyahu debated the false prophets of Ba'al, he challenged them to a test: He and they would separately bring sacrifices and the G-d that accepted the offering would be recognized by all as the true G-d. The oxen were willing to be Eliyahu's sacrifice but refused to be used by the false prophets of Ba'al. Eliyahu whispered to an ox that he should agree to be used by the false prophets, because the failure of their efforts would prove the falsehood of Ba'al worship, and through the ox there would be a great *Kiddush Hashem (Yalkut Shimoni,* I Kings, 18).

Moshe told Pharaoh, "Even if we should agree to let our cattle remain in Egypt, it will be of no avail. For even if we do not take them, *mikneinu yeilech imanu* — our cattle will go with us of their own volition — due to their deep desire to be used as sacrifices for Hashem."

(תורת משה - חת"ס)

"כשלחו כלה גרש יגרש אתכם מזה"

"When he lets you go, he will drive you out from here altogether." (11:1)

QUESTION: Why did Hashem tell Moshe that Pharaoh would *drive* the Jews out?

ANSWER: Hashem told Avraham, "Your children will be enslaved in a strange land for 400 years and afterwards leave with great wealth." The Jewish people slaved indeed for many years under Pharaoh without any compensation. As the time for their departure was arriving, Hashem instructed Moshe to tell the Jewish people to borrow gold and silver from the Egyptians. Eventually, they would keep this as payment for 400 years of work and as a fulfillment of the promise of great wealth.

Moshe hesitated since it resembled as trickery. "After all," he argued, "they did not complete their servitude, and thus, are not entitled to such wealth."

Hashem explained to Moshe, "According to *halacha,* when one hires a worker and fires him in the middle of the day, he is obligated to pay him for the full time. Similarly, Pharaoh will drive out the Jewish people in the middle of their period of service. Therefore, they are rightfully entitled to be paid for 400 years of serving Egypt."

(חנוכת התורה)

"דבר נא באזני העם וישאלו איש מאת רעהו ואשה מאת רעותה כלי כסף וכלי זהב"

"Speak in the ears of the people. Each man should borrow from his friend and a woman from her friend silver and gold vessels." (11:2)

QUESTION: The word *"rei'eihu"* means friend. 1) Since when are Egyptians considered friends of the Jews? 2) Why was it necessary to speak "in the ears" of the people, i.e. to keep it secret?

ANSWER: Hashem wanted the Jews to leave Egypt laden with gold, silver, and valuables, which they would borrow from the Egyptians. But how could this be easily accomplished? Wouldn't an Egyptian ask, "How do I know I can trust you?"

Therefore, Hashem told Moshe that first the Jewish males should borrow from their *Jewish* friends and that the females should borrow from their *Jewish* friends. When the Egyptians would see the friendship and trust among the Jews, the Jews would find favor in their eyes and the Egyptians would readily agree to lend them gold and silver.

Since this was a scheme to get the gold and silver from the Egyptians, it was necessary that the message be "spoken into the ears of the people" and kept discreet.

(שער בת רבים - מלבי"ם)

"ולכל בני ישראל לא יחרץ כלב לשנו"

"But against any of the children of Israel no dog shall whet it's tongue." (11:7)

QUESTION: Why did Hashem specify dogs instead of simply saying, "No wild beast will harm them"?

ANSWER: The *Gemara (Sanhedrin* 105a) declares that Lavan, Bilam, and Cushan-rishatayim are the same person. Lavan chased after Yaakov, wanting to destroy him and the future of the Jewish people. Years later he returned in the form of Bilam and advised Pharaoh to drown the Jewish children, and later, in the days of Balak, he came to curse the Jewish people. In the time of the Judges, when the Jewish people angered Hashem through their improper behavior, He exiled them for eight years under the regime of Cusham-rishatayim, King of Aram. He, too, was a reincarnation of Lavan. (See Judges 3:7-11.)

The acronym of the names "Cushan," "Lavan," and "Bilam" spells the word *"kelev"* — "dog." Hashem told Moshe, "Throughout history, the wicked will always reappear and attempt to annihilate the Jewish people. However, be assured that neither

Lavan in all his disguises *(kelev)* nor any other enemies will succeed, G-d forbid, in destroying the Jewish people."

(שער בת רבים פ׳ בלק)

"ויאמר ד׳ אל משה ואל אהרן...החדש הזה לכם ראש חדשים"

"And G-d said to Moshe and Aharon...'This month (Nissan) shall be for you the head of the months.'" (12:1-2)

QUESTION: Why did Hashem convey the laws of establishing the Jewish calendar to Moshe and Aharon together?

ANSWER: The Jewish calendar follows the lunar system. Every month the *Beit Din* declares *Rosh Chodesh,* based on testimony of witnesses who have seen the new moon. In order to reconcile the lunar year and the solar year, it is necessary once every few years to add an extra month. Otherwise, *Pesach* could end up in the fall, and *Sukkot* in the spring.

According to the *Gemara (Sanhedrin* 18b), a King or a *Kohen Gadol,* because of personal interest, cannot be part of the *Beit Din* that decides a leap year. The King would always want a leap year, because his army is paid on an annual basis, and thus he would get a month of free labor. The *Kohen Gadol,* who has to perform the service on *Yom Kippur* barefoot, would rather there not be a leap year, so that *Yom Kippur* would be in the summer. However, since the *Kohen Gadol* and the King have complimentary interests, it would be proper to have a *Beit Din* with *both* of them participating together.

In view of the above, Moshe, being a King, would not be permitted to be a participant in the *Beit Din* on his own, nor would Aharon, because he was the *Kohen Gadol.* Therefore, Hashem spoke to the two of them together, saying, "This month shall be for *you* the beginning of months — should *you* want to determine the calendar and decide about a new year, it can only be done if the *two* of you are in the *Beit Din together."*

(ילקוט האורים - ר׳ נפתלי כ״ץ זצ״ל)

* * *

QUESTION: What lesson can we learn from a leap year?

ANSWER: The secular calendar follows the solar year, the cycle of the sun, and consists of 365 days. The Jewish calendar follows the lunar system, the cycle of the moon, and is approximately 354 days. To make up the deficiency of close to 11 days, every few years we have a leap year, after which we actually end up a few days ahead of the solar year.

The leap year serves as a reminder that everyone has an opportunity from time to time to make up for what he has failed to accomplish in the past. Furthermore, just as the leap year not only makes up for the deficiency, but provides an "advance" on the future, a Jew must also intensify his efforts in his service of Hashem and store up additional merits.

(לקוטי שיחות חכ״א ע׳ 480)

"החדש הזה לכם ראש חדשים"

"This month (Nissan) shall be for you the head of the months." (12:2)

QUESTION: Why was the lunar calendar the first *mitzvah* given to the Jewish people as a whole?

ANSWER: When Hashem created the world, the two luminaries, the sun and the moon, were of equal strength. The moon complained, "It is not proper for two 'kings' to have the same type of crown." In response, Hashem made the moon smaller. When *Mashiach* comes, the moon will return to its original strength *(Bereishit* 1:16 Rashi, Isaiah 30:26).

The unique quality of the moon is that up to the middle of the month, it continuously grows, becoming smaller thereafter. By the end of the month, it is not seen anymore — but suddenly it reappears.

The history of the Jewish People is similar to the stages of the moon: Throughout our history we have had rising and falling fortunes. We have been expelled from various countries, and when we were thought to be extinct, suddenly, a new Jewish community arose in another part of the world. Like the moon, the Jewish people will never disappear, and will eventually be, in the days of *Mashiach,* the most glorious and respected people in the world. This essential quality of the Jewish people is thus indicated by the first *mitzvah* given to them.

(כ"ק אדמו"ר)

* * *

The last letters of the words *"Hachodesh hazeh lachem"* (החדש הזה לכם) — "this month shall be for you" spell the word "Moshe," which is the name of the person through whom Hashem gave us the Torah. Moreover, the words *"Hachodesh hazeh lachem"* have the numerical value of 424, which is also the numerical value of the word *"kadat"* (כדת), meaning in the fullest accordance with *halachic* requirements.

In the first *mitzvah* Hashem gave the Jewish people, He emphasized the importance of fulfilling *kadat* — properly — the Torah which He gave us through Moshe. This will merit them the ultimate redemption through משיח בן דוד *(Mashiach Ben David),* whose name is also numerically equivalent to 424.

(חיד"א - פני דוד)

"החדש הזה לכם ראש חדשים"

"This month *(Nissan)* shall be for you the head of the months." (12:2)

QUESTION: The word *"lachem"* — "for you" — seems extra?

ANSWER: *Nissan* was and will always be the month of miracles and redemption *(Rosh Hashanah* 11b). With the word *"lachem"* the Torah is emphasizing that the coming of *Mashiach* and ultimate redemption depends on *you* — the Torah study and good deeds of each and every individual Jew.

(עיטורי תורה)

"אל תאכלו ממנו נא ובשל מבשל במים כי אם צלי אש"

"Do not eat of it partially raw, or cooked in water, only roasted over fire." (12:9)

QUESTION: The meat of the sacrifices may be eaten by *Kohanim* in whatever manner suits their palates. They may eat it cooked, broiled or roasted, etc. (Rambam, *Ma'aseh haKarbanot* 10:10). Why did Hashem insist that the *karban Pesach* be eaten only roasted with fire?

ANSWER: Partially raw and fully cooked meat hardly have an aroma. Roasted meat, however, can be smelled at a distance.

The Jews slaved in Egypt for many years and were petrified of their Egyptian masters. Hashem's command to offer a sheep, the animal worshipped by the Egyptians, as a *karban Pesach* frightened them. In order not to arouse the wrath of the Egyptians, they were going to eat it partially raw or fully cooked, hoping that the Egyptians would not notice.

Consequently, Hashem told Moshe to tell the people, "Enough is enough! Stop walking with your heads bowed down. Lift them up and be proud of the fact that you are Jews and free people. *Roast* the sacrifice on fire, let the aroma be smelled from one end of Egypt to the other, and let the entire country know that you are proudly worshipping your G-d."

(דעת זקנים מבעלי התוספות)

"והיה הדם לכם לאת על הבתים אשר אתם שם"

"The blood shall be a sign for you upon the houses where you are." (12:13)

QUESTION: The *pasuk* should have said *"li"* — "for me" — instead of *"lachem"* — "for you." What token did the Jewish people need?

ANSWER: The prophet prophesied: גדול יהיה כבוד הבית הזה" האחרון מן הראשון" — "Greater shall be the glory of the latter house than the former" (Haggai 2:9).

The Sages of the Talmud explain this to mean that the second *Beit Hamikdash* would be structurally taller than the first *Beit Hamikdash* and also last longer *(Bava Batra* 3a).

A Gentile once asked the *Rashba,* Rabbi Shlomo Ben Aderet (Responsa 187), "Since the prophet referred to the second *Beit Hamikdash* as *'acharon'* — 'last' — how do the Jews believe that when *Mashiach* comes there will be a third *Beit Hamikdash?"*

The Rashba told him that *"acharon"* does not necessarily mean "last," but can also mean "second." He proved it to him from Hashem's dialogue with Moshe: When Hashem asked Moshe to go down to Egypt and tell the Jewish people about their imminent redemption, Moshe responded, "What will be if they doubt that you have spoken to me?" Hashem gave him three signs with which to prove his authenticity to the Jewish people. The first was the staff becoming a snake, and the second was his hand becoming leprous.

Before showing him the third sign, Hashem said to Moshe, "It shall be that if they do not believe you and do not heed the voice of *ha'ot harishon* — the first sign — they will believe the voice of *ha'ot ha'acharon* — the latter sign" (4:8). It is clear that although there was a third sign, He referred to the second sign as *"acharon."* Thus, *"acharon"* does not necessarily mean "last," but can also mean "second."

Before the Jews left Egypt, Hashem told them that the blood, i.e. the sign of water turning to blood (which was the *third* of the signs given to Moshe to present to the Jewish people), would be *"lachem le'ot"* — "for you a sign" — *"al habatim"* — that there would be *three Batei Mikdash,* although the prophet referred to the second as *"acharon."*

(פנינים יקרים)

"והיה היום הזה לכם לזכרון וחגתם אתו חג לד' לדרתיכם"

"And this day shall be to you for a remembrance; and you shall celebrate it as a feast to G-d for your generations."
(12:14)

QUESTION: Why do we add the cup *"kos shel Eliyahu"* when we celebrate the *Pesach seder?*

ANSWER: Eliyahu once complained to Hashem that the Jewish people were not faithfully observing the *mitzvah* of circumcision. Hashem did not receive this complaint very well and told Eliyahu, "My children are trustworthy, and from now on you will be present at every Jewish *brit* to witness their dedication." For this reason, at every *brit* a special chair is set aside for Eliyahu (*Pirkei DeRabbi Eliezer* 20).

According to *halacha,* the uncircumcised may not partake of the *Pesach* offering. Therefore, Eliyahu, who is present at all *britim,* appears in each home to testify that the participants of the *seder* are all eligible to eat from the *karban Pesach,* and a cup is prepared in his honor.

* * *

Additionally, in Egypt, the Jews neglected the *mitzvah* of circumcision, and thus on the night of *Pesach* all the Jews circumcised themselves in order to be eligible to partake of the *karban Pesach.*

Undoubtedly, the prophet Eliyahu was in Egypt that night, because he is the messenger of redemption (see Malachi 3:23). Thus, he witnessed all the *britim* and is also invited to participate in our freedom celebration every year.

* * *

There is a popular question: A *brit* must be performed during the day. How did the Jews in Egypt perform their *britim* during the night?

The answers include the following: 1) The law of performing a *brit* during the day took effect *after* the Torah was given. 2) A *brit* which is not performed on the 8th day after birth may be performed either day or night. 3) According to the *Zohar,* when Hashem revealed Himself at midnight to smite the firstborn, suddenly, the night became illuminated, to the extent that *"velaila kayom ya'ir"* — "the night shined like the day" (Psalms 139:12). In view of this, it was permissible to perform a *brit* at night.

(הגש"פ כ"ק אדמו"ר)

"ולא יתן המשחית לבא אל בתיכם לנגף"
"And He will not permit the destroyer to enter your homes to smite." (12:23)

QUESTION: The *Haggadah* of *Pesach* explains the passage, "I will smite every firstborn in the land of Egypt" (12:12) to mean *"Ani velo seraf"* — "I and not a fiery angel." Why was it necessary to make a sign for the destroyer, since the plague of the firstborn was inflicted by Hashem Himself?

ANSWER: In Egypt there lived a few million Jews and millions of Egyptians. In such a populace, it is normal that some people die each day. If the *malach hamavet* (Angel of Death) had killed a Jew during the night of the plague of the firstborn, Pharaoh would not have agreed that a miracle had taken place. He would have claimed that there was an epidemic which claimed Egyptians and Jews alike. Therefore, it was the will of Hashem that the destroyer *(malach hamavet)* not kill even one Jew on that night.

(הגר"א)

"והיה כי יאמרו אליכם בניכם מה העבדה הזאת לכם"
"And it shall come to pass when your children will say to you, 'What is this service to you?'" (12:26)

QUESTION: In the *Haggadah* of *Pesach* this *pasuk* is associated with the wicked son. What indication is there for this in the *pasuk?*

ANSWER: Children must respect and honor their parents. They should seek their guidance and follow their instruction. A good child does not tell his parents *his* decision and expect them to listen to him.

Since the Torah mentions a child who *tells* the parent his opinion, the *Haggadah* deduces that we are not dealing with a good child, but unfortunately the opposite.

(הדרש והעיון)

"ויהי בחצי הלילה וד' הכה כל בכור בארץ מצרים"
"At midnight G-d struck all the firstborn in the land of Egypt." (12:29)

QUESTION: In the *Haggadah* of *Pesach* there is a listing of the ten plagues, and afterwards we are told that Rabbi Yehudah referred to them by acronyms: "דצ"ך, עד"ש, באח"ב."

Rabbi Yehudah was one of the great sages of the Talmud. What genius is there in making an acrostic out of the first letters of the ten plagues?

ANSWER: In Psalms (136:10), Hashem is praised for *"lemakeih Mitzraim bivchoreihem"* — "striking the Egyptians through their firstborn." It does not say that Hashem struck the firstborn of Egypt, but rather that He struck the Egyptians *through* their firstborn. This is explained in the *Midrash (Yalkut Shimoni)* as follows:

Upon hearing that they would be victims of the last plague, the *"bechorim"* — "firstborn" — insisted of Pharaoh and their parents that the Jews be released immediately. When their pleas were refused, a civil war broke out and the desperate firstborn attacked and killed their parents and fellow Egyptians. Thus, the tenth plague dealt a double blow to Egypt, killing both firstborn and non-firstborn.

In the *Haggadah,* the ten plagues are listed as *"dam, tzefardei'a...makat bechorot"* — "Blood, frogs...plague of the firstborn." The word *"makat"* is not mentioned for any of the plagues except for *"bechorot"* — why?

It can be explained that Rabbi Yehudah *argues* with the author of the *Haggadah* as to what was the major part of the double-blow plague. According to the author of the *Haggadah,* the main part was *"makat"* — the smiting of the Egyptians by their own angry and violent *"bechorim"* — firstborn.

Rabbi Yehudah's third acronym is "באח"ב". The final "ב" stands for *"bechorot."* He did not make the acronym "באח"מ," which would have meant *"Makat bechorot,"* because in his opinion the major part of the plague was *Hashem's* slaying of the firstborn, and not the smiting of the Egyptians by their own firstborn.

(הגש"פ צוף אמרים בשם יסוד התורה)

"ותהי צעקה גדלה במצרים כי אין בית אשר אין שם מת"
"There was a great cry in Egypt, for there was not a house where there was not one dead." (12:30)

QUESTION: Even in a home where there were no firstborn, the eldest of the household perished (Rashi). Why did Moshe only warn that the firstborn would die without warning about the eldest of the house?

ANSWER: Some Egyptians thought they could outsmart Hashem and Moshe. Warned of the oncoming plague, they took their firstborn and placed them into Jewish homes. Hashem killed those firstborn and also the eldest of the household from which each firstborn originated. Had Moshe warned them of this, they would have kept the firstborn home, and thus the eldest in the household would have survived.

Moshe intentionally did not warn them, so that their punishment would be twofold. The firstborn were killed to punish the Egyptians for not listening to Hashem to free the Jews, and the eldest because the Egyptians tried to outsmart Hashem.

(עדות ביוסף)

"וַיִּקְרָא לְמשֶׁה וּלְאַהֲרֹן לַיְלָה וַיֹּאמֶר קוּמוּ צְאוּ מִתּוֹךְ עַמִּי"

"And he called for Moshe and Aharon [at] night and he said, 'Rise up, go out from among my people.'" (12:31)

QUESTION: The word *"laila"* — "[at] night" — seems extra. It would be sufficient to say, "He called for Moshe and Aharon and told them to rise and leave Egypt"?

ANSWER: When Moshe came before Pharaoh after the plague of darkness, Pharaoh angrily said to him, "I am warning you not to see my face anymore, because in the day when you will see my face you shall die." Moshe responded, "You have spoken correctly: I shall never see your face again" (10:28-29). Thereafter, Moshe did not return to Pharaoh.

After the plague of the firstborn, there was an uproar in the land of Egypt. Pharaoh called for Moshe, but he refused to come, saying, "Pharaoh made a promise that I should not see his face and that if I did, I would be killed." Pharaoh, knowing that he needed to see Moshe, began to plead, *"Laila"* — "Now it is night and I only promised *'beyom'* — that 'on the day' you would see my face you would die. Since it is dark and it is hard to see my face, please come speak to me and take the Jewish people out of the country."

(אור החיים)

* * *

Alternatively, when Moshe asked Pharaoh to release the children of Israel, he refused, arguing, "The people have to be here 400 years and only 210 have passed." Moshe responded, "You enslaved them inhumanely; they toiled for you both day and night. Their unceasing work for 210 years was equivalent to 400 years of slavery under normal conditions." Nevertheless, Pharaoh remained stubborn and did not let the Jews go.

After being punished with the tenth plague, the killing of the firstborn, Pharaoh finally yielded. Hastening to the Jewish neighborhood, he cried the word, *"Laila"* — "Night" — "I admit that Moshe is correct: Their laboring during the night completes the 400 years, and they are entitled to leave Egypt to serve Hashem."

* * *

In The Book of Job (28:3), Job praises Torah very highly and encourages man to be righteous. He contrasts Torah with night, stating that Torah is infinite while, *"keitz sam lachoshech"* — "Hashem has made a limit to darkness." The word *"keitz"* (קץ) has the numerical value of 190. Possibly, Job was alluding that Hashem deducted 190 years from the original 400 years of Egyptian bondage due to *choshech,* the laboring of the Jewish people during the darkness of the nights.

(בית יעקב)

"בבית אחד יאכל לא תוציא מן הבית מן הבשר חוצה ועצם לא תשברו בו"

"It must be eaten in one house, do not remove any of the meat from the house to the outside, and you shall not break a bone in it." (12:46)

QUESTION: Why in regard to taking meat outside is the violation said in the singular, *"lo totzi"* — and the violation of breaking the bone in the plural — *"lo tishberu"?*

ANSWER: According to *halacha,* it is forbidden for a member of a group eating the *karban Pesach* together to take a *kezayit* of meat to another house. If someone does and afterwards a second person takes this same piece of meat to another house, it is not considered a transgression. However, if a member of a group breaks a bone of the *karban Pesach,* and then another member breaks the same bone, he is to be punished for transgressing "Do not break a bone in it."

Therefore, the prohibition of taking meat out is expressed in the singular because it is violated only by the first person who carries it out. The prohibition of breaking the bone is stated in the plural because it can be violated by more than one person.

(ילקוט הדרוש בשם ספר תולדות אדם)

"שבעת ימים תאכל מצת... מצות יאכל את שבעת הימים"

"Seven days you shall eat *matzot*...*matzot* shall be eaten seven days." (13:6-7)

QUESTION: 1) Why does the first *pasuk* say *"tochal"* — "you shall eat"? — while the second *pasuk* says *"yei'acheil"* — "shall be eaten" (passive)? 2) Why in the first *pasuk* is *matzot* written without a "וי" and in the second with a "וי"?

ANSWER: It is incumbent upon each person to give *ma'ot chittim* before *Pesach* so that the poor will be able to properly celebrate the Yom Tov (*Shulchan Aruch, Orach Chaim* 429).

The first *pasuk* is referring to the giver and commands that *"tochal"* — he eat *matzot* to celebrate *Pesach*. The second *pasuk* is teaching that in addition to *your* celebrating, you must make sure that *matzot* is eaten *("yei'acheil")* by those who cannot afford it. They too must celebrate the festival for seven days.

A person may skimp on his own portion of *matza*, but he has no permission to skimp on the poor man's portion. The poor must be provided with everything in the fullest measure in order to have a happy and joyous *Yom Tov*. Consequently, when the Torah mentions *your* eating *("tochal")*, the word *"matzot"* is written without a "וי". However, to indicate that a person should make sure that the poor are able to eat *("yei'acheil")*, the word *"matzot"* is spelled with a "וי", alluding that the needs of the poor be provided in the fullest measure.

(הגר"א)

"והיה כי ישאלך בנך מחר לאמר מה זאת ואמרת אליו...."

"If your child asks you tomorrow 'What is this?' you should say to him...." (13:14)

QUESTION: The word *"machar"* — "tomorrow" — seems superfluous?

ANSWER: Rashi explains, יש מחר שהוא עכשיו ויש מחר שהוא לאחר זמן — "Sometimes the word '*machar*' (tomorrow) means 'now,' and sometimes it means 'in a time to come.'"

Rashi is not just offering an explanation of the term *"machar,"* but is also teaching an important lesson about rearing children. The term *"machar"* is not just a relative period of time, but a description of two types of *"bincha"* (sons).

There is a son who is *"achshav"* — "now" — he lives in the same spirit that you do and is a Torah observing Jew as yourself. There is also another son, who is *"achar zeman"* — "of a later time." He considers his Torah-observant father an "old timer" and considers himself a progressive denizen of a different spiritual era.

The Torah is instructing every father, "Even if you have a son who presently does not agree with your Torah way of thinking, you must bear in mind that he is *"bincha"* — *"your son."* Moreover, you as a father have to help him and give him the answers which will make him *"achshav"* — a Torah observant Jew like yourself

(לקוטי שיחות ח"ו ע' 268)

*   *   *

The previous Lubavitcher Rebbe, Rabbi Yosef Yitzchak Schneersohn (who passed away *Shabbat Parshat Bo, Yud Shevat* 5710), was like a father to many Jews and helped many non-observant Jews find their way back to *Yiddishkeit.* When asked why he spent so much time with nonreligious people, he explained that when a father has two children one of whom is healthy and the other sick, although he definitely loves the two of them equally, he usually spends more time trying to cure the sick one.

"והיה לאות על ידכה"

"It shall be for a sign upon your hand." (13:16)

QUESTION: What is the significance of the seven coils on the forearm?

ANSWER: The *tefillin* consist of two parts, one placed on the left arm facing the heart, the other on the head, the seat of intellect. One of the basic teachings implied in this, is that the head should rule the heart. The heart is considered the seat of emotions, *(midot)* which are generally divided into seven branches. Of the seven, the following three, namely: love *(chesed)*, fear *(gevurah)* and mercy *(tiferet)*, are the basic ones, and the other four (endurance *(netzach)*, splendor *(hod)*, bond *(yesod)*, sovereignty *(malchut)*, see Mystical Concepts in Chassidism, are secondary offshoots of the first three. Hence, the seven coils on the forearm are symbolic of these seven emotions, which should be controlled by the intellect.

("טאקס", מרחשון, תשי"ח)

* * *

The above may give an insight into the custom of Chabad when wrapping the seven coils on the forearm, there is a space made between the upper three and the lower four. (See notes of Rabbi Sholom Dovber Schneersohn, Fifth Lubavitcher Rebbe, on *Siddur, Torah Ohr.)*

"והיה לאות על ידכה"

"It shall be for a sign upon your hand." (13:16)

QUESTION: What is the meaning of the three coils on the middle finger?

ANSWER: One of the symbols of *tefillin* is that of the devotion and affection between G-d and Israel, which are frequently spoken of in terms of betrothal. Hence the coils around the finger are symbolic of the wedding ring, and one of the explanations of the triple coil is the triple reference to the betrothal between G-d and Israel in Hosea 2: 21-22. In fact, it is customary in many Jewish communities to quote this Scriptural text as one winds the straps around the finger, after having put on the head *tefillin.*

("טאקס", מרחשון, תשי"ח)

"וְלְטוֹטָפֹת בֵּין עֵינֶיךָ"

"And frontlets between your eyes." (13:16)

QUESTION: What is the significance of the two straps hanging down from the head *tefillin?*

ANSWER: The two straps that hang down from the head *tefillin* symbolize the flow of influence from the head to the rest of the body, on the right and left side of it. Hence, the two straps are a continuation of the strap that surrounds the head, and that begin to branch off from the special knot at the back of the head, which is the meeting place of the cerebrum and cerebellum, which is also the beginning of the spine.

All this is to indicate that, just as physically, the brain is the most vital nerve center that vitalizes and controls the entire body, so, spiritually, the intellect is to vitalize and guide the entire life of the Jew, and the body with all its limbs and organs must be functionaries to carry out the Divine commandments and precepts in daily life.

("טאקס", מרחשון, תשי"ח)

"וְהָיָה לְאוֹת עַל יָדְכָה וּלְטוֹטָפֹת בֵּין עֵינֶיךָ"

"It shall be for a sign upon your hand and frontlets between your eyes." (13:16)

QUESTION: Why does the *shel yad* — hand *tefillin* — have only one compartment while the *shel rosh* — head *tefillin* — has four?

ANSWER: *Tefillin shel rosh* are placed on the head, the seat of the human intellect, while the *tefillin shel yad* are placed on the hand, which represents the source of action.

Faculties of people vary greatly. Some are better in their studies and some are poorer. Some comprehend the subject matter profoundly and others superficially. Therefore, to recognize the differences between one head and another, the Torah portions of the *tefillin shel rosh* are put in separate compartments.

However, *mitzvot* have to be performed by everyone equally, regardless of whether one has a good head or a poor head, much understanding or little understanding. Thus, the Torah portions of *tefillin shel yad* are all in one compartment, because all are equally obligated to perform *mitzvot*.

(לקוטי בתר לקוטי ח״א)

* * *

The fact that the hand *tefillin* are put on before the head *tefillin,* represents the great and basic principle of the Jewish religion, that practice must come before theory. One must first fulfill the Divine commandments without question, and only then try to understand as much as possible their significance.

(״טאקס״, מרחשון, תשי״ח)

ෆ ෨

BESHALACH • בשלח

"ויהי בשלח פרעה את העם"

**"And it came to pass when Pharaoh sent out the people."
(13:17)**

QUESTION: The *Gemara (Megillah* 10b) states that the word *"vayehi"* often denotes a time of distress. Leaving Egypt was indeed an event that the Jewish people eagerly anticipated. After slaving for many years, undoubtedly, they wanted to become free people. Thus, why the use of *"vayehi"?*

ANSWER: Moshe pleaded with Pharaoh to release the Jewish people from Egyptian bondage. He stubbornly refused till Hashem performed many miracles. As strange as it may seem, there were still some Jews who thanked Pharaoh for *"beshalach Paroh et ha'am"* — permitting them to leave and sending them away. The Torah uses the expression *"vayehi"* to portray the sad situation that after all the sufferings under Pharaoh, some gave credit to Pharaoh for sending them away instead of praising and thanking Hashem.

(פניני התורה)

"ויהי בשלח פרעה את העם"

**"And it came to pass when Pharaoh sent out the people."
(13:17)**

QUESTION: Why is the cantillation *("trope"* printed above the Hebrew text) *revi'i munach* on the words *"vayehi beshalach"?*

ANSWER: Regrettably, there existed among the Jewish nation a group of wicked people uninterested in leaving Egypt. Had Hashem punished them publicly, the Egyptians would have erroneously thought that the suffering affected everyone, both the Jews and themselves. Therefore, during the plague of darkness, when the Egyptians were unable to see anything and were literally tied to their places, these unworthy Jews died and were buried.

The Torah relates, *"vachamushim alu B'nei Yisrael"* — "and B'nei Yisrael went up armed" (13:18). Rashi explains that the word *"chamushim"* alludes to the fact that only one fifth of the people left Egypt, while the other four fifths died.

Consequently, the words *"vayehi beshalach"* have the cantillation of *"revi'i munach"* (which can be read as meaning "four remains") to indicate that four of the five portions remained, and that only one fifth of the people left when Pharaoh sent them out.

(זר הצבי)

"ויקח משה את עצמות יוסף עמו"
"And Moshe took the bones of Yosef with him." (13:19)

QUESTION: The *Gemara (Sotah* 13a) says that while all the Jews were occupied with acquiring the gold and silver of the Egyptians, Moshe was occupied with the *mitzvah* of the "bones of Yosef." The *Gemara* connects this with the *pasuk "chacham-leiv yikach mitzvot"* — "The wise-hearted takes *mitzvot"* (Proverbs 10:8).

What wisdom did Moshe show here?

ANSWER: Moshe was considered a *Kohen* (for the 40 years the Jews were in the desert or at least until after the seven days of inauguration, see *Zevachim* 102a). It is forbidden for a *Kohen* to defile himself by contact with a corpse. However, a corpse no one is taking care of is considered a *meit mitzvah* and even a *Kohen* should defile himself for its sake.

All the Jews were occupied with gathering the gold and silver of the Egyptians, and no one took care of the bones of Yosef. Moshe, in his wisdom, occupied himself with the *mitzvah* of caring for the bones of Yosef because it was a case of *meit mitzvah,* for which even a *Kohen* may defile himself.

(תוספת ברכה)

"ויקח משה את עצמות יוסף עמו"
"Moshe took the bones of Yosef with him." (13:19)

QUESTION: In the *Gemara (Sotah* 13a) there is a dispute as to where Yosef was buried. According to one opinion he was interred in the crypt where the Kings of Egypt are buried, whereas another opinion is that he was buried in the Nile river. Yosef was definitely one of the greatest personalities of his time. It would be logical to assume that his burial place was a national monument; how then is it possible for such diverse opinions as to where he was buried?

ANSWER: The name "Yosef" can refer to the Jewish people. As the Psalmist says, "O Shepherd of Israel (Hashem), You who leads Yosef (the Jewish people) like a flock" (80:2). Since Yosef provided for his brothers and their families throughout the years of the Egyptian famine, all of Jacob's descendants who survived by Yosef's benevolence are called by his name (Rashi).

The views expressed in the *Gemara* can be explained as a metaphor for the survival of the Jewish people throughout the *galut.*

The issue is the source of strength of the Jewish people. What secret power is "buried" within them that helps them endure and survive all the persecutions they encounter throughout their lengthy exile? One opinion is that it is due to the "crypt of Kings" — their political connections to the highest officials in government. Fortunately, often the intelligence, wisdom, and contribution for the betterment of the country made by members of the Jewish people has been recognized, gaining them access to government. In turn, these individuals used their influence on behalf of their brothers.

Another view claims that their source of strength is the "Nile river" — a body of water completely separate from the land. This symbolizes that the Jewish people have nothing to do with the inhabitants of the country in which they dwell. Their absolute detachment and isolation from Egyptian society helped preserve their identity and ultimately enable them to survive the alien forces which sought their destruction.

In reality, both views are correct. Even when the Jew rises in government circles and in the eyes of its leaders, he must always remember to maintain his identity and his uniquely Jewish spirituality. This was actually *"Atzmut Yosef"* (lit. the bones) — the "essence" of Yosef, and the philosophy he embodied. Moshe "carried" this legacy and imparted it to Klal Yisrael.

(מצאתי בכתבי אבי הרב שמואל פסח ז"ל באגאמילסקי)

"ואמר פרעה לבני ישראל נבכים הם בארץ"

**"Pharaoh will say to the Jews: 'They are lost in the desert.'"
(14:3)**

QUESTION: All the Jews left Egypt or died during the days of darkness. To which Jews will Pharaoh speak?

ANSWER: Moshe told Pharaoh that the Jews wanted to leave Egypt to serve Hashem and that the trip would take only three days. Afterwards, they would return. Prior to their leaving, Hashem said to Moshe, "Speak into the ears of the people that they should borrow gold and silver" (11:2). This was to be kept secret so that Pharaoh should not find out that the Jews did not intend to return. Datan and Aviram, the infamous troublemakers, were not told so that they could not inform Pharaoh.

Thus, when it came time to leave Egypt, Datan and Aviram decided not to go because it was not worth the effort to make such a big trip in three days. When the Jewish people failed to return, Pharaoh said to Datan and Aviram, "It seems *your* people are lost in the desert."

(תרגום יונתן בן עוזיאל)

"ויגד למלך מצרים כי ברח העם ויהפך לבב פרעה ועבדיו"

"And it was told to the King of Egypt that the people fled; Pharaoh and his servants had a change of heart." (14:5)

QUESTION: The people did not *run* away. Were they not asked to leave?

ANSWER: In *Parshat Beshalach* the term *"am"* — "people" — refers to the *"eirev rav"* — a mixed multitude of Egyptians who left Egypt together with the Jewish people, and the expression *"B'nei Yisrael"* refers to the members of the Jewish community.

When Pharaoh asked the Jewish people to leave Egypt, he sent along with them a contingency of his own Egyptians. He anticipated that this "fifth column" would assure the return of the Israelites to Egypt. Suddenly, word reached Pharaoh that *"barach ha'am"* — his *own* people whom he sent along with the Jewish people had fled.

Pharaoh now had a change of heart for permitting the children of Israel to leave, because not only did he lose his free slaves, but he also lost his own subjects who enriched his coffers with taxes.

(אור החיים)

* * *

The children of Israel were originally destined to be slaves for 400 years in Egypt, but were only there 210 years. The word *"barach"* (ב ח) — "fled" — has the numerical value of 210. When the Egyptians began to complain to Pharaoh that *"barach ha'am"* — the Jews were there only 210 years — again his heart hardened and he regretted sending out the Jewish people prematurely.

(רבינו בחיי)

"ויאמר משה אל העם אל תיראו...ד' ילחם לכם ואתם תחרישון"

"Moshe said to the people, 'Do not fear...G-d will fight for you, and you shall be silent.'" (14:13-14)

QUESTION: Moshe should have only said, "Do not fear. G-d will fight for you." Why did he add "You shall be silent"?

ANSWER: The *Midrash* says: Continuously Hashem has an argument with Satan. Satan complains to Hashem that the Jewish people commit various crimes. Hashem tells Satan, "Instead of speaking evil about the Jewish people, let us compare their record with that of the Gentile world, and you will see how upright the Jewish people are."

However, Hashem has a problem when Satan complains that the Jewish people speak in *shul* during *davening* and the reading of the Torah. It is difficult for Him to defend them because in church the Gentiles are very quiet and well behaved.

Moshe was alluding to this and told the Jews, "Do not worry about any problem Satan tries to create, because Hashem will fight him and defend you. However, the condition is *"Ve'atem tacharishun"* — "You should be silent in *shul* during *davening* and the Torah reading. Do not speak any *devarim betteilim* — idle talk — because Hashem finds it difficult to defend us from *this* complaint of Satan."

(ילקוט האורים בשם חידת שמשון)

"וישם את הים לחרבה ויבקעו המים"
"Hashem made the sea dry land and the water split." (14:21)

QUESTION: Water normally flows, and only Hashem can alter the laws of nature and split the sea. Interestingly, according to the *Gemara (Sotah* 2a), pairing two people in marriage is as difficult as splitting the sea, and earning a *parnasah* — livelihood — is also as difficult as splitting the sea *(Pesachim* 118a).

What is the connection between the splitting of the sea, marriage, and *parnasah?*

ANSWER: When the children of Israel saw Pharaoh pursuing them into the wilderness, they formed a number of plans of action. One group favored a battle with the Egyptians, another group advised leaping into the sea, a third said to surrender and return to Egypt, and a fourth said to cry out to Hashem for help. Nobody dreamt of the possibility that the sea would split and that they would march through valiantly on dry land (see *Mechilta* 14:13).

Frequently, young people fantasize about their most suitable match. However, despite their plans, they meet their *"bashert"* in a totally unanticipated way, and often one marries someone from a distant place never originally envisioned. Similarly, in earning one's livelihood, an individual may have many plans and calculations, but ultimately Hashem often provides him an unanticipated source of income.

(שמעתי מדודי הרב ברוך הכהן ז"ל כהן מח"ס קול תודה)

"ויסר את אפן מרכבתיו וינהגהו בכבדת"

"And He took off the wheel of their chariots, and He made them drive heavily." (14:25)

QUESTION: Why does the *pasuk* say *"ofan"* — "wheel" — in the singular, although a chariot has four wheels?

ANSWER: Had Hashem removed all four wheels of their chariots, the horses could have exerted themselves and dragged the chariots on the ground. However, by removing only *one* wheel, Hashem caused their ride to be turbulent and agonizing with the chariots violently swaying from side to side. Thus, the riders were pummeled and pounded by the damaged chariots.

(שער בת רבים)

"ויושע ד' ביום ההוא את ישראל מיד מצרים"

"Thus G-d saved Israel that day out of the hand of the Egyptians." (14:30)

QUESTION: It would have been sufficient to state, "Thus G-d saved Israel out of the hand of the Egyptians." What do the words "that day" signify?

ANSWER: Pharaoh commanded that the Jewish boys be drowned in the river, but when Moshe was born, his mother managed to hide him for three months. Unable to conceal his whereabouts any longer, she was compelled to place him in the river and leave his fate to Hashem. That day was the twenty first of *Nissan* (the seventh day of *Pesach*). Angels in heaven witnessing this pleaded before Hashem, "The one who will be reciting praise to you on this day should be smitten on this day?!" Their plea was accepted: Moshe's life was spared *(Sotah* 12b).

Arriving at the shores of the sea on the twenty first of *Nissan,* the people feared for their lives when they saw the Egyptians pursuing them. Hashem came to their rescue and saved them from the hands of the Egyptians. However, in reality it had all started many years earlier when on *that day,* He accepted the plea of the angels and spared the life of Moshe, who ultimately redeemed the Jews from Egypt.

(מלא העומר)

"וירא ישראל את היד הגדלה אשר עשה ד' במצרים...ויאמינו בד' ובמשה עבדו"

"And Israel saw the big hand which G-d made in Egypt...and they believed in G-d and his servant Moshe." (14:31)

QUESTION: What "big hand" did they see, and how did this cause them to believe in Moshe?

ANSWER: Pharaoh ordered the drowning of newborn Jewish boys. When Moshe was born, his mother managed to keep his birth a secret for three months. Afterwards, she put him in a box and placed it at the river's edge.

Pharaoh's daughter came to bathe and noticed the box. The Torah relates that she stretched out her arm and took it. Rashi (2:5) explains that when she stretched out her hand, it miraculously elongated and she was able to retrieve the box. When the Jewish people learned about "the big hand" which Hashem made many years ago in Egypt to save Moshe, they recognized his stature and believed in him.

(ילקוט האורים בשם לב ארי')

"זה א-לי ואנוהו...מרכבת פרעה...ומבחר שלשיו טבעו בים סוף"

"This is my G-d and I will glorify Him...The chariots of Pharaoh and his chosen captains sank in the sea." (15:2-4)

QUESTION: What is the connection between glorifying G-d and the drowning of "his chosen captains" *(shalishav)?*

ANSWER: Based on the words *"zeh Keili ve'anveihu"* — "this is my G-d and I will glorify Him" (15:2), the *Gemara (Shabbat* 133b) learns that when one performs a *mitzvah*, it should be done *behiddur* — in a beautiful way. According to an opinion in *Gemara (Bava Kamma* 9b) this means one should allow himself to spend an "outside" third extra, i.e., one should spend an amount equal to a third of the price of the *more* expensive *tefillin, Sefer Torah,* etc.

According to the *Targum Yonatan Ben Uziel* 14:7, the word *"shalishav"* refers to three horses. Originally it was a custom for a chariot to be drawn only by one horse; in the days of Yosef, Pharaoh changed it to two. Wanting to overtake the Jewish people quickly, Pharaoh now used three prize horses to pull each chariot.

Upon being saved by Hashem from the vicious Pharaoh, who added a "third" in his effort to destroy them, the Jewish people declared that in appreciation they would perform *mitzvot behiddur,* by adding up to an additional third.

(בני יששכר מאמרי שבתות מא' ב' אות ה')

"תבאמו ותטעמו בהר נחלתך"

"You will bring them and plant them on the mount of your inheritance." (15:17)

QUESTION: By saying, "You will bring *them,*" instead of "You will bring *us,*" Moshe unknowingly prophesied that *he* would not enter *Eretz Yisrael* (Rashi).

Why did Moshe say that *anyone* would come to *Eretz Yisrael,* since they would all die in the wilderness due to the sin of the *meraglim* — spies? (See Rashi.)

ANSWER: Eighty years earlier, Pharaoh decreed that all Jewish baby boys be thrown into the river. To circumvent this, the Jewish women would go out to the fields to give birth and leave the babies there. Hashem provided for them two stones out of which flowed milk and honey. When the Egyptians were out in the fields, the ground would crack open, allowing the children to fall in, and then close up and hide them. When the Egyptians would leave, the ground would open up to let them breathe the fresh air. When Hashem appeared at the splitting of the sea, they sang, "This is my G-d," recognizing the G-d who cared for them when they were little babies *(Sotah* 11b).

Only those people who were between the ages of 20 and 60 when the Jews left Egypt died in the wilderness due to the sin of the *meraglim.* Anyone younger or older survived *(Bava Batra* 121b). Thus, the people who sang the *shirah* were 80 years old at that time, and they all merited to come to *Eretz Yisrael.*

The only exception was Moshe. He too, was 80 years old, but he did not enter *Eretz Yisrael.* Consequently, Rashi correctly says that Moshe unknowingly prophesied that *he* would not come into *Eretz Yisrael,* but all the others his age, who had sung the *shirah,* did indeed come to *Eretz Yisrael.*

(ילקוט האורים)

"ותקח מרים הנביאה אחות אהרן את התף בידה"

"Miriam the prophetess, the sister of Aharon, took the tambourine in her hand." (15:20)

QUESTION: 1) Instead of saying *"et hatof"* — *"the tambourine"* — indicating a specific one — could it not have just said *"tof"* — "a tambourine"? 2) Why does the Torah mention here that she was a prophetess?

ANSWER: Eighty years before *Kriat Yam Suf* — the splitting of the Red Sea — Pharaoh issued a decree to drown Jewish children. At that time, Amram, apprehensive about being married and having children, divorced his wife, Yocheved. His daughter Miriam implored him to remarry Yocheved and also prophesied that her mother would give birth to a child who would take the Jewish people out of *galut.* Due to Miriam's insistence, he remarried Yocheved at a very happy wedding celebration in which Miriam and her younger brother, Aharon, danced and entertained *(Sotah* 12a). Throughout all the years Miriam cherished the tambourine she used at the wedding and carried it with her.

When Moshe crossed the sea with the Jewish people, the redemption from Egypt reached its fruition. Experiencing the fulfillment of her prophecy, Miriam joyously took out *the* wedding tambourine and called on everyone to rejoice.

(שמעתי מהרב מנחם מענדל שיחי׳ אלפערין)

"ותקח מרים הנביאה אחות אהרן את התף בידה ותצאן כל הנשים אחריה בתפים ובמחלת ותען להם מרים שירו לד׳"

"And Miriam the prophetess, the sister of Aharon, took the tambourine in her hand, and all the women went out after her with tambourines and dancing. And Miriam answered them, 'Sing to G-d.'" (15:20-21)

QUESTION: Whom did Miriam answer?

ANSWER: Upon witnessing the great miracles at the Red Sea, Moshe and the Jewish people sang praise to Hashem. Soon afterwards, Miriam led a group of Jewish women with instruments. The men noticed this and told them that women are forbidden to sing in the presence of men. Miriam *answered* them, "We will only play the music, and you men will be the ones to sing."

This fits in very well with the words of the *pasuk: "vata'an"* — "and she answered" — *"lahem"* — "to them" (masculine plural). If Miriam were telling the women to sing, grammatically it should have said *"vetomar lahen"* — "and she said to them" (feminine plural).

(שמעתי מזקני הרב צבי הכהן ע״ה קפלן)

* * *

There are opinions that Miriam led the women in song (Rashi). In order not to violate Torah law, they played musical instruments so that their voices would be drowned out and not heard by men.

(פרדס יוסף)

"ותען להם מרים שירו לד' כי גאה גאה סוס ורכבו רמה בים"

"Miriam told them 'Sing to G-d: He is mighty and exalted; the horse and it's rider He threw into the sea.'" (15:21)

QUESTION: Why did she emphasize to the women the drowning of the horse and rider?

ANSWER: The ultimate purpose of the Exodus from Egypt was to receive the Torah, which all men are obligated to study. According to the *Gemara (Sotah* 21a), although women are not obligated to fulfill the *mitzvah* of Torah study, they are rewarded for helping their husbands and children study.

When Hashem drowned the Egyptians and their horses, Miriam wondered why the unfortunate horses were punished. What wrong had they done? She concluded that since the horses were assisting the riders in their evil plans, they too deserved punishment. From this she deduced how great the reward would be for women who assist and inspire their husbands and children to study Torah.

(פרדס יוסף)

"ויאמר אם שמוע תשמע לקול ד' אלקיך והישר בעיניו תעשה והאזנת למצותיו ושמרת כל חקיו כל המחלה אשר שמתי במצרים לא אשים עליך כי אני ד' רפאך"

"And He said, 'If you will surely listen to the voice of G-d and do what is right in His eyes, hear His commandments, and keep all His statutes, then any of the diseases I placed upon Egypt I will not bring upon you; for I am G-d your healer.'" (15:26)

QUESTION? What is the connection between obeying Torah and Hashem being the healer?

ANSWER: Unfortunately, there are people who refuse to fulfill *mitzvot* with the argument that they do not understand their purpose. The response to them is: When one, G-d forbid, is ill, he visits a doctor who prescribes medication. Though the patient is not a pharmacist and has no knowledge of the effect of the medication, he puts his trust in the doctor and eventually becomes healthy. Likewise, Hashem is our doctor. He "prescribes" Torah and *mitzvot* to keep us spiritually "healthy." We must follow His instructions regardless of whether we understand how they can benefit us.

(נחל קדומים)

* * *

Spiritual illness is caused by our *"yeitzer"* (יצר) — "evil inclination." The word *"yeitzer"* has the numerical value of 300. G-d is fire *(Devarim 4:24)* and so is his Torah (Jeremiah 23:29). The Hebrew word for fire — *"eish"* (אש) — numerically adds up to 301 as does *"rofecha"* (רפאך) — "your healer." Thus, the fire of Torah (301) is stronger and nullifies the *"yeitzer"* (300). Consequently, through Torah study and observance, we merit *"rofecha"* (301) — a healing from Hashem.

(נחל קדומים)

"ויראו בני ישראל ויאמרו איש אל אחיו מן הוא כי לא ידעו מה הוא
ויאמר משה אלהם הוא הלחם אשר נתן ד' לכם לאכלה"

"The children of Israel saw it, and they said one to another, 'It is *mann*,' for they did not know what it was. Moshe said to them, 'This is the bread which G-d has given you to eat.'" (16:15)

QUESTION: Why did they name it *"mann"* if they were unsure what it was ?

ANSWER: The *Gemara (Ta'anit* 24a) relates that when the *gabba'ei tzedakah* (people in charge of charity collecting) would see Elazar of Birta, they would run away because he would donate everything he had. Once he went to the market to buy a wedding gift for his daughter. When the *gabba'ei tzedakah* tried to avoid him, he ran after them and asked what cause they were collecting for. When they told him they were raising money for a poor bride and groom, he gave them all his money but one coin, with which he bought some wheat. He put the wheat in his storeroom and went to the *Beit Midrash* to learn.

When his wife came home, she asked her daughter, "What did your father bring?" She replied, "Whatever he brought is in the storeroom." They were unable to open the door because the storeroom was filled with wheat from corner to corner, so his daughter ran to the *Beit Midrash* and excitedly told him, "Come see what the G-d who loves you did." He immediately said, "I forbid you to use it for anything more than your bare necessities." Rashi explains that he was harsh to his daughter because he realized that the wheat had multiplied miraculously and it is forbidden for a person to derive benefit from a miracle.

When the Jews went out in the morning and saw on the ground "something fine and scaly," they did not know what it was. Puzzled, one said to the other, "Undoubtedly, this is something derived from a miracle." Therefore, they called it *"mann"* (מן) which is the abbreviation for *"ma'aseh nissim"* (מעשה נסים) "something made miraculously" — and they resolved not to benefit from it.

Moshe told them, "This is the bread which Hashem has given you to eat — since in the desert there are no means of obtaining food, without this bread from heaven your lives are in jeopardy. In a case of mortal danger it is permitted to benefit from a miracle."

(בית יעקב)

**"ויאמרו איש אל אחיו מן הוא כי לא ידעו מה הוא ויאמר משה אלהם
הוא הלחם אשר נתן ד' לאכלה"**

"They said one to another, 'It is *mann,*' for they did not know what is was. Moshe said to them, 'This is the bread G-d has given you to eat.'" (16:15)

QUESTION: What more did they know about the *mann* after Moshe had spoken than they knew before?

ANSWER: When the Jews first saw the *mann,* they were in doubt as to what *berachah* to make over it. Bread requires *"hamotzei,"* and cake *"mezonot."*

The word *mann* (מן) means "food," and is also an acronym for *"Mah Nevarech?"* — "What blessing should we recite?" Upon seeing the *mann,* they said one to another *"mann hu"* — "obviously it is food." However, *"Mah nevarech"* — "What blessing should we recite?" — *"ki lo yadu"* — "because they did not know" — *"מיהי הוא?"* — "is it המוציא or מזונות?"

Moshe said to them, *"Hu halechem"* — "It is bread which Hashem gave you from heaven — and since it does not grow from the ground, you should make the blessing *'Hamotzi lechem min hashamayim'* — 'who brings forth bread from Heaven.'"

(בני יששכר שבתות מאמר ג' סי' ג')

"ובני ישראל אכלו את המן ארבעים שנה"

"And the children of Israel ate the manna forty years." (16:35)

QUESTION: In the desert, all the needs of the Jewish people were provided by Hashem. Food came from heaven, and their clothing grew with them. How was one able to fulfill the *mitzvah* of *tzedakah* (helping those in need)?

ANSWER: The manna that the Jews received in the desert tasted like the particular food each eater had in mind *(Yoma* 75a). A poor person had never tasted expensive foods, so the *tzedakah* of a rich person was to recommend to a poor person what to have in mind while eating so that his palate would enjoy hitherto untasted delicacies.

"ויבא עמלק וילחם עם ישראל"

"Amalek came and fought with the Jews." (17:8)

QUESTION: How was Amalek able to attack the Jews when they were protected from all sides with *ananei hakavod* — clouds of glory?

ANSWER: According to the *Midrash Tanchuma (Parshat Teitze* 10), some members of the tribe of Dan worshipped idols which they took with them from Egypt. The clouds cast out these people, and thus, they were vulnerable to attack. Moshe called on Yehoshua to gather together a group of righteous people and fight Amalek on behalf of these Jews.

From this we can learn a lesson of cardinal importance: Even when a Jew has stooped, G-d forbid, to the extent of worshipping idols, it is incumbent even on *tzaddikim* to do everything possible to help save him and return him to the Jewish fold.

(כ"ק אדמו"ר)

"ויאמר משה אל יהושע בחר לנו אנשים וצא הלחם בעמלק...ומשה אהרן וחור עלו ראש הגבעה"

"Moshe said to Yehoshua, 'Choose people for us to go do battle with Amalek'...Moshe, Aharon and Chur ascended to the top of the hill." (17:9-10)

QUESTION: Why was it necessary to have a team consisting of Moshe, Aharon, Yehoshua, and Chur to fight Amalek?

ANSWER: Under normal circumstances, when the Jewish people behave properly, Amalek is unable to attack them. However, he attacked the Jews in the city of Rephidim, whose name indicates two reasons for their vulnerability to attack:

1) *"Rafu yedeihem min hamitzvot"* — their involvement in *mitzvot* became weakened." 2) *"Pirud"* — lack of unity (see *Keli Yakar*).

The first letters of the names "Aharon," "Chur," "Yehoshua," and "Moshe" form the acronym for *"achim"* (אחים) — "brothers." Moshe's call to the Jewish people was to act as brothers, live in brotherly harmony and be united in the study of Torah and observance of *mitzvot*. This would assure that Amalek would be unable to penetrate the Jewish camp.

(ילקוט ראובני)

"ויאמר כי יד על כס י-ה מלחמה לד' בעמלק מדר דר"

"And he said: 'The hand upon the throne of G-d; G-d maintains war against Amalek from generation to generation.'" (17:16)

QUESTION: Why is Hashem so angry at Amalek that He commanded us to wipe out his remembrance entirely?

ANSWER: The Jews who left Egypt witnessed the glory of Hashem and the miracles He performed. This brought them to the highest level of *emunah* (faith in Hashem). Amalek's attack on the Jewish people was not merely intended to destroy them physically, but to detach them from Hashem spiritually.

The name "Amalek" has the numerical value of 240, which is the same numerical value as *"safek"* (ספק) — "doubt." Amalek wanted to chill the Jewish people's enthusiasm for Hashem by putting doubts in their minds about Hashem. Since Amalek is our greatest adversary, Hashem swore He will not rest till he is eradicated. Whenever a Jew has doubts about *Yiddishkeit,* Amalek is at work.

(כתר שם טוב, הוספות סי' צ"ג)

CSEO

SHABBAT SHIRAH • שבת שירה

"ויהי ביום השביעי יצאו מן העם ללקט ולא מצאו"

"On *Shabbat* some people went out to pick manna and they did not find any." (16:27)

QUESTION: The word *"matza'u"* — "find" — is used in regard to finding a lost object. Since no manna was lost, the text should read *"velo haya"* — "and there wasn't any"?

ANSWER: Moshe told the Jews that on Friday there would be a double portion of manna, one for Friday and one for *Shabbat*, when no manna would be delivered. The infamous troublemakers, Datan and Aviram thought this would be a good opportunity to "prove" to the people Moshe's dishonesty. Friday evening they secretly put out manna in the field and invited people to come with them *Shabbat* morning to collect it. The birds, upon hearing this evil plan, quickly ate it up. Consequently, when Datan, Aviram, and their faction came out to the fields, they did not *find* any manna.

(ר׳ מאיר מפרימישלאן זצ״ל)

* * *

QUESTION: What is the reason for the custom to put out food for the birds on *Erev Shabbat Shirah?*

ANSWER: On *Shabbat Shirah,* when we read about the manna that Hashem provided for the Jewish people, it is customary to put out food for the birds on *Erev Shabbat* as a reward for the *Kiddush Hashem* they brought about.

(ר׳ מאיר מפרימישלאן זצ״ל)

* * *

Alternatively, the *Maharal* of Prague would instruct the teachers of young children to gather their students in the *shul* yard on *Shabbat Shira* and relate to them the story of the splitting of the sea. They were also to tell the children that at the time of *Kriat Yam Suf* (splitting of the Red Sea) Hashem performed a miracle and trees with beautiful fruit grew in the sea (see *Midrash* Rabbah 22:1). When the Jews sang the *Shirah,* the birds sang and danced. The little Jewish children picked fruits from the trees and fed the birds. To commemorate this event, we put out food for the birds *Erev Shabbat Shirah.*

* * *

The teachers would give them *kasha* (buckwheat) to throw to the birds. And afterward the *Maharal* would bless the children and also the parents that they should merit to see them enter to Torah, marriage and good deeds.

(ספר השיחות תש״ב ע׳ 73 - לקוטי שיחות ח״ב ע׳ 522)

* * *

Some have the custom to feed *wheat* to the birds on *Shabbat Shirah.*

(מגן אברהם שכ״ד, ז׳ וספר תוספת שבת)

It is the custom of *Chabad* to eat *kasha* on *Shabbat Shirah.*

(היום יום י״ז שבט)

This custom is based on the *pasuk:* "Hasam gevuleich shalom cheilev chitim yasbi'eich" — "He has made peace within your borders; He satiated you with the finest of wheat" (Psalms 147:14). Thus, on *Shabbat Shirah,* when we read that Hashem emancipated the Jewish people from Egyptian bondage and prepared them to be in their own geographical boundaries and also the boundaries of Torah, it is customary to eat wheat (buckwheat).

The word *"beshalach"* (בשלח) is an acronym for the words "בשבת שירה לאכל חטים" — "On *Shabbat Shirah* to eat wheat (buckwheat)."

(עוללות אפרים)

૯૩ ૪૭

ט"ו בשבט • TU BESHEVAT

"באחד בשבט ראש השנה לאילן כדברי בית שמאי בית הלל אומרים
בחמשה עשר בו"

**"On the first day of *Shevat* is the new year for the tree
according to *Beit Shamai. Beit Hillel says* it is on the 15th of
Shevat." (Rosh Hashanah 2a)**

QUESTION: Why is it necessary for us to know the date of
the New Year for the trees?

ANSWER: The Hebrew calendar is set up according to a
seven year cycle, the seventh year is known as the *shemittah* year,
in which the land is left idle and no work is done in the fields.
During the six year, the first, second, fourth and fifth year of the
cycle, the farmers have to set aside *ma'aser rishon* (first tithe) for
the Levi, and *ma'aser sheini* (second tithe) is brought to Jerusalem
to be eaten. On the third and sixth year, *ma'aser oni* is given to the
poor people in lieu of *ma'aser sheini.*

Ma'aser must be given from the fruits which grow on the tree
each year. One cannot give from produce of the current year for
another year. For purposes of *ma'aser* from trees, the new year is
reckoned from the time when the fruits of the trees begin to
blossom. *Tu BeShevat* is the cut-off date between one year and the
next. In the year which follows *shemittah,* fruits which blossomed
before *Tu BeShevat* belong to the first year of the cycle, and fruits
which blossom after *Tu BeShevat* belong to the second year of the
cycle.

"באחד בשבט ראש השנה לאילן כדברי ב"ש, ב"ה אומרים בט"ו"

"On the first day of *Shevat* is the new year for the tree according to *Beit Shamai*. *Beit Hillel* says, it is on the 15th of *Shevat.*" *(Rosh Hashanah* 2a)

QUESTION: What is the basis of their dispute?

ANSWER: The *Mishnah (Rosh Hashanah* 16a) states that on the festival of *Sukkot* (15th *Tishrei*) the world is judged in regard to water. This is not a contradiction to the opinion in the *Gemara* which states that on *Rosh Hashanah* (1st *Tishrei*) the entire world is judged, because the judgment on *Rosh Hashanah* is general, but the details regarding water are determined on *Sukkot*.

According to the *Talmud Yerushalmi (Rosh Hashanah* 1:2), the significance of the New Year for trees is that until then all trees live on the water of the previous year. After *Rosh Chodesh Shevat* the trees derive their life source from the water of the new year. Thus, the effect of the new water occurs four months after the period of judgment.

Thus, *Beit Shamai* and *Beit Hillel* are disputing which has a greater significance, the potential (בכח) or the actual (בפועל). *Beit Shamai* is of the opinion that the potential is of primary significance. Consequently, according to *Beit Shamai,* since in potential the judgment of water took place on the first of *Tishrei,* four months later we celebrate the New Year of the trees, because they are now potentially deriving their life source from the waters which were included in the judgment of the entire world four months ago.

However, according to *Beit Hillel,* primacy is given to that which is actual. Thus, the actual decision on water takes place on the fifteenth of *Tishrei.* Therefore, four months later, on the fifteenth of *Shevat,* the trees start actually living from the new waters.

(לקוטי שיחות ח"ו)

"באחד בשבט ראש השנה לאילן כדברי ב"ש, ב"ה אומרים בט"ו"

"On the first day of *Shevat* is the new year for the tree according to *Beit Shamai*. *Beit Hillel says* it is on the 15th of *Shevat*." (Rosh Hashanah 2a)

QUESTION: The Torah states, *"ki ha'adam eitz hasadeh"* — "Man is like the tree of the field" *(Devarim* 20:19). The Jewish people have often been compared to different trees; what lesson can man learn from trees?

ANSWER: Trees teach us the following:

1) A tree is planted by first putting a kernel (seed) in the ground. Afterwards it is necessary to constantly water the ground and remove all weeds. In each and every Jew, Hashem planted a Divine seed — his soul. It is man's obligation to water it with Torah study and protect it by weeding out bad friends and influences.

2) A healthy tree continues to grow and grow. A healthy Jew must continuously grow spiritually. This is accomplished through studying Torah and performing *mitzvot.*

3) To assure that a young tree will grow straight, it is tied to two supports, one on each side. To ensure that a young child grows beautifully, the parents must always be at his side and constantly supervise him.

4) The strength of the tree depends on how well it is rooted in the ground. The root of the Jew is his *emunah.* The stronger our *emunah,* the better Jews we are.

5) The beauty of a tree is the fruit it produces. *Mitzvot* and *ma'asim tovim* — good deeds — are man's fruits. The more one does, the more beautiful a Jew one is.

(ספרים)

"באחד בשבט ראש השנה לאילן כדברי ב"ש, ב"ה אומרים בט"ו"

"On the first day of *Shevat* is the new year for the tree according to *Beit Shamai*. *Beit Hillel says* it is on the 15th of *Shevat*." (*Rosh Hashanah* 2a)

QUESTION: All the different New Years discussed in the *Mishnah* are mentioned in plural. Why is this New Year mentioned in singular "for the *tree*" (אילן) instead of "for the *trees*" (אילנות)?

ANSWER: The Torah commands that on the *yom tov* of *Sukkot* we take a *"peri eitz hadar"* — "a beautiful fruit of a tree" (*Vayikra* 23:43). Our sages say this refers to the *etrog* — the citron. People go through great expense to purchase a beautiful *etrog* in order to fulfill the *mitzvah* in an exceptional way. The *Mishnah* tells that *Tu BeShevat* is the New Year for the tree, and by using a singular term it alludes that we should pray particularly *"la'ilan"* — "for *the* tree" — namely the *etrog* tree, which is particularly important to us. On this day, one should beseech G-d to be granted a beautiful *etrog* with which to perform the Torah's command.

(בני יששכר)

* * *

The word *"ilan"* (אילן) — "tree" — has the numerical value of 91, which is also the numerical value of א-ד-נ-י י-ה-ו-ה (The L-rd G-d). This emphasizes that the trees of the field are not the work of man, but that of A-mighty G-d.

(נטעי גבריאל)

"נוהגין האשכנזים להרבות במיני פירות של אילנות"

"[On *Tu BeShevat*] Ashkenazi Jews are accustomed to eat many different fruits from trees." (*Magen Avraham* 131:16)

QUESTION: When one eats new fruits which one did not eat throughout the year, one makes a *berachah shehechiyanu*. Should it be recited before the *berachah* of *"borei pri ha'eitz"* or after?

ANSWER: It should be recited before. The reason why *"shehechiyanu"* precedes *"borei peri ha'eitz"* is the following:

"shehechiyanu" is made when one experiences joy. In reality, joy is experienced at the time one sees the new fruits on the trees or displayed in the store, and it would be proper to make the *"shehechiyanu"* at that time. However, it is our custom to wait with the *"shehechiyanu"* till we actually eat the fruit. Therefore, since the obligation to recite the *berachah shehechiyanu* came some time ago, and now when one want to eat the fruit one is obligated to make a *"borei peri ha'eitz,"* *"shehechiyanu"* is recited first because it is an earlier obligation.

(סדר ברכת הנהנין פי״א סעי׳ י״ב - פמ״ג שו״ע או״ח סי׳ רכ״ה)

℣ ™

YITRO • יתרו

"וישמע יתרו"

"And Yitro heard." (18:1)

QUESTION: Rashi writes, "Yitro had seven names; one was 'Yeter' because he 'added' a *parshah* in the Torah: *"ve'atah techezeh"* — "and you should seek out" (18:21).

When Yitro saw how hard Moshe was working, the first thing he said was, *"Lo tov hadavar asher atah oseh"* — "What you are doing is not good" (18:17). The *pasuk "ve'atah techezeh"* is four *pesukim* later. Why isn't the *parshah* Yitro added called *"Lo tov hadavar"*?

ANSWER: Some people are quire critical and ready to say "what you are doing is not good." It is easy to criticize, so Yitro is not entitled to credit for finding fault with Moshe's judicial procedure. He receives credit, rather, for his constructive suggestion.

(ליקוטי יהושע)

"וישמע יתרו כהן מדין חתן משה"

"Yitro the High Priest of Midian, the father-in-law of Moshe, heard." (18:1)

QUESTION: Why does the Torah *now* cite Yitro's already-mentioned relationship to Moshe and his position?

ANSWER: In the times of Kings David and Shlomo the Jews did not accept converts because the Jewish people were then at the height of their glory, and it was suspected that the motivation of the would-be convert was not Torah and *mitzvot,* but the prosperity and glory of the Jewish people.

If so, why did King Shlomo accept the daughter of Pharaoh as a convert and then marry her? The answer is that she was an exception to the rule. As the daughter of a king, she already had no lack of glory, and therefore her only intent in converting was her love for Torah and *mitzvot (Yevamot* 24b, see *Tosafot).*

When the Jews left Egypt and the sea split, the entire world witnessed the greatness of the Jewish people. From all over, people wanted to convert and become a part of the Jewish nation. Since their intent was to share the glory of the Jewish people and not sincere love for *Yiddishkeit,* they were rejected.

However when Yitro decided to convert, he was accepted because, as the famous High Priest of Midian, he could not be suspected as a seeker of glory. In addition, it was not likely that he was converting out of fear of the Jewish people, because nobody would harm the father-in-law of Moshe.

(ילקוט האורים)

"וישמע יתרו את כל אשר עשה אלקים למשה...ויקח יתרו את צפרה אשת משה אחר שלוחיה"

"Yitro heard what G-d had done to Moshe...and Yitro took with him Tzipporah, Moshe's wife, after he had sent her away." (18:1-2)

QUESTION: What had Yitro heard that Hashem had done to Moshe that prompted him to come with Tzipporah?

ANSWER: When Hashem appeared to Moshe for the first time and asked him to be his messenger to Pharaoh and redeem the Jews from Egypt, Moshe was reluctant. Hashem became angry and told Moshe, "Originally I had planned for you to be a *Kohen;* now that you are refusing your mission, Aharon will be the *Kohen* in your stead" *(Zevachim* 102a).

When Moshe finally agreed, he divorced his wife Tzipporah before going to Egypt so that he could be entirely dedicated to the mission of redeeming the Jewish people. The word *"shilucheha"* can mean "after he divorced her," as in the term *"veshilchah"* in connection with divorce *(Devarim* 24:1).

After Yitro heard what Hashem had done to Moshe, he decided to bring back Tzipporah. Now that Moshe was no longer a *Kohen,* it was permissible for him to marry a divorcee and he could, thus, remarry Tzipporah.

(נחל קדומים)

"ויאמר אל משה אני חתנך יתרו בא אליך ואשתך"

"And he said to Moshe, 'I, your father-in-law Yitro, am coming to you along with your wife.'" (18:6)

QUESTION: He should have merely said *"chotencha ba eilecha"* — "your father-in-law is coming to you"; the words *"ani"* — I — and "Yitro" are superfluous?

ANSWER: According to the Arizal, Yitro was originally Kayin and Moshe was Hevel. Tzipporah, the wife of Moshe, was originally Hevel's twin sister and Kayin killed Hevel to obtain her for himself.

The first letters of the words "אני חתנך יתרו" are an acronym for *"achi"* (אחי) — "my brother." Yitro informed Moshe that he was the *gilgul* — reincarnation — of Kayin, and that since Moshe was the reincarnation of Hevel, they were brothers. To atone for the crime that he committed by killing him and taking away his twin sister, he was bringing him back Tzipporah, who was the reincarnation of that sister.

(בית יעקב)

"ויחד יתרו על כל הטובה אשר עשה ד' לישראל אשר הצילו מיד מצרים"

"Yitro was happy for all the good that G-d did for the Jews for saving him from the hand of the Egyptians." (18:9)

QUESTION: Why did Yitro use a singular expression *"hitzilo"* — saving *him* — and not the plural *"hitzilam"* — "saving *them"?*

ANSWER: Pharaoh had three advisors, Job, Yitro and Bilam. Considering the Jewish people a serious threat to him and the land of Egypt, he called his advisors and consulted with them. At the conference, Bilam suggested the idea of drowning all newborn Jewish boys. Job was silent. Yitro not wanting to be present when plans were being made against the Jewish people, ran away. In the end, Bilam was killed, Job endured his famous sufferings, and Yitro, who ran away, was rewarded to have Moshe as his son-in-law and his descendants as members of the *Sanhedrin (Sotah* 11a).

When Yitro heard of the rescue through the drowning of Egyptians, he was happy for the good Hashem did for the Jewish people. In addition, he was happy and grateful that Hashem had given *him* the idea to run away from Pharaoh's conference. Thanks to this, *he* was prevented from suffering or perishing with the Egyptians.

(באר מים חיים)

"עתה ידעתי כי גדול ד' מכל האלהים"

"Now I know that G-d is the greatest of all deities." (18:11)

QUESTION: Why did Yitro *now* come to this realization?

ANSWER: When Hashem told Moshe about the coming plague of the killing of the firstborn, He also said, "and against all the gods of Egypt I will execute judgment" (12:12). Ultimately, all the idols were destroyed except for one — Ba'al Tzefon (see Rashi 14:2).

Yitro was a theologian and very familiar with all deities. Upon learning the fate of all the idols, he was convinced of their worthlessness. However, he remained with some doubts in regard to Hashem's supremacy due to the survival of Ba'al Tzefon.

Actually, Hashem permitted Ba'al Tzefon to remain in order to mislead the Egyptians. When they chased after the Jews and found them camping at the shores of the Red Sea, they were certain that the power of the Ba'al Tzefon was aiding them. Consequently, they thought, they would conquer and retrieve the gold and silver the Jews had taken from them. Eventually, the

Egyptians were drowned in the sea and Ba'al Tzefon, too, was destroyed.

The miraculous splitting of the sea encouraged Yitro to join the Jewish people. He declared, *"Now* that *all* the gods of the Egyptians, including Ba'al Tzefon, have been destroyed, I no longer have any doubts and am totally convinced that your G-d is the true and only one."

(מלא העומר)

"עתה ידעתי כי גדול ד' מכל האלהים"

"Now I know that G-d is the greatest of all deities." (18:11)

QUESTION: To say that Hashem is *greater* than all the gods is heresy because it implies that other gods have some substance too; why would Yitro say such a thing?

ANSWER: This statement is not one of relative comparison, but of total rejection. Yitro was the High Priest of Midian and a very prominent theologian. He was familiar with all the gods the pagan world worshipped. After learning of the miracles Hashem performed, he was convinced of the nothingness and worthlessness of all the other deities and of Hashem's identity as the one and only G-d of the world.

Hence, he proudly proclaimed, "Now I know that G-d is great! I have reached this conclusion *'mikal ha'elohim'* — through realizing the falsehood of all the gods of the pagan world. I know that they are indeed nothing and that Hashem is omnipotent."

(אלשיך)

"ויקח יתרו חתן משה עלה וזבחים לאלקים ויבא אהרן וכל זקני ישראל לאכל לחם עם חתן משה"

"Yitro brought a burnt offering and sacrifices to G-d. Aharon, and all the elders of Israel came to eat bread with the father-in-law of Moshe." (18:12)

QUESTION: Yitro was the guest; why did Aharon and the elders not make the meal and invite him?

ANSWER: Yitro came to visit Moshe because he wanted to convert and become a member of the Jewish people. A convert must be circumcised, and Yitro was so overjoyed at his conversion that he made a *seudat mitzvah* similar to the one usually given when a Jewish child has his *brit milah* — circumcision. Aharon, together with all the elders of Israel, participated in the *seudat mitzvah*.

* * *

A hint for the making of a festive meal at the time of a *brit* is found in the word *"milah"* (מילה). It is an acronym for ימשתה "יעשה לכל הקהל" — "a meal should be made for all assembled."

(שער בת רבים)

Another hint is in the *pasuk* ״ומלתה אתו אז יאכל בו״ — *"Umalta oto az yochal bo"* — "You shall circumcise him; then he shall eat of it" (12:44). The word *"az"* (אז) has the numerical value of 8, which alludes that following a *brit* on the eighth day, there should be a meal.

(שו״ת חות יאיר סי׳ ע׳, וע׳ שערי תשובה סי׳ תקנ״א ס״ק ל״ג)

״ויבא אהרן וכל זקני ישראל לאכל לחם עם חתן משה״
"Aharon and all the elders of Israel came to eat bread with the father-in-law of Moshe." (18:12)

QUESTION: Why didn't Moshe participate in the festive meal?

ANSWER: After receiving the Torah on Mt. Sinai, Moshe went up to heaven three times and came back the last time on *Yom Kippur.* On the following day, he sat in judgment and also conveyed the Torah to the people (see *Rashi*). Since Moshe already knew about fasting on *Yom Kippur,* he did not participate in the meal. However, all the other Jews, who first learned the Torah on the following day, were able to eat, because they did not yet know the laws of fasting on *Yom Kippur.*

(לקוטי בתר לקוטי בשם השר שלום מבעלז זצ״ל)

"מה הדבר הזה אשר אתה עשה לעם מדוע אתה יושב לבדך וכל
העם נצב עליך מן בקר עד ערב"

**"What is this thing you are doing to the people? Why do you
sit alone and all the people stand about you from morning
until evening?" (18:14)**

QUESTION: It was well known that Moshe was the judge for
all matters. Why did Yitro ask Moshe, "What are you doing?"

ANSWER: There are two approaches that a *beit din* can use in
deciding a *din-Torah*. One is *pesharah* — compromise — and the
other is *"din"* — a decision according to the letter of the law. A
compromise can be made even by a *beit din* consisting of one
judge. In addition, the defendant and plaintiff do not have to stand
while they are discussing the issues. When the *beit din* is using the
approach of absolute *din,* there should be three judges and the
defendant and plaintiff must stand while the *din-Torah* is taking
place.

Yitro knew that Moshe was conducting a *beit din* and handling
din-Torahs. However, he was somewhat puzzled by the procedure.
Therefore, he asked Moshe, "I notice that while you conduct *din-
Torahs* the defendant and plaintiff are standing, which seems to
indicate that your approach is absolute *din* and not compromise. If
so, why do you conduct the *din-Torah alone* without two
additional judges?"

Moshe explained to Yitro that even when the approach is *din*
and not compromise, if the judge is a *mumcheh* — an outstanding
expert — he is permitted to handle the *din-Torah* alone: "Since I
was in heaven and personally taught by Hashem, I am considered
an expert. Consequently, the people must stand."

(פרדס יוסף - שארית יעקב)

"ויאמר משה לחתנו...כי יהיה להם דבר בא אלי ושפטתי בין איש ובין רעהו"

"Moshe said to his father-in-law, 'When they have a matter, it comes to me, and I judge between a man and his friend.'" (18:15-16)

QUESTION: The *pasuk* begins in plural: "When *they* have a matter"; why does it not continue *"ba'im eilai"* — "*'they'* come to me"?

ANSWER: Often questions or *din-Torahs* come before a Rabbi which seem very similar to those he has previously handled. It is improper for a judge to compare one case to another and not go again through all the details. For though on the surface the two cases appear identical, in each issue there may be slight differences which can lead to an entirely different outcome (see *Choshen Mishpat* 10:2).

Yitro asked Moshe why he was so involved from morning to evening deciding questions and not quick to issue answers based on previous decisions. Moshe replied, "When they have a matter of dispute, even if *'ba eilai'* — a matter similar to this has *already* come before me and I rendered a decision — I do not rely on that. I judge anew and go through all the details. Therefore, it takes much time to come up with fair and just decisions."

(עיטורי תורה)

"כי יהיה להם דבר בא אלי ושפטתי בין איש ובין רעהו"

"When they have a matter, it comes to me, and I judge between a man and his friend." (18:16)

QUESTION: 1) In the *midbar* — the wilderness — all the needs of the Jewish people were provided by the A-mighty. Their clothing grew with them and their food came from heaven. Over what were there so many *din-Torahs?* 2) Yitro's plan to appoint judges was logical and simple; why didn't Moshe think of it himself?

ANSWER: When the Jews left Egypt, a group of Egyptian's known as the *"eirev rav"* — "the mixed multitude" — joined them. When the Egyptians drowned in the sea, their jewelry washed up on the shore and the Jews took it. The people of the *eirev rav* fought with the Jews, arguing that the drowned people were their relatives and that they were their heirs. Therefore, there were many *din-Torahs* taking place over this issue. (The term *"rei'eihu"* can refer to an Egyptian, see 10:2).

A judge is qualified to preside over a *din-Torah* only if he has no personal interest in the matter. *All* the Jews except Moshe took the wealth of the Egyptians. Therefore, he was the *only* judge qualified to handle all the *din-Torahs*.

(בנין אריאל)

"כי יהיה להם דבר בא אלי ושפטתי בין איש ובין רעהו והודעתי את
חקי האלקים ואת תורתיו"

"When they have a matter, it comes to me, and I judge between man and his friend and I make them know the statutes of G-d and His laws." (18:16)

QUESTION: It would have been sufficient just to say, "I judge between man and his neighbor." What is the reason for the additional phrase "I make them know the statutes of G-d and His laws"?

ANSWER: Approximately 250 years ago, in the city of Frankfurt, a member of the Jewish community opened his business on *Shabbat*. Reb Avraham Abish, the Rabbi of Frankfurt, was very upset and sent for him to appear at his office. When the individual refused to appear, the Rabbi called the President of the community and instructed him to purchase a large amount of goods on credit from the *Shabbat* desecrator and refuse to pay when payment became due unless he came to a *din-Torah*.

When the two appeared before the Rabbi, Reb Avraham Abish told the *Shabbat* desecrator, "It was my idea that he not pay you because I wanted to discuss with you the holiness of *Shabbat*." The storekeeper became upset and said, "This is trickery; I am surprised that a Rabbi uses such tactics."

The Rabbi opened the *Chumash* and showed him this *pasuk*. "From here we can learn that when people come to a Rabbi for their personal matters, the Rabbi should use the opportunity to 'make them know the statutes of G-d and his laws' — discuss with them how to further their Torah study and observance of *mitzvot*. In order for me to enlighten you about *Shabbat* observance, I was compelled to create a situation which would bring you before me for a *din-Torah*."

(וישמע משה)

"ושפטו את העם בכל עת את הדבר הקשה יביאון אל משה וכל הדבר הקטן ישפוטו הם"

"They administered justice on a regular basis, bringing the difficult cases to Moshe and judging the easy cases by themselves." (18:26)

QUESTION: Yitro advised Moshe to judge *"kal hadavar hagadol"* — "every *big* case" — and to let the judges consider *"kal hadaver hakatan"* — "the *small* cases" (18:12). Why did Moshe speak of *"hadavar hakasha"* — "difficult cases" — and *"hadavar hakatan"* — "easy cases" — while Yitro spoke of big and small ones?

ANSWER: In many countries the importance of a case is decided by how much money it involves. There is a small claims court for disputes over small amounts of money and a civil court which handles cases involving larger amounts. Yitro advised Moshe that he personally handle the "big cases" — the ones involving large sums of money — and the newly appointed judges should deal with the "small cases" — the ones involving small amounts of money.

According to Jewish law, a case involving a penny and a case concerning hundreds of dollars are both to be approached with the same seriousness *(Sanhedrin* 8a). Therefore, Moshe instructed that he would handle the difficult cases, regardless of the amount of money involved, and the easier cases would be under the jurisdiction of the judges.

(פרדס יוסף)

"And Moshe went up to G-d." (19:3)

QUESTION: According to the *Gemara* (Shabbat 86b) when Moshe came up to heaven to take the Torah, the angels objected: *"Tenah hodecha al hashamayim"* — "Set your glory (Torah) above the heavens." Hashem told Moshe to tell them why Torah was not for them. Moshe said, "The Torah says 'I am the L-rd your G-d who brought you out of Egypt' — were you ever in Egypt? It says 'You shall not murder' — Do you have a *yeitzer hara?"* The angels conceded, but why did they think the Torah was for them to begin with?

ANSWER: Once a great Torah scholar assumed the position of Rabbi in a large city. After a short while, he realized that the position would not leave him ample time for his own Torah study. Thus, he decided to resign his position and look for a small city. He approached a nearby small city and as soon as they were convinced that he was serious, immediately they hired him. Concerned that his townspeople might object to his leaving, he returned home to seek their permission. Realizing that he was adamant about dedicating more of his time to Torah study, they reluctantly agreed.

When the small community received word that their new Rabbi was ready to come, they sent an entourage of the most prominent people to bring him to the city. Upon arrival in the large city, the townspeople met them with sticks and stones and assaulted them for having the audacity to take away their Rabbi. In amazement, the Rabbi asked, "Why are you hitting them? Did I not discuss my leaving with you and receive your consent?!"

The townspeople told their Rabbi, "If we did not show our opposition to your leaving, they might think us not satisfied with you and happy to see you leave. Consequently, they would not hold you in the high regard you deserve. When however, they notice that we are fighting over you and not wanting to let you go, they will highly esteem you.

The angels really knew that Torah was appropriate for human beings and not for them. However, to assure that man keep Torah in the highest regard and dignity, they fought over it so that when a man acquires Torah, he will cherish it dearly.

(מצאתי בכתבי אבי הרב שמואל פסח ז״ל באגאמילסקי)

"ומשה עלה אל האלקים"
"And Moshe went up to G-d." (19:3)

QUESTION: What took place in heaven when Moshe appeared?

ANSWER: According to the *Midrash Rabbah* (28:1), the angels wanted to attack Moshe for coming to take the Torah down to earth. Hashem altered his face to resemble Avraham's and said to them, "Aren't you ashamed to attack the person from whose hospitality you benefited?" Consequently, thanks to the food that Avraham gave the angels, we were able to receive the Torah.

This is alluded to in *Pirkei Avot* (3:17): *"Im ein kemach, ein Torah"* — Were it not for the food that Avraham had given to the angels, we would not have been able to take the Torah away from them. *"Im ein Torah, ein kemach"* — Were it not for Avraham's desire that his children should learn Torah, he would not have offered food to his angelic guests.

(מהר״ם שי״ף)

* * *

In the *Gemara (Pesachim* 68b) there is a dispute concerning whether on *Yom Tov* one should dedicate himself entirely to Torah study and worship, or whether one must also set aside time for the physical enjoyment of eating and drinking. Nevertheless, all the Sages agree that on the festival of *Shavuot* one has a meal because it commemorates the day that the Torah was given.

However, since *Shavuot* commemorates the giving of the Torah, shouldn't it be celebrated entirely with study of Torah and G-dly matters?

In view of the above, that the Jews received the Torah thanks to Avraham's feeding the angels, it is easily understood why a festive meal is obligatory on *Shavuot*.

(שער בת רבים)

‏"כה תאמר לבית יעקב ותגיד לבני ישראל"

"Thus say to the House of Jacob and tell to the Children of Israel." (19:3)

QUESTION: It would be sufficient to say only *"Beit Yaakov"* or only *"B'nei Yisrael"*; why the redundancy?

ANSWER: Women are usually in the home. They see to it that their children go to *yeshivah* and encourage their husbands to study Torah, so they have a merit in the study of their husbands and children *(Sotah* 21a).

"Beit Yaakov" refers to women who are *akeret habayit* — the foundation of the home. Hashem told Moshe to speak to the women and tell them that *"vetageid livnei Yisrael,"* each and every woman should tell her sons to study Torah. In addition, each and every woman should tell her husband that the spiritual aspects of life are more important to her than the material, and thus, encourage him to set aside time for Torah study.

(מהרש"א)

‏"אתם ראיתם אשר עשיתי למצרים ואשא אתכם על כנפי נשרים ואביא אתכם אלי"

"You have seen what I did to Egypt and that I carried you on eagles' wings and brought you to me." (19:4)

QUESTION: Why did Hashem single out the eagle as an example of his connection with the Jewish people?

ANSWER: In Hebrew an eagle is known as *"nesher,"* because the word *"nesher"* means "falling off." The eagle's feathers are constantly falling off and being replaced (Psalms 103:5 Rashi); therefore, the choice of the eagle to symbolize *His* relationship with the Jewish people alludes that even if a Jew should, G-d forbid, "lose his feathers" — fail in his observance of Torah and *mitzvot* — his case is not hopeless. Immediately, he has a chance to do *teshuvah* and grow "new feathers."

(ר' לוי יצחק זצ"ל מברדיטשוב)

"ויענו כל העם יחדו ויאמרו כל אשר דבר ד' נעשה"

"And all the people answered together and said, 'All that G-d has spoken we will do.'" (19:8)

QUESTION: Each individual Jew should have responded *"e'eseh"* — *"I* will do." Why did all answer in the plural, *"na'aseh"*?

ANSWER: When the Jews heard about the Torah and realized its beauty and importance, each individual took upon himself not only to observe it, but also to be responsible for all other Jews doing so. Each one responded in the plural *"na'aseh,"* meaning "I will do, and also see to it that *other* Jews will do."

This may be an additional source for the Talmudic dictum כל" ישראל ערבין זה לזה" — "Each Jew is a guarantor for his fellow" *(Shavuot* 39a).

(חידושי הרי"ם)

"ויהי קלת וברקים וענן כבד על ההר...ויחרד כל העם אשר במחנה"

"There was thunder and lightning and a thick cloud on the mountain...and the people trembled." (19:16)

QUESTION: Why didn't Hashem give the Torah on a calm and serene day?

ANSWER: When Hashem offered the Torah to the Jewish people, they immediately accepted it without hesitation. Some Jews responded eagerly, thinking that Torah would make life pleasant and effortless.

To dispel this theory, Hashem brought thunder and lightning, alluding that in the years that lay ahead, there would be difficult periods. Jews would suffer and be tortured for their adherence to Torah. However, the perpetual existence of the Jewish people would not be through forsaking the Torah, G-d forbid. Keeping the

Torah tenaciously would help the Jewish people endure the most difficult times and be the source of salvation.

(פרי לבנון)

"וירד ד' על הר סיני"
"And G-d descended upon Mount Sinai." (19:20)

QUESTION: In the *Haggadah* of *Pesach* we say "Had He brought us before Mount Sinai and not given us the Torah, *dayeinu* — It would have sufficed us." Of what value would Mount Sinai be without the Torah?

ANSWER: The Torah consists of 613 *mitzvot*, and the word Torah (תורה) has the numerical value of 611. The first two commandments were uttered by Hashem Himself, unlike the rest of the Torah, which was given through Moshe. Thus we proclaim, "Had He brought us before Mount Sinai only to hear from G-d Himself the two commandments and not given us the Torah (the other 611 *mitzvot*), it would have sufficed us."

(הגש"פ ברכת השיר)

"וידבר אלקים את כל הדברים האלה"
"And G-d spoke all these words." (20:1)

QUESTION: Why is the giving of the Torah recorded in *Parshat Yitro?*

ANSWER: Regarding the Torah it is stated: *"Ein tov ela Torah* — The true good is only Torah. As it is written, *'Ki lekach tov natati lachem'* — 'I have given you a good teaching — the Torah.'" *(Pirkei Avot* 6:3). The word *"tov"* (טוב) has the numerical value of 17. Counting from the first *parshah* of the Torah (Bereishit), Yitro is the 17th *parshah*. Thus, it is most appropriate that the ultimate good be expounded in the 17th *parshah*.

"וידבר אלקים את כל הדברים האלה לאמר"
"And G-d spoke all these words, saying." (20:1)

QUESTION: The Sages in the *Gemara (Shabbat* 86b) maintain that the Torah was given on the 6th day of the month of *Sivan*. Rabbi Yossi, however, claims that it was given on the 7th of *Sivan*.

The Torah is precise in listing the exact dates of all *yamim tovim*. Why does it not specify on which day the Torah was given?

ANSWER: Hashem, by not stating the exact date of the giving of the Torah, conveys to us that Torah is not restricted to or connected with any specific time. Twenty four hours a day, every day of the year, a Jew must live in accordance with the Torah.

(כ"ק אדמו"ר)

"וידבר אלקים את כל הדברים האלה לאמר אנכי..."
"And G-d spoke all these words, saying, I am..." (20:1,2)

QUESTION: The *Gemara (Avodah Zarah* 2b) relates that prior to giving the Torah to the Jewish people, Hashem offered it to the nations of the world, who refused it because some of its laws did not please them.

Why did Hashem reveal to the Jewish people that He offered the Torah to the nations of the world and that they refused to accept it? Doesn't this cast the Jewish people in a bad light?

ANSWER: By imparting this to the Jewish people, Hashem intended to convey a very important message regarding the sanctity of Torah.

The people of Yishmael refused to accept the Torah because it contained the commandment "You shall not steal," and the character trait of Yishmael was "His hand will be extended against all people" *(Bereishit* 16:12). The people of Eisav declined the Torah because it included the commandment "You shall not kill," and Eisav was told by Yitzchak "You will live by your sword" *(Bereishit* 27:40).

Apparently, the entire Torah suited these nations, except for one commandment. If so, should they not have accepted the Torah and disregarded the single law which they could not contend with?

Hashem was thus emphasizing that the other nations realized that the Torah is comprised of 613 totally unified *mitzvot*, and the slightest omission takes away from the Torah in its totality: A Torah of 612 *mitzvot* is not an abbreviated Torah, but no Torah at all! After this introduction Hashem's question to the Jewish people concerned their willingness to accept the whole Torah of 613 *mitzvot,* to which they unequivocally responded, "We will do and we will listen — we accept the Torah in its entirety."

(הרב פנחס מ. ז"ל טייץ)

"אנכי ד' אלקיך אשר הוצאתיך מארץ מצרים"
"I am the Lord your G-d, who brought you out of the land *Mitzraim."* (20:2)

QUESTION: Why didn't Hashem introduce Himself as the One who created heaven and earth?

ANSWER: The redemption from Egyptian bondage is something which the Jews had just experienced and it had a personal meaning to each and every one of them.

Moreover, the word *"Mitzraim"* can also be read as *"meitzarim"* — boundaries and limitations. Torah gives a person the capability to elevate himself over all physical limitations. Hashem is telling the Jews that He is the One who is giving them the Torah, which gives them the ability to go out of *Mitzraim — meitzarim* — spiritually and physically. Through the study of Torah and observance of *mitzvot,* a Jew can control the nature of heaven and earth, instead of being subject to its control.

(חסידות חב"ד)

"אנכי ד' אלקיך...לא יהיה לך אלהים אחרים..."
"I am the L-rd your G-d...You shall not have any other gods..." (20:2-3)

QUESTION: Why did Hashem personally say only the first two commandments and convey the others through Moshe?

ANSWER: Though it is incumbent upon every Jew to observe all the precepts of the Torah, a prophet is permitted to tell the community to sometimes temporarily violate a Torah precept. Exempted from this rule is idolatry. No one has the authority to tell any Jew at any time to transgress this prohibition *(Sanhedrin 90a)*.

The way Torah was given to the Jewish people may give insight into the reason for the above-mentioned rule. The entire Torah was given through Moshe, who was the greatest of all prophets. Since he, as a prophet, was imbued with the power to convey the Torah, Hashem vested in Moshe and his successors the strength to temporarily supersede a *mitzvah* of the Torah. However, the first two commandments, which forbid idolatry, were given directly from Hashem. Hence, these laws are eternal and totally unchangeable.

(אמרי רש"ד, הרב שמעון דובער אנאליק ז"ל)

"כבד את אביך"
"Honor your father." (20:12)

QUESTION: The verse could have stated *"kabed avicha"* — "honor your father"; the word *"et"* (את) is superfluous?

ANSWER: According to *halacha,* a person is obligated to honor his father at all times. However, the father cannot order his child to violate a law of the Torah. The first letters of the words "כבד את אביך" have the numerical value of 22. This alludes that one should only honor his father when his requests are in accordance to the Torah, written with the twenty two letters of the *alef-beit.*

Moreover, the last letters of the words "כבד את אביך" — spell the word *"kedat"* (כדת). This comes to further emphasize that one must honor his father when the request is *"kedat"* — in harmony with *halacha*.

(בית יעקב)

"כבד את אביך ואת אמך"

"Honor your father and your mother." (20:12)

QUESTION: The *Gemara* (*Kiddushin* 30b) states, "There are three partners in the forming of man: Hashem, his father, and his mother. When one honors his father and mother, Hashem considers it as though He abided in their midst and they rendered honor to Him." What allusion is there in our *pasuk* to this equation?

ANSWER: The word "אביך" in *mispar katan* (single numerals, disregarding the zero in the numerical value of the Hebrew letter so that "כ"=2, "ל"=3, etc.) — has the numerical value of six. The word "אמך" in single numerals has the numerical value of seven. Together they add up to 13, which is the numerical value of "אחד," which alludes to the One and Only — Hashem. When a person honors his father and mother, he merits to have *"echad"* — Hashem with him.

(שפתי כהן)

"כבד את אביך ואת אמך למען יארכון ימיך על האדמה אשר ד'
אלקיך נתן לך"

"Honor your father and your mother so that your days will be lengthened upon the land that the L-rd your G-d gives you." (20:12)

QUESTION: In the *Gemara* (*Kiddushin* 31a) Rabbi Eliezer is asked "To what extent is the *mitzvah* of honoring parents obligatory?" He answers, "Take a lesson from a Gentile named Dama Ben Netina. Once there was a need to purchase stones for the *efod* (the apron worn by the *Kohen Gadol*). It was an opportunity for him to earn a vast sum of money, but he refused to make the sale because the key to the safe was under his father's pillow and he did not want to awaken him. A year later G-d rewarded him: A red heifer was born to a cow in his herd, and the Sages offered to buy it. He replied, 'I know that you will gladly give whatever price I will ask for the heifer. However, I only request that you pay me the amount of money I lost through honoring my father.'"

Couldn't Rabbi Eliezer have found a Jew to emulate who extended himself to honor his father?

ANSWER: Rabbi Eliezer was conveying to his students a profound message on the subject of honoring parents:

Many are under the impression that honoring parents is something which our human comprehension dictates: Since our parents struggle to raise us and give us the best of everything, it is our obligation to reciprocate by honoring and respecting them.

According to Rabbi Eliezer this is an erroneous approach, and he was using the story of Dama Ben Netina to discredit this attitude. He was *not* telling his students to emulate him and learn from him the extent of honoring parents, but rather to learn from the reward he received the profundity of the *mitzvah.*

If Hashem wanted to help him recover his loss, why was it necessarily in the form of red heifer?

The Torah is divided into three categories *eidot* (testimonies) *mishpatim* (civil laws) and *chukim* (statutes, laws with no apparent rationale). The ultimate statute is the law of red heifer. It is totally incomprehensible according to our limited intellect, and we obey it only because it is G-d's will.

Likewise, the message to be learned from Dama Ben Netina's *reward* is that honoring parents is a must even if our thinking cannot find a rationale for it. The *mitzvah* of honoring parents is a super-rational law; we must do it because it is G-d's will.

"למען יארכון ימיך על האדמה אשר ד' אלקיך נתן לך"

"So that your days will be lengthened upon the land that G-d your G-d gives you." (20:12)

QUESTION: The word *"Lema'an"* — "in order that" — seems superfluous, it could have just said, *"veya'arichun yamecha"*?

ANSWER: The Jewish people is eagerly awaiting *Mashiach's* coming, which is referred to as the *"keitz"* (קץ). The word *"lema'an"* (למען) is numerically equivalent to 190, which is also the numerical value of the word *"keitz."* This teaches us that through honoring our parents we will hasten the coming of *Mashiach* and live an extended life.

The last letters of the words "כבד את אביך" add up numerically to 424, which is the same numerical value as *Mashiach Ben David* (משיח בן דוד), who will speedily be revealed through this great *mitzvah* of honoring parents.

(בית יעקב)

"לא תרצח"

"You shall not kill." (20:13)

QUESTION: Why is it, that when reading the *Aseret Hadibrot* in private, *"lo tirtzach"* is read with a *patach,* and when it is read in public — in *shul* — it is pronounced with a *kamatz* (*"lo tirtzawch"* in the *Ashkenazi* pronunciation)?

ANSWER: The act of killing can be performed in two ways:

1) Actual shedding of blood.

2) Shaming a person in public which is equated to killing him, because his blood drains from his face, leaving him pale as a corpse *(Bava Metzia* 58b).

The two pronunciations of *"lo tirtzach"* of the *Aseret Hadibrot* allude to these two forms of killing. The *patach,* (literally "open") which is pronounced with an open mouth, represents the type of killing where a wound is opened in the person and blood is shed.

This is forbidden even in private. The *kamatz* (literally "close") is pronounced with the mouth closed, and it alludes to the form of killing that is committed by shaming a person, in which superficially, everything is "closed up" on the person, yet he is like a dead man. Such an act of killing takes place only in public.

(שי לחגים ומועדים בשם הרב י. צירלסאן ז״ל מקעשינוב)

"אנכי...אשר לרעך"
"I am...which belongs to your friends." (20:2-14)

QUESTION: Why are there 620 letters in the *Aseret Hadibrot?*

ANSWER: In the Torah there are 613 *mitzvot*. In addition to this, there are seven *mitzvot* which were added by our sages. Each letter in the *Aseret Hadibrot* is for one of the *mitzvot*.

The last two words, "אשר לרעך," have seven letters, representing the seven *mitzvot* instituted by Rabbinic ordinance:

א = **א**בילות, the laws of mourning.

ש = **ש**מחת חתן וכלה, the seven days of celebration for a groom and bride.

ר = **ר**חיצה, the laws of *nitilat yadayim* — washing of hands before a meal.

ל = **ל**חם, the laws of saying a *berachah* before eating food and also that breads and foods baked or cooked by Gentiles are forbidden to us, even if there is no problem about the *kashrut* of the ingredients.

ר = **ר**שויות, the laws regarding different types of domains where it is permissible to carry on *Shabbat* and where not, and also the distance permissible to walk out of residential area.

ע = **ע**מלק, the laws pertaining to reading the *Megillah* on *Purim,* and the other *mitzvot* of *Purim* — Haman was a descendant of Amalek, and *Purim* commemorates the victory over him.

ך = **כ**הנים, the miracle of *Chanukah,* which was brought about through the *Kohanim* of the family of Mattityahu.

(חתם סופר)

"וכל העם ראים את הקולת"

"The entire people saw the thunder [that issued from the mouth of Hashem — Rashi]." (20:15)

QUESTION: The *Midrash Rabbah* (28:5) states that the voice was unique in that it had no echo. Usually, the stronger the voice, the stronger the echo. Isn't the lack of echo from the voice of Hashem a sign of weakness?

ANSWER: The distance the voice can travel depends on the strength of the person. When the voice reaches a wall, it rebounds, causing an echo. The *Midrash* is implying that the voice of Hashem was so powerful that it penetrated and permeated every person and every physical part of the universe, so that there was no echo.

(לקוטי שיחות חלק ה')

"לא תעשון אתי אלהי כסף"

"You shall not make idols of silver." (20:20)

QUESTION: This prohibition also includes a warning that if one makes the *keruvim* which stood on the Ark from silver instead of gold, it is as though one made idols (Rashi).

In time of need it is permissible to make the vessels of the *Mishkan* with other metals (Rambam, *Beit Habechirah* 1:19). Why is it forbidden to make *keruvim* of anything else but gold?

ANSWER: The *keruvim* had the faces of children. Placing them on the Ark, which had in it the Torah, alludes to the fact that Jewish children must receive a Torah education.

The law that *keruvim* can be made *only* from gold teaches a very important lesson: It is permissible to substitute anything with a cheaper metal, but we must give our children the best Jewish education (gold). Anything inferior is forbidden.

(הרב מאיר ז"ל שפירא מלובלין)

"לא תעלה במעלת על מזבחי"
"You shall not ascend my altar on steps." (20:23)

QUESTION: The *Gemara (Menachot* 29a) states that there was a stone in front of the *menorah* having three steps upon which the *Kohen* would stand upon when lighting the *menorah*. Why was it forbidden however to have steps to ascend the altar?

ANSWER: The altar represents the concept of *teshuvah*. On it were brought offerings through which one would gain atonement. The *menorah* exemplifies Torah. Its purpose was to give off light, and Torah is light, as it is written; "A *mitzvah* is a candle and Torah is light" (Proverbs 6:23). The twenty two cups represented the twenty letters of the *alef-beit* with which the Torah was written (see Rabbeinu Bachya).

A step is for gradual ascent and a ramp is for rapid movement. Consequently, in the study of Torah, one needs to progress gradually, step by step. However, *teshuvah* can be accomplished instantly, moving from one status to another in a single moment. Thus, one can become a *ba'al teshuvah* instantaneously, while it requires many laborious years to reach the degree of *talmid chacham* — Torah scholar.

* * *

Rabbi Menachem Mendel of Kotzk once said to his students, "We say of A-mighty G-d" [that thanks to our *teshuvah*] "as far as east from west, has he distanced our transgressions from us" (Psalms 103:12). Perhaps one of your can tell me how far east is from west."

The students deliberated and grappled with this problem. Each one came up with a different astronomical figure. Suddenly, the Kotzker Rebbe interrupted them and declared, "You are all in error!" From east to west is only one swerve. When one stands facing east and turns around, instantly, he is in the west. This is the immediacy of *teshuvah*.

(שמעתי מאחי הרב שמואל פסח שי' באגאמילסקי)

৪৩ ৪০

MISHPATIM • משפטים

"ואלה המשפטים אשר תשים לפניהם"
"And these are the laws that you must set before them." (21:1)

QUESTION: Rashi states: "Like a set table which is ready for the person to partake of the feast." How is the *halacha* governing monetary matters like a set table?

ANSWER: Admirably, many people are very particular about the *kashrut* of the food they eat. When they are invited to a party, before partaking of the foods laid out on the table, they will inquire about the *shechitah* of the meat and the bakery that produced the baked goods, etc. Only if the food on the table meets their *kashrut* standards will they eat of it. Unfortunately, in monetary matters they are often not so stringent and they may even engage in questionable business practices.

Rashi is alluding that in money matters, one should be as strict as with the food on one's table.

* * *

The Code of Jewish Law is known as the *Shulchan Aruch*, which literally means "a set table." This, too, emphasizes that in all issues of *halacha* one must act with total integrity, as one demands the highest standards of *kashrut*.

(ר' משה ליב מסאסוב זצ"ל)

"ואלה המשפטים...כי תקנה עבד עברי שש שנים יעבד ובשבעת
יצא לחפשי חנם"

"And these are the laws...If you buy a Jewish slave, he shall work for six years, and in the seventh he shall go free." (21:1-2)

QUESTION: Why do the laws concerning a thief sold as a Jewish servant immediately follow the giving of the Torah?

ANSWER: If Jews would constantly bear in mind that Hashem is the Master of the world and its inhabitants, no one would ever sin. We mortals tend sometimes to forget this basic principle and, thinking that Hashem is not looking, furtively transgress His will.

To protect us from this misconception, the laws of the Jewish slave follow the giving of the Torah to emphasize that each individual should strive to be a totally dedicated servant of G-d.

The period of six years of a Jewish slave's servitude represents the six millennium of this world. During this stage we should submit ourselves to serving Hashem through performing Torah and *mitzvot*. Adhering to this guideline, a Jew can be certain that in the seventh year, which represents the seventh millennium, he will merit everlasting tranquillity.

(כ"ק אדמו"ר)

"כי תקנה עבד עברי"

"If you will buy a Jewish slave." (21:2)

QUESTION: The person becomes a slave only *after* he is purchased. It should have said *"Ki tikneh Ivri le'eved"* — "If you buy a Jew to be a slave."

ANSWER: All Jews have Hashem as their master: They must serve *Him*. The Torah is telling the individual who buys another Jew to realize that his relationship with such a Jew cannot be one of master and slave, because every Jew is *already* a slave belonging to another master — Hashem.

In addition, the master should bear in mind that the servant has obligations towards his true Master and that it is imperative to grant him the time to fulfill them.

(לקוטי רצב"א)

"והגישו אל הדלת או אל המזוזה ורצע אדניו את אזנו במרצע"
"He shall bring him to the door or to the door post, and his master shall bore his ear with an awl." (21:6)

QUESTION: Why was the ear of the slave pierced near the door or the door post?

ANSWER: After a slave works for six years, the "doors are opened" to him and he can go out free. When a slave does not use the "open door," he is put up against the door to have his ear pierced.

On the door post, moreover, there is a *mezuzah,* in which it is written, "You shall love your G-d." Since the slave, instead of saying "I love my G-d who took me out of Egypt and made me free," is saying "I love my master and want to remain *his* slave," his ear is pierced near the *mezuzah.*

(כלי יקר)

"ורצע אדניו את אזנו במרצע"
"And his master shall bore his ear with an awl." (21:6)

QUESTION: Why was a *martzei'ah* (awl) used and not another tool?

ANSWER: The Jewish people were slaves for 400 years, and Hashem freed them. The word *"martzei'ah"* (מרצע) adds up to 400. In the case of a slave who does not want to go free, the awl reminds him of the 400 years of slavery and the freedom that Jews should enjoy.

(מסכת קידושין דף כ"ב ע"ב תוד"ה מה)

"ורצע אדניו את אזנו במרצע ועבדו לעלם"
"And his master shall bore his ear with an awl, and he shall serve forever." (21:6)

QUESTION: The ear was selected to be pierced because it heard on Mt. Sinai, 'You shall not steal,' and nevertheless the person stole. In addition, the ear heard on Mt. Sinai that *B'nei Yisrael* are to be servants of Hashem, and the person acquired a different master for himself (Rashi).

According to these explanations, why do we delay boring the ear till the person decides to stay on as a slave after six years, instead of boring immediately when he is sold or sells himself as a slave?

ANSWER: When a Jew acquires anything, he must do an action *(kinyan)* to demonstrate his ownership. Originally, the slave was bought for a period of six years. At the time of the sale the buyer paid money, which is a way of acquiring ownership. If the slave desires to stay after the original six years, the owner must make a new *kinyan* to establish new continued ownership. The *Mishnah (Kiddushin* 14b) states, *"hanirtza nikneh biretziah"* — "the slave whose ear is bored is *acquired* through the boring of the ear." Thus, the boring of the ear is not a punishment, but a form of *kinyan.*

Since this form of *kinyan* is not found anywhere else, we have to search for a reason for such a strange method. Therefore, Rashi quotes the above explanations to help us understand the reason for boring the ear.

(עי' משנה למלך עבדים פ"ג, הל"ז)

"וכי יזיד איש על רעהו להרגו בערמה מעם מזבחי תקחנו למות"
"If a man shall act intentionally against his fellow to kill him with guile — from My altar shall you take him to die." (21:14)

QUESTION: What is the connection between killing the one who murders intentionally and the altar?

ANSWER: A physically ill person who is unable to live even for the duration of a year, is called a *"treifa,"* and, according to *halacha,* one is not put to death for killing such a person. An animal can also be considered a *treifa,* in which case it may not be used as a sacrifice on the altar.

Since the majority of animals are not *treifa,* however, we need not be concerned with the minority that are, and we are allowed to bring all animals as sacrifices.

A person who intentionally killed, can claim *"be'armah"* — with guile — that the person he killed was a *treifa* (one already mortally wounded) and thus avoid the penalty. The Torah responds to this by mentioning the altar: Just as in regard to animals fit to be brought on the altar, we follow the "majority principle," so in the instance of intentional killing, we affirm that the majority of people survive far beyond a year and assume that the victim was not a *treifa.*

(נחל קדומים)

"ורפא ירפא"

"And he shall provide for healing." (21:19)

QUESTION: Why in *Parshat Beshalach* (15:26) does it state *"Ani Hashem rofecha"* — "I am G-d your healer" — with a soft "פ", and here with a hard "פ"? Moreover, why is the word repeated twice in this case, while there it is only stated once?

ANSWER: When a doctor endeavors to heal a patient, often the patient experiences pain. Moreover, at times a doctor may make mistakes, and regardless of his good intentions, complicate the illness, before healing the patient.

Hashem's method of healing is with a soft touch, and He never errs. Thus the *pasuk* uses a soft "פ", and there is no need for repetition of the word.

(בעל הטורים - רבינו בחיי)

"ורפא ירפא"
"And he shall provide for healing." (21:19)

QUESTION: From this *pasuk* the school of Rabbi Yishmael learned that the A-mighty gives doctors permission to heal *(Berachot* 60a). The *Gemara (Kiddushin* 82a) says, *"Tov sheberofim leGeihinom"* — "The best of doctors will go to *Geihinom."* How can we comprehend this *Gemara* in light of the fact that some of our greatest sages, such as the Rambam, the Ibn Ezra, and others, were doctors?

ANSWER: The *Shemonah Esrei,* which is recited thrice daily, originally consisted of 18 *berachot.* One of them is *"Refa'einu, Hashem, veneirafei,"* in which we pray to Hashem for healing. Unfortunately, there are doctors, who otherwise have faith in Hashem, but take all the medical credit for themselves and forget that they are His emissaries.

The numerical value of the word *"tov"* (טוב) is 17. The *Gemara's* statement *"Tov sheberofim ligeihinom"* refers to the doctor who recites the *Shemonah Esrei* but only believes in 17 of the *berachot.* A doctor who lacks full faith in *"Refa'einu, Hashem"* belongs in *Geihinom;* however, doctors who are righteous and believe that it is Hashem who gives them the power to heal will be rewarded with *Gan Eden.*

(פרדס יוסף)

* * *

Alternatively, it is incumbent upon doctors to give the best of their professional knowledge for their patients. The doctor must follow his teachings and adhere to them accurately. When a doctor diagnoses a patient and instructs him as to what he may eat or may not eat, or what he may do and may not do, he must be strict in his orders.

Sometimes the patient may say, "But doctor I cannot exist without this..." The doctor, feeling sorry for the patient may say, "Okay, I'll be lenient with your diet and permit you to eat small portions of the forbidden foods or I will only restrict your activities for two days instead of seven." In reality, he is endangering the welfare of the patient. This kind of doctor who is permissive and wants to be a 'good' person, endangering the patient's life by yielding to his wishes, deserves *Geihinom*.

(פרדס יוסף)

"עין תחת עין"

"An eye for an eye." (21:24)

QUESTION: Rashi explains that he *pays* the value of an eye. What indication is there in the *pasuk* that it means a cash payment and not the actual taking of an eye?

ANSWER: When one writes the letters of the *alef-beit* from *alef* to *tav,* one under the other with *alef* on top, the letter under "ע"is "פ", the one under "י" is "כ", and the letter under "נ" is "ס". Thus the three letters *under* the letters of the word *"ayin"* (עין) — "eye" — spell the word *"kesef"* (כסף), which means "money." Hence, the Torah is teaching us that *"Ayin"* — if a person blinded another's eye — he must give *"tachat ayin"* — what is spelled by the letters *under "ayin"* — and that is *"kesef"* — money.

(קול אליהו)

"וכי יפתח איש בור או כי יכרה איש בר ולא יכסנו ונפל שמה שור או חמור"

"If a man shall uncover a pit, or if a man shall dig a pit and not cover it, and an ox or a donkey fall into it...." (21:33)

QUESTION: Why is the first *"bor"* (pit) written with a "ו" and the second *"bor"* without a "ו"?

ANSWER: The law of responsibility for digging a pit in the ground which caused fatal damage applies only to a pit ten handbreadths deep.

A person who uncovers a pit ten handbreadths deep is considered as having dug the entire pit, and he is responsible for the damages. Similarly, one who adds a handbreadth to an already-existing pit nine handbreadths deep is also fully responsible as if he had dug the entire pit.

According to our Sages *(Bava Kamma* 51a) the first part of the *pasuk* is referring to the instance where a pit ten handbreadths deep was uncovered, while the latter part refers to the case where one digs the tenth handbreadth. Therefore, in the first part of the *pasuk,* in which one makes the entire pit, *"bor"* is written with a "וי". But where one only digs the one handbreadth (and becomes responsible for the pit), it is written without a "וי".

(קול אליהו)

"אם המצא תמצא בידו הגניבה...שנים ישלם"
"If the stolen object shall be found in his possession...he shall pay double." (22:3)

QUESTION: Why does a *ganav* pay double?

ANSWER: When a thief steals $100, his intention is to gain $100 for himself at the expense of $100 to his victim. The punishments in the Torah are measure for measure. Therefore, by paying double the thief ends up losing $100 *and* making the victim *gain* $100. What is done to him is exactly what he planned to do to his fellow.

(פרדס יוסף)

"אם כסף תלוה את עמי"
"When you lend silver to My people." (22:24)

QUESTION: In ancient times currency was made of gold or silver; why does the Torah specify *"kesef"* (כסף) — silver?

ANSWER: The letters that comprise the word *"zahav"* (זהב) decrease in numerical value (7,5,2), while the letters which spell the word *"kesef"* (כסף) increase (20,60,80).

The Torah is conveying an important lesson — *"im kesef"* — when a person wants his assets to increase, it can be achieved through *"talveh et ami"* — extending interest-free loans to My people because charging interest causes a decline of ones' assets *(Shulchan Aruch, Yoreh Dei'ah* 160:2).

(בית יעקב)

* * *

King Shlomo says about Torah study, *"Im tevakshenah chakesef...veda'at Elokim timtza"* — "If you seek her as silver...you will find the knowledge of G-d" (Proverbs 2:4-5). Superficially, the analogy is difficult to comprehend. More effort is made to find gold than silver, why doesn't the wisest of all men preach to seek Torah as one seeks gold? The above-mentioned concept can provide insight into Shlomo's wisdom. He is saying: To succeed in Torah study one must take the approach of *"kesef"* — continuously increase and intensify diligence. Thus, one will eventually find (understand) the knowledge of Hashem.

(בית יעקב)

"אם כסף תלוה את עמי את העני עמך"
"When you lend money to My people, the poor among you." (22:24)

QUESTION: A *gemilat chesed* (loan) is both for the rich and the poor. Why does the Torah single out "the *poor* among you"?

ANSWER: According to the *Gemara (Bava Metzia* 75b) giving someone a loan without witnesses is equivalent to placing a stumbling block before the blind because the borrower may be tempted to deny the loan. However, when one gives *tzedakah* (charity), it should be done discreetly so that the poor man will not become embarrassed.

Our *pasuk* alludes to this important rule: *"Im kesef talveh"* — "when you are giving a loan" — *"et ami"* — "[do it] before my people." However, *"et he'ani"* — "[if you are helping] a poor person [with charity]" — *"imach"* — "[it should be] between you and him."

(אוצר חיים בשם גור ארי')

"אם כסף תלוה את עמי את העני עמך"

"When you lend money to My people, the poor among you." (22:24)

QUESTION: The words *"et he'ani imach"* — "the poor among you" — seem extra?

ANSWER: Helping a person in need is a great *mitzvah*. One should give at least one tenth of one's earnings for *tzedakah*. Unfortunately, sometimes people do not have money readily available when they are called upon for a worthy cause. Others, do not want to dip into their reserves, and consequently, they lose a great *mitzvah*.

The *pasuk* gives advice on how to give *tzedakah* easily and wholeheartedly. When a person brings home his earnings, he should immediately take off *at least* ten percent and put it away in a *"tzedakah* account." Thus, he will no longer consider the money as his, but rather the property of the poor. When a poor man or a charitable cause comes to him for help, he will not feel as if he is giving *his* own money, but rather *"et he'ani imach"* — [the money of] the poor man which is in his possession.

(לקוטי בתר לקוטי מדו"ת - שערי שמחה)

* * *

Another important lesson the Torah is teaching on *tzedakah* is the following: One Jew must help the other when he has been blessed with abundant wealth. Moreover, even one who is experiencing financial difficulties should not hesitate to help another in need. The Torah alludes to this with the words *"et he'ani imach"* — even when *you* experience poverty ("poverty is with *you*") — make an effort to help a fellow Jew in need.

(לקוטי בת לקוטי - ר' שמעלקא מניקלשבורג זצ"ל)

"אם כסף תלוה את עמי את העני עמך"

"When you lend money to My people, the poor among you." (22:24)

QUESTION: The word *"imach"* — "with you" — seems superfluous. Would it not have been sufficient to say "If you lend money to My people, the poor"?

ANSWER: Many people establish an amount they will give to a particular charity and are very careful not to exceed it. Although in the interim their wealth has increased many times over, they still continue to give their original allocations. The Torah abhors this behavior and instructs us that when we give to the poor, we should always consider them *"imach"* — to be on our level. When we are enriched and do more for ourselves, we should accordingly do more for them.

* * *

King David in Psalms (112:3) writes: *"Hon va'osher beveito vetzidkato omedet la'ad"* — "Wealth and riches are in his house, and his righteousness *(tzidkato)* lasts forever." According to a homiletic interpretation he is referring to people in whose home there is continuous beautification thanks to increased wealth, but *"tzidkato"* (the donations for *tzedakah*) remain the same forever.

(לקוטי בתר לקוטי מהדו"ת)

"אם כסף תלוה את עמי את העני עמך...לא תשימון עליו נשך"

"When you lend money to My people, the poor among you — do not place upon him usury." (22:24)

QUESTION: Why is the Torah adamant about charging interest?

ANSWER: A rich man does not necessarily deserve his wealth, nor a poor person his poverty. Affluence and poverty derive from acts of Hashem designed to test the person. The rich man should think that he is merely the caretaker of money which rightfully belongs to the poor man. It is placed in his custody to test him, to see if he will be blinded by riches.

This is implied in the words *"et he'ani imach"* — "The poor man's money is with you." When you extend him a loan, in reality you are granting him access to *his* money. Consequently, charging him interest on *his* money is adding insult to the suffering of poverty and a grave iniquity.

(אלשיך)

"אם חבל תחבל שלמת רעך עד בא השמש תשיבנו לו...הוא שמלתו לערו במה ישכב"

"If you take as collateral your friend's garment, you must return it to him before sunset...it is his garment for his skin; in what shall he sleep?" (22:25-26)

QUESTION: Why is the word for "garment" spelled differently in each *pasuk* (שלמה and שמלה)?

ANSWER: The word "שמלה" is composed of two words "שם לה" — *"shem lah"* — an item of importance with its own name — and the word "שלמה" is also composed of two words "של מה" — *"shel mah"* — of what value is it?

When a person gives a loan and takes an item as collateral, he may think that it is a *"shel mah"* — not of great value — and that it will not make a difference if he returns it before sunset or not. The Torah warns, however, that this seemingly meager garment may be the poor man's only one, and to him it may be *"shem lah"* — a valuable possession.

(שער בת רבים)

"ואנשי קדש תהיון לי ובשר בשדה טרפה לא תאכלו לכלב תשלכון אתו"

"Be holy men to Me, do not eat *treifah* [torn-off flesh] in the field; cast it to the dogs." (22:30)

QUESTION: Why does the Torah specify *"basadeh"* — in the fields? Should it not say *"babayit"* — in the home?

ANSWER: Many people are meticulous in the laws of *kashrut* in their homes. They only eat food that has reliable Rabbinic supervision, etc. However, when they go out to the "fields" for vacations, they are very lax in the laws of *kashrut*. They may stay in hotels and purchase food in establishments without high *kashrut* standards.

Therefore, the Torah emphasizes that even when out in the "fields," it is necessary to observe the laws of *kashrut* strictly.

"אחרי רבים להטת"

"A case must be decided on the basis of the majority." (23:2)

QUESTION: The Gentile world is the majority and the Jews are the minority. Why don't we, G-d forbid, join them in respect to idolatry?

ANSWER: A heathen once asked Rabbi Yehoshua ben Korcha this question and his answer was the following: 'In the case of Eisav six souls are mentioned in Torah, and yet the word used of them in Torah is "souls" *(nefashot)*, in the plural, as it is written, "And Eisav took his wives, and his sons, and his daughters, and all the souls of his house *(Bereishit* 36:4).

In Yaakov's family, on the other hand, there were seventy souls, and yet the word used of them in Torah is "soul", as it is written, "And all the nefesh [sing., soul] that came out of the loins of Yaakov," *(Shemot* 1:5). The reason is that Eisav worshipped many deities, while Yaakov worshiped one G-d.

Though the Gentiles are many in number and we are few, they practice polytheism. Thus, since we are all united and worship only one G-d, in reality we are the majority and they the minority.

(ויקרא רבה ד:ו - ע״י מתנת כהונה)

Alternatively, in the olden days debates would take place between priests and rabbis. The priests would attempt to prove the correctness of their faith and force the Jews to convert. Once, a priest asked the above question of a rabbi. The rabbi wisely responded, "The law of following the majority applies only when there is doubt. However, though we are a minority, we Jews have no doubts about our faith and are convinced that our G-d is the one and only G-d and Master of the entire world."

(אוצר חיים)

"ודל לא תהדר בריבו"
"Do not glorify a destitute person in his grievance." (23:3)

QUESTION: What is the grievance of the poor man?

ANSWER: Often, the poor man may express his frustration and anger against Hashem: "Why does He take care of everyone and forsake me?"

When one extends charity to the needy, he refutes the contention of the poor man. On the other hand, when one refuses to give charity, he is confirming the poor man's complaint. Therefore, the Torah cautions to give charity so as not to provide support for the poor man's grievance about his economic situation.

(אור החיים)

"כי תראה חמור שנאך רבץ תחת משאו וחדלת מעזב לו עזב תעזב עמו"
"If you see your enemy's donkey lying under its load, you might want to refrain from helping him; [however], you must surely help with him." (23:5)

QUESTION: Only a wicked person would think this way; why is it necessary for Torah to caution against it?

ANSWER: Before Rabbi Shneur Zalman of Liadi, known as the *"Alter Rebbe,"* became the leader of Chabad, he once traveled to raise money for an important charitable cause. He came to the home of a wealthy man who, sensing that he was not one of the ordinary collectors, offered to have him stay and teach his children in return for the entire sum he hoped to raise.

After a short stay, he informed his host that he was leaving because he could not tolerate the conduct of the people of the city. His host asked him what he meant, and Rabbi Shneur Zalman replied, "You torture the poor." The host thought that he was referring to a recent meeting to determine how to raise the money for a tax. It was decided that first the poor should give as much as they were able, and whatever was missing would be made up by the rich. He realized that Rabbi Shneur Zalman was right: the poor should not be bothered at all. Let the rich give as much as they can, and the poor won't have to give anything. Immediately he arranged a second meeting, and it was decided that the rich should first give what they could afford.

A few days later, Rabbi Shneur Zalman again gave notice that he was leaving, exclaiming again, "You torture the poor." Amazed, the host told his guest of the second meeting and that the poor would not be bothered at all. Rabbi Shneur Zalman told him that he was not aware of the meetings and had been referring to a different matter:

In the human body there are 'rich' organs and a 'poor' organ. The 'rich' organs are the mind and the heart, and the 'poor' organ is the stomach. "In this city," he explained, "instead of putting emphasis on the rich organs and engaging them in the study of Torah and concentrating on prayer to Hashem, the approach is to constantly fast; thus, the 'poor' organ, the stomach, is deprived and made to suffer for the person's iniquities. I cannot tolerate this approach!"

This new philosophy was very intriguing to the host, and he asked Reb Shneur Zalman its source. He told him of the Ba'al Shem Tov and his teachings, which accentuate working with the mind and heart and not punishing the body.

"The Ba'al Shem Tov," he continued, "bases his theory on a *pasuk* in *Parshat Mishpatim* and interprets it as follows: *'Ki tireh'* — when you will come to the realization that — *'chamor'*— the physical matter of the body is — *'sonacha'*— your enemy — because he is engaged in attaining physical pleasures, and thus, hates the *neshama* who is striving for G-dliness and a high spiritual level — and the body is *'roveitz tachat masa'o'* — lying under his burden not wanting to get up and serve Hashem — *'vechadalta mei'azov lo'* — you may think that you will begin to torture him and deny him the food he needs. Be advised that this is a wrong approach. Instead, *'azov ta'azov imo'* — help him! Give him his bodily needs and attune your mind and soul to worship Hashem. Eventually, your body will become purified and cooperate in your worship."

(שמעתי מאבי חותני הרה"ח הרה"ת ר' אליהו משה ע"ה ליס - עי' היום יום, כ"ח שבט)

"וחג האסף בצאת השנה באספך את מעשיך מן השדה"

"The festival of ingathering *[Sukkot]* should be celebrated at the *end* of the year." (23:16)

QUESTION: In *Parshat Ki Tissa* (34:22) it is written, *"vechag ha'asif tekufat hashanah"* — "the festival of ingathering at the turn of the year." Rashi explains this to mean *"bitchilat hashanah haba'ah"* — "the *beginning* of the coming year."

Is *Sukkot* at the end or the beginning of the year?

ANSWER: Rabbi Levi says *(Yalkut Shimoni, Pinchas* 29): Hashem planned to give the Jewish people a *yom tov* every month of the spring and summer. Thus, *Pesach* falls in *Nissan, Pesach Sheini* in *Iyar,* and *Shavuot* in *Sivan.* When the Jewish people sinned in *Tammuz* with the golden calf, Hashem canceled *yamim tovim* for the months of *Tammuz, Av* and *Elul.* In *Tishrei,* however, He gave *Rosh Hashanah, Yom Kippur* and *Sukkot,* which were really supposed to be during *Tammuz, Av* and *Elul* respectively, and also *Shemini Atzeret* for the month of *Tishrei.*

In this *parshah,* Hashem is talking about the *yom tov* of *Sukkot, before* the Jews sinned with the golden calf. At that time the festival of *Sukkot* was designated to be at the end of the year, during the month of *Elul.* The sin of the golden calf is recorded in *Parshat Ki Tissa.* After the sin was committed, the *yom tov* of *Sukkot* was moved up to the beginning of the new year — the month of *Tishrei.*

(פנינים יקרים - ספר קנה אברהם)

"ראשית בכורי אדמתך תביא בית ד' אלקיך לא תבשל גדי בחלב אמו"

"Bring your first fruits *[bikurim]* to the house of G-d, your G-d; you shall not cook a kid in the milk of its mother." (23:19)

QUESTION: What is the connection between *bikurim* and cooking meat with milk?

ANSWER: The festival of *Shavuot* is also known as "the festival of *Bikurim*," being the preferred time for bringing *bikurim*. On the first day of *Shavuot* it is customary to eat a *milchig* meal. Thus, the Torah reminds us that when we bring the *bikurim* on *Shavuot*, we should be very careful while cooking for *Yom Tov* not to mix any meat together with milk.

(של"ה מס' שבועות)

* * *

In the olden days, if a farmer wanted his field to produce good fruits he would cook a kid in the milk of its mother. Pouring the milk on the field would fatten the soil. According to *halacha*, one is not only forbidden to eat a mixture of milk and meat, but also to derive and benefit from it. Therefore, the Torah tells us that if one properly fulfills the *mitzvah* of bringing the first fruits to the *Beit Hamikdash*, the produce of your fields will be blessed, making it unnecessary to violate this law in order to fatten the soil.

(שער בת רבים)

"ועבדתם את ד' אלקיכם וברך את לחמך ואת מימיך"

And you shall serve G-d, your G-d, and He shall bless your bread and your water." (23:25)

QUESTION: Why does the *pasuk* begin *"va'avadetem"* — "you [plural] shall serve" — and conclude *"lachmecha ve'et meimecha"* — "your [singular] bread and water"?

ANSWER: Our Sages speak very highly of *tefilah betzibur* — *davening* with a *minyan*. The word *"tzibur"* (צבור) is an acronym for "צדיקים בינונים ורשעים" — "righteous, intermediate, and wicked." Individually, one may not be worthy that Hashem grant him his desires. However, the *zechut* of the multitude can help pull through even those who in their own rights are lacking merit.

The Torah is advising that if *you* want Hashem to bless *"lachmecha"* — "your bread" — with abundance, this can be accomplished through *"va'avadetem"* — praying *betzibur* — and the *zechut* of the many will stand you in good stead.

"ונגש משה לבדו אל ד' והם לא יגשו"

"And Moshe alone shall approach G-d, but they shall not approach." (24:2)

QUESTION: The word *"levado"* — "alone" — seems superfluous, since it states *"veheim lo yigashu"* — "but they shall not approach"?

ANSWER: The *Gemara (Bava Metzia* 85b) relates that Rabbi Chaviva Bar Surmaki knew a Rabbi whom the prophet Eliyahu would visit regularly. Once he requested Eliyahu to show him the [departed] Sages as they ascend to the heavenly academy. He responded, "You may look upon all of them except for the carriage of Rabbi Chiya." The Rabbi inquired, "How will I know to distinguish between the carriage of Rabbi Chiya and the others?" Eliyahu replied, "All are accompanied by angels when they ascend and descend excepting Rabbi Chiya who ascends of his own accord."

The greatness of Moshe was that he was able to approach Hashem *"levado"* — "on his own" — while all the others were unable to do so. Therefore, the *pasuk* uses the expression *"veheim lo yigashu"* (יִגָּשׁוּ) in the passive, instead of *"veheim lo yigshu,"* (יִגְּשׁוּ) to teach that they could not approach, even with assistance. Moshe, however, had direct access to Hashem; as Torah states, *"UMoshe alah el haElokim"* — Moshe, on his own, ascended to G-d (19:3).

(שער בת רבים - שפתי כהן)

"ויאמרו כל אשר דבר ד' נעשה ונשמע"

"And they said, 'All that G-d has spoken we will do and we will obey.'" (24:7)

QUESTION: In the previous *parshah,* it is written, *"Vaya'anu chol ha'am yachdav"* — "And the people answered together, 'All that G-d has spoken, *na'aseh* — we will do'" (19:8). 1) Why is the word *"nishmah"* — "obey" — not mentioned? 2) Why in our *parshah* is there no mention that they responded *"yachdav"* — "together"?

ANSWER: It is really impossible for every Jew on his own to fulfill all the 613 *mitzvot.* Some *mitzvot* can only be performed by a king, others only by a *Kohen,* etc. Nevertheless, there are ways for every Jew to receive credit for the fulfillment of all the 613 *mitzvot:* 1) Through learning about the *mitzvot,* it is considered as though he performed them. 2) When the Jews are united, they are considered one entity. Thus, through togetherness, they fulfill all the *mitzvot* and share the rewards.

Therefore, in our *parshah,* since it says, *"na'aseh"* — "we will do" — and also *"nishmah"* — "we will obey" — which means to study and learn about the *mitzvot,* each Jew on his own is doing *"kol asher diber Hashem"* — "everything which Hashem has spoken." However, in *Parshat Yitro* only *"na'aseh"* — "we will do" — is mentioned, not *"nishmah,"* which means obeying and learning. Therefore, fulfilling *everything* G-d commands is *only* possible through *"yachdav"* — togetherness and unity.

(פרדס יוסף)

"ויחזו את האלקים ויאכלו וישתו"

"They gazed at G-d and they ate and drank." (24:11)

QUESTION: What is the connection between the spiritual delight of seeing G-d and physical eating and drinking?

ANSWER: Unfortunately there are people who are lax in their observance of *kashrut.* They eat in many establishments without really checking their reliability.

A story is told of a stranger who entered a "kosher" restaurant and began to inquire about its standards. The proprietor directed the visitor to a picture on the wall: "You see that man up there with the long beard and *peiyot;* he was my father." The visitor said to him, "If your father with the beard and *peiyot* was standing here behind the counter and your picture was hanging on the wall, I would not ask any questions. Since the opposite is true, I have doubts and must investigate before I can eat here."

The Torah is implying that before eating and drinking at any home or restaurant, one should check for a sign of a G-dly environment. Only after *seeing* that a G-dly and Torah spirit prevails should one partake of the food.

(פרדס יוסף)

附 ぬ

TERUMAH • תרומה

"ויקחו לי תרומה"
"Let them take for Me an offering." (25:2)

QUESTION: The word *"li"* — "for Me" — is superfluous. Would it not be sufficient to say *"Veyikchu terumah"*?

ANSWER: The first offering the farmer separates from his harvest is *terumah,* which he gives to the *Kohen.* According to the Torah, one can fulfill the *mitzvah* of *terumah* by giving a very small portion, even one grain of wheat for a huge pile. However, the Rabbis instituted that a generous person should give 1/40th (two and one half bushels of every 100), an average person should give 1/50th (two bushels of every 100), and a stingy person should give at least 1/60th (one and two thirds bushels of every 100).

The word *"li"* (לי) has the numerical value of 40. Hashem is telling Moshe that when a Jew gives *terumah* to the *Kohen,* he should be generous and give him one fortieth.

(פנינים יקרים)

"ויקחו לי תרומה"
"Let them take for Me an offering." (25:2)

QUESTION: According to Rashi, the word *"li"* teaches *"lishmi"* — "for My name." What is the connection between *terumah* and Hashem's name?

ANSWER: In *Bamidbar* (5:11-31) there is a discussion of the laws of a *sotah* — a woman suspected of being unfaithful to her husband. When she denies any wrongdoing, the husband is required to bring her to the *Kohen.* To determine her guilt or innocence, the *Kohen* erases this portion of the Torah, in which there is also written Hashem's name, mixes it with water, and gives it to the woman to drink.

Immediately preceding this is a discussion of giving gifts to the *Kohen*. Rashi explains that when a person does not recognize the *Kohen* to give him what the Torah allocates, he will eventually have to come to him with a suspected wife.

Thus, giving the *Kohen* his portions eliminates the possibility of having to erase Hashem's name for the *sotah*. Therefore, Rashi says that the giving of *terumah* is *"lishmi"* — "for the sake of not erasing My name."

(ילקוט האורים)

* * *

The *Gemara (Pesachim* 50a) says that the name of Hashem is not to be pronounced as written. However, in the *Beit Hamikdash* Hashem's name was in fact uttered.

The purpose of the collections discussed in the *parshah* was to build a sanctuary for Hashem; therefore, Hashem told Moshe, "Take up a collection so that they can build a sanctuary *'lishmi'* — for the sake of being able to recite My name as written."

(באר מים חיים)

* * *

The four-lettered name of Hashem is spelled "ה-ו-ה-י," and it teaches the correct manner of offering *tzedakah*. The "י" represents the coin being given. The "ה" is the hand (five fingers) giving the coin. The "ו" is the poor man stretching out his hand to receive the coin, and the final "ה" is the receiving hand. However, if a poor man first stretches his hand out and asks for *tzedakah,* the name of Hashem is not in order (ה,ה,ו,י).

Rashi is teaching that the proper way to give *tzedakah* is *"lishmi"* — in the order of the spelling of My name.

(של"ה)

"ויקחו לי תרומה"

"Let them take for Me an offering." (25:2)

QUESTION: The people *gave* donations to the building of the *Mishkan*. Why does it not say *"veyitnu"* — "and they should *give"*?

ANSWER: When a Jew gives *tzedakah* he is not only giving but also receiving, because when the poor man accepts the *tzedakah,* the giver receives a *zechut* for the *mitzvah,* through which he will get back from Hashem ten times as much as he gave. On the words *"Aser te'aser"* — "You shall give a tithe," *(Devarim* 14:22) the *Gemara (Ta'anit* 9a) says, *"Aser bishvil shetitasheir"* — "By giving ten percent to *tzedakah,* you will become rich."

Thus, by giving for the *Mishkan,* the Jews were "taking" from Hashem much more than they actually gave.

(אפריון)

"ויקחו לי תרומה מאת כל איש אשר ידבנו לבו תקחו את תרומתי"

"Let them take for Me an offering, of every man whose heart is willing, you shall take My offering." (25:2)

QUESTION: Why does the *pasuk* start with the word *"terumah"* — *an* offering — and conclude with the word *"terumati"* — *My* offering?

ANSWER: Sometimes people do not contribute to charitable causes wholeheartedly because they have to use money designated for another purpose when a collector for charity arrives unexpectedly.

It is therefore advisable to have a special box or account in which one deposits at least 10 percent of one's earnings earmarked "charity distributions." Thus, when a collector comes for a charitable cause, one will contribute willingly, because the money was already set aside exclusively for *tzedakah.*

The Torah imparts in this *pasuk* the following important advice: Hashem told Moshe to tell the Jewish people that the first thing each Jew should do is *"Veyikchu li"* — "Take from their earnings a portion for Me and set it aside as *'terumah'* — money to go for *tzedakah* causes. After doing this, you can be sure that when the time comes to take from them an offering for the *Mishkan* (or any other charitable cause), they will give it with the graciousness of their hearts. Because *'tikchu et terumati'* — they will not feel that you are taking theirs, but instead they are giving *tzedakah* from that which was already designated as *My* offering."

(כלי חמדה)

"ויקחו לי תרומה מאת כל איש אשר ידבנו לבו...וזאת התרומה אשר תקחו מאתם זהב וכסף ונחשת...שמן למאור בשמים...."

"Let them take for Me an offering, from everyone whose heart is willing...and this is the offering that you shall take from them: gold and silver and copper...oil for lighting, spices...."
(25:2-3)

QUESTION: 1) The word *"veyikchu"* means "they shall take," and it sounds as though Hashem is the giver and we are taking it from Him?

2) Why are each of the first items enumerated connected to the next with a *"vav"*: "זהב וכסף ונחשת ותכלת" — "gold *and* silver *and* copper" while there are no *"vav"*s connecting שמן למאור "בשמים לשמן המשחה...אבני שהם" — "oil for lighting, spices... *shoham* stone" (25:6)?

ANSWER: According to *Targum Yonatan Ben Uziel* (35:27), Hashem sent heavenly clouds to the Nile river in order to bring up the stones from the sands under the water and throw them near the Jewish camp. He also sent heavenly clouds to *Gan Eden* to bring the spices and olive oil. The heads of the tribes picked them up and brought them for the *Mishkan*.

Therefore, Hashem is saying the following: *"veyikchu li"* — "you should *take* from Me" — *"terumah"* — my contribution to the *Mishkan*. In addition, *"mei'eit kol ish asher yidvenu libo"* —

"[You shall also take] from every Jew whose heart directs to contribute gold and silver, etc."

The first eleven items mentioned all have a *"vav"* connecting one with another, because all these items were contributed by the people. Starting with *shemen lama'or* — oil for lighting — there are no *"vav"'s* because the items mentioned from there on were contributed by Hashem.

(נחל קדומים)

"וזאת התרומה אשר תקחו מאתם זהב וכסף ונחשת"
"And this is the offering you shall take from them: gold and silver and copper." (25:3)

QUESTION: Why is the most valuable metal, gold, called *"zahav"* (זהב), the cheaper metal, silver, named *"kesef"* (כסף), and the least valuable metal, copper, called *"nechoshet"* (נחשת)?

ANSWER: The word "זהב" is an acronym for זה הנותן בריא — one who gives his contribution while in good health. "כסף" is an acronym for כשיש סכנת פחד — he who contributes due to fear caused by danger. The word "נחשת" is an acronym for נתינת חולה שאמר תנו — a severely ill person who directs his family to give. He is unfortunately very sick and unable to give himself, but he instructs his family to give for him after he passes on.

In regard to giving *tzedakah* it is important not *what* one gives, but *how* one gives. Giving *tzedakah* just for the sake of the *mitzvah* and without any ulterior motive is similar to gold. When one is motivated by deep fear and gives money to diminish his fears, it is of lesser significance and considered like silver. Bequeathing charity is the lowest level of charity and therefore equivalent to copper.

(ר' מאיר מפרימישלאן זצ"ל)

Alternatively: *"Zahav"* (זהב) — "gold" — is an acronym for "זה המביא בעצמו" — the person knows of a charitable endeavor, and *before* even being asked, he brings his contribution; *"kesef"* (כסף) — "silver" — is an acronym for "כשהגבאים סובבים פתחו" —

the individual makes pledges but is not prompt in redeeming them. Only after the supervisors of the charity fund come to his house to collect, does he pay his pledge; *"nechoshet"* (נחשת) — "copper" — is an acronym for "נתן חלקו, שכפאוהו תחילה" — he gives only after being forced.

(משכנותיך ישראל)

"וזאת התרומה אשר תקחו מאתם זהב וכסף ונחשת...ועשו לי מקדש ושכנתי בתוכם"

"And this is the offering you shall take from them: gold and silver and copper...and let them make for Me a sanctuary and I will dwell among them." (25:3,8)

QUESTION: Why were our forefathers instructed to use silver and brass and not exclusively gold?

ANSWER: G-d commanded the Jews to build the *Mishkan* in order that *"veshachanti betocham"* — "I will dwell in them." Grammatically it should have said *"veshachanti betocho"* — "I will dwell in it." According to the *Shelah (Sha'ar Ha'otiot* 30) this indicates that in addition to building the physical *Mishkan,* Hashem wants each and every Jew to make himself and his home a holy place so that He can be among every Jew.

Among the Jewish populace there exists various levels. Some Jews are very pure (holy) like gold; others are compared to inferior metals such as silver and brass. The building of the *Mishkan* was for *all* Jews; regardless of a person's level, he must make himself a proper dwelling for Hashem.

(כ"ק אדמו"ר)

"ועשו לי מקדש ושכנתי בתוכם"

"They shall make for Me a sanctuary and I will dwell among them." (25:8)

QUESTION: Presently, they were building the *Mishkan* (tabernacle) and not the *Beit Hamikdash*. It should have said *"ve'asu li Mishkan"?* Furthermore, it should have said *"betocho"* — "in it" — instead of *"betocham"* — "in them"?

ANSWER: The first *Beit Hamikdash* lasted 410 years, and the second *Beit Hamikdash* 420 years. This *pasuk* is hinting this by saying *"ve'asu li Mikdash"* — "They shall make for Me a *Beit Hamikdash.*" The word *"veshachanti"* (ושכנתי) — "and I will rest" — can be read as two words: "ושכן" — "and I will rest [in it]" — "ת"י" — 410 years (ת = 400, י = 10). The word "ושכנתי" can also be rearranged to read "ושני ת"כי" — "and the second, 420."

Since the *pasuk* is alluding to Hashem's dwelling in the first and second *Beit Hamikdash*, it says *"betocham"* — "in them."

(בעל הטורים)

"ועשו לי מקדש ושכנתי בתוכם: ככל אשר אני מראה אותך את
תבנית המשכן ואת תבנית כל כליו וכן תעשו"

"And let them make Me a Mishkan that I may dwell among them. Like everything that I show you, the form of the Mishkan and the form of all its vessels, so shall you do." (25:8-9)

QUESTION: The words *"vechein ta'asu"* — "so shall you do" — seem superfluous — how else?

ANSWER: When Hashem conveyed through Moshe the command of building a *Mishkan*, He said, "They shall make a Sanctuary for Me — so that I may dwell *"betocham"* — "among them" (25:8). Grammatically, *"betocho,"* in the singular, should be used. The *Shelah* explains that in addition to the physical *Mishkan*, Hashem requests that each Jew should transform himself into a Sanctuary, so that He can dwell in them — in each and every Jew. Thus the Torah adds, *"vechein ta'asu,"* to indicate that in addition to the construction of the physical *Mishkan*, "so shall *you* do" — make yourself a Sanctuary for Hashem.

This is accomplished by living a life in accordance with the significance of all the details of the *Mishkan*. The Sanctuary contained the Ark, *menorah*, table, and altar. The Ark represents Torah study, the *menorah* depicts *mitzvot (neir mitzvah)*, the table alludes to hospitality and *kashrut*, and the altar signifies *mesirut nefesh* — dedication. Likewise, the home of every individual must have *seforim* and Torah study, the performance of *mitzvot,* a table with Kosher food and guests, and *mesirut nefesh* to maintain the highest standards of *Yiddishkeit.*

The Jew who builds such a home can be assured that just as G-d abides in the *Mishkan,* so He will also dwell in the home.

(שפתי כהן)

"ועשו ארון"
"And they shall make an Ark." (25:10)

QUESTION: Why for all the vessels made for the *Mishkan* such as the table, *menorah,* etc. does the Torah command in a singular form — *"ve'asita"* — "And you shall make," while only for the Ark and *efod* (apron) does it say *"ve'asu"* — "And *they* shall make?" (28:6)

ANSWER: The Ark contained the tablets and represents the idea of studying and observing Torah. The word *"efod"* (אפד) has the numerical value of 85, which spells the word *"peh"* (פ=80, ה=5) — "mouth" — and is a hint for the *Torah Sheba'al Peh* — the Oral Torah. With the plural expression Hashem is alluding that both the Written and Oral Torah belong to *Klal Yisrael.* Each and every Jew has a share in it and no individual can claim ownership of Torah.

(קרבן העני)

* * *

Alternatively, it is incumbent upon every Jew to learn Torah full-time — day and night. Since this is impossible for everyone to accomplish, two Jews can enter into an agreement: One will learn Torah full time and the other will work and support him and receive a share in his *mitzvah* of learning Torah. This is known as the "Yissachar-Zevulun" arrangement. Yissachar learned Torah full time, and Zevulun did business and supported him. The Ark which housed the tablets, represents Torah study. Since most individuals cannot achieve maximum Torah study on their own, the command is in the plural.

(כלי יקר)

* * *

In the Torah there are 613 *mitzvot*. Some *mitzvot* can only be performed by *Kohanim,* others only by *Levi'im* and others only by *Yisra'eilim.* Since it is impossible for a single Jew to fulfill all 613 *mitzvot,* the making of the Ark, which represents Torah, is commanded in the plural.

(אור החיים)

"ועשו ארון עצי שטים אמתים וחצי ארכו ואמה וחצי רחבו ואמה וחצי קמתו"

"They shall make an Ark 2 1/2 cubits in length, 1 1/2 cubits in width, and 1 1/2 cubits in height." (25:10)

QUESTION: Why did all the measurements of the Ark include fractions?

ANSWER: The Ark, which contained in it the *tablets,* represents Torah study. The measurements teach that people who learn Torah must always bear in mind that regardless of how much they learn, they do not master it all. The extent of their knowledge is only a fraction of the vast teachings and depth of the Torah.

(כלי יקר)

* * *

It is also for this reason that the first page of every *Gemara* is *daf beit* (folio 2) and not *daf alef* (folio 1). This reminds the Torah student not to conceitedly think that he has mastered it, for he still lacks knowledge of the first page.

"ועשו ארון...ועשית שלחן...ועשית מנורת זהב טהור"

"You shall make an Ark...a table...a menorah." (25:10,23,31)

QUESTION: Why are the items for the *Mishkan* listed in this order?

ANSWER: In the *pesukim* concerning the making of the Ark every letter of the *alef-beit* is used except the letter *gimel.* An explanation for this is that *"gimel"* in Hebrew alludes to *"gemul"* which means "reward" (see *Shabbat* 104a). Since the Ark represents Torah study, the *gimel* is omitted to emphasize that a person should not study Torah to receive a reward.

The table and the bread on it represent material affluence. The *menorah* represents spiritual light and warmth.

The order in which these three items are listed in the Torah conveys an important lesson. When one learns Torah *lesheim Shamayim* — without anticipation of personal gain, but only to fulfill Hashem's command — eventually he will be rewarded with a table and *menorah* — material and spiritual abundance.

(כלי יקר)

"ועשו ארון...וצפית אותו זהב טהור...ועשית בדי עצי שטים וצפית אתם זהב"

"And you shall make an Ark...and cover it with pure gold. And you shall make poles of cedar wood and cover them with gold." (25:10-11,13)

QUESTION: Why were the poles which carried the Ark covered with ordinary gold, while the Ark itself was covered with pure gold?

ANSWER: The Ark, which housed the tablets, alludes to the one who studies Torah. The poles, which carry the Ark, represent the people who support the scholars dedicated to Torah study.

Torah should be studied *lishma* — for the sake of Hashem and without ulterior motives. *Tzedakah,* however, may be given with personal gain in mind. According to the *Gemara,* even if one gives charity on the condition that his child should live, it is *"tzedakah gamurah"* — the highest form of charity — and the giver is considered a *"tzaddik gamur"* — a "perfect *tzaddik*" (*Rosh Hashanah* 4a, see *Rabbeinu Chananeil*).

Consequently, when speaking of the Ark, which represents Torah study, *pure* gold is required, to emphasize that Torah study should be totally pure of ulterior motives.

(קרבן העני)

"בטבעת הארן יהיו הבדים לא יסרו ממנו"

"In the rings of the Ark shall be the poles; they shall not be removed from it." (25:15)

QUESTION: Instead of *"mimeno"* — "from him" — why does it not say "They shall not be removed, *meihem"* — from *them* (the rings)?

ANSWER: The Ark housed the *tablets* and represents the Torah scholar. The poles represent the philanthropists who support the Torah scholar and enable him to study in tranquillity.

At all times it is incumbent upon the benefactors to stand alongside the Torah scholar and never leave *him* without financial resources. *(Mimeno* can mean either "from him" or "from it.")

(אלשיך)

"ועשית שנים כרבים זהב מקשה תעשה אתם ...אל הכפרת יהיו פני הכרבים"

"And you shall make two *keruvim* of gold...toward the ark cover shall the faces of the *keruvim* be." (25:18-20) "They had the form of the face of a child." (Rashi)

QUESTION: When Adam transgressed and ate from the tree of knowledge, the Torah relates, "So He drove out the man and He placed at the east of the Garden of Eden the *keruvim,* and the flaming sword which turned every way." *(Bereishit* 3:24). Rashi comments that the *keruvim* were "destructive angels." It is enigmatic that the same exact term should have such contrasting interpretations; here, the *keruvim* express the innocence of a small child, yet regarding the exile from the Garden of Eden, they are described as "destructive angels?"

ANSWER: Rearing children has always been a challenging and difficult task over which parents have struggled and agonized. In contemporary times, we live in an atmosphere of turbulence and confusion, in an era when statistics indicate gloomy prospects for children continuing their parents' religious lifestyles. We hear of a generation gap and the estrangement and alienation of our youth.

Many parents ponder the question, "What have I done wrong? Why was I unsuccessful with my children?"

Keruvim are children. They can be wonderful faultless angels, or vicious and destructive. It is important to always bear in mind that it depends on where we put them, and to what we expose them.

If we choose to expose the child to the *"cherev hamithapechet"* — the contemporary "swinging swords" of materialism, secularism, and modernism — we must then be prepared to suffer the consequence that the *keruvim* — the faultless children — may turn into destructive angels.

However, if one resolves to attach his children to the Holy Ark, teaching them to look toward the Ark and the Torah for guidance, he can then anticipate the reward of the *keruvim* — spiritually pure children who will be a source of *"Yiddishe nachas"* to their parents, family, and the entire Jewish people.

"מן הכפרת תעשו את הכרבים על שני קצותיו"

"From the Ark-cover you shall make the *keruvim* on its two ends." (25:19)

QUESTION: The *keruvim* were to be hammered out simultaneously with the making of the Ark-cover (Rashi). Why weren't they made separately and attached afterwards to the cover?

ANSWER: The *keruvim* were statues which had the faces of small children (Rashi). They were placed on the cover, gazing down at the Ark. Their message was that Jewish children should be exposed to and directed to the teachings of the Torah.

A father and mother of a two-year-old child once argued about when should they begin the Torah education of their child. The father contended that when the child reached school age, they would send him to *yeshivah*. The mother argued, however, to wait until he matured. Unable to resolve their argument, they agreed to consult a Rabbi. They presented their views and the Rabbi then inquired, "How old is your child?" They responded, "Two years old." The Rabbi looked at them and said, "I regret to tell you that you are already two years late."

The Torah is teaching that as soon as the child is born, there should be no delay, and he should immediately be exposed to a Torah education so that he can lead a Torah-true life. Do not wait to "attach" him at some later date.

(לקוטי בתר לקוטי מהדו״ת)

"וּפְנֵיהֶם אִישׁ אֶל אָחִיו אֶל הַכַּפֹּרֶת יִהְיוּ פְּנֵי הַכְּרֻבִים"

"And their faces shall look one to another; towards the Ark-cover the faces of the *keruvim* shall be." (25:20)

QUESTION: The *Gemara (Bava Batra* 99a) asks why in the *Mishkan* the *keruvim* faced each other, whereas in the *Beit Hamikdash "ufeneihem labayit"* — their faces were to the walls of the house" (II Chronicles 3:13). The *Gemara* answers: When the Jews fulfilled Hashem's wish, the *keruvim* faced each other. When they conducted themselves contrary to His will, then the *keruvim* faced the wall.

What is the connection between the direction of the *keruvim* and the will of Hashem?

ANSWER: The *Gemara's* explanation of the direction the *Keruvim* faced may be explained as a metaphor: "Each man facing his brother" (the literal translation of *"ish el achiv"*) can be taken as a symbol of the relationship between one Jew and another when in compliance with the will of Hashem. He desires that a Jew always be concerned for a fellow Jew.

"Facing the walls of the house" means that one turns his back on the other and is totally preoccupied with what takes place within the walls of his home. Such selfish behavior is contrary to G-d's will.

(פרדס יוסף)

"ועשית שלחן עצי שטים אמתים ארכו ואמה רחבו ואמה וחצי קמתו"

"You shall make a table of acacia wood two cubits long, one cubit wide, and one cubit and a half in height." (25:23)

QUESTION: Why was the width of the table less than the height?

ANSWER: Inviting guests and feeding the needy is highly commendable. Unfortunately, often people go overboard on lavish table expenses in order to make an impression. Their extravagance causes them huge debts and may be at the expense of giving *tzedakah* or paying tuition. The Torah teaches us that the width *("breitkeit"* — expansiveness) of one's table should not exceed one's "material height."

(פון אונזער אלטען אוצר)

"ונתת על השלחן לחם פנים"

"Set upon the table *lechem happanim* — show-bread." (25:30)

QUESTION: Rashi explains that *"panim"* means "face" — the bread's sides faced and saw the sides of the *Mishkan.* (Some explain *"panim"* to mean "sides" because each loaf had 12 sides, and others explain it to mean "hollow inside" — see commentaries on *Mishnah Menachot* 11:6.)

Why were the *lechem hapanim* "U"-shaped (like a square "U," an open box with both ends removed)?

ANSWER: The table represents the *mitzvah* of hospitality and feeding the needy. Unfortunately, often when a person is blessed and sated, he is insensitive to the needs of others. His success and wealth prevent him from seeing and understanding the needs of the poor. The Torah therefore prescribes that the bread on the table be "U"-shaped. A normal loaf of bread is a solid, opaque mass, but one could look through the hollow *lechem hapanim* loaf. This alludes that one's bread, i.e. one's success, should not block one's vision. The needs of the poor must always be visible.

"Lechem hapanim" can be translated literally as "bread of the face," possibly alluding to the importance of "seeing" the poor man's imploring face.

"ונתת על השלחן לחם פנים"
"On the table you shall place showbread be for Me always." (25:30)

QUESTION: The show-bread was prepared on Friday and rested on the table until the following *Shabbat.* Miraculously, it maintained its warmth and freshness. This miracle was a sign of Hashem's love for the Jewish people. When Jews made the pilgrimage on *Yom Tov,* the table would be uplifted for everyone to view the miracle of fresh loaves of bread *(Chagigah* 27b). There were many miracles that occurred in the *Beit Hamikdash,* as mentioned in *Pirkei Avot* (5:5); why was this miracle (which is not mentioned among the others in *Pirkei Avot*) demonstrated to those who made the pilgrimage?

ANSWER: When King David was in the wilderness of Yehudah, he sang to Hashem, "My soul thirsts for you, my flesh yearns for you in a land barren and with no water. Just as I have beheld you in the Sanctuary to see your might and glory" (Psalms 63:2-3). Simply, this is understood as King David expressing his yearning now to be as close to G-d as he was within the Sanctuary.

The Ba'al Shem Tov provides a Chassidic explanation that King David is actually praying that he should retain this thirst and yearning he now has for Hashem while in a barren and distant land also when he is actually within the Sanctuary.

People typically yearn for things that seem distant and inaccessible. Once obtained, however, the object of desire often loses its appeal. Thus, a child away from home yearns to see his parents, and as the days approach for his return home, his excitement increases greatly. However, when he is finally home, he neglects his parents and takes them for granted.

Therefore, King David expresses the wish that even after he is granted the opportunity of again being close to G-d and beholding

G-dliness in the Sanctuary, his aspiration and strong desire for G-dliness should not be lessened.

The Jews were shown the show-bread to demonstrate that just as the freshness of the show-bread was constantly maintained, so the desire and longing that they have for Hashem before the pilgrimage should be retained once they are in Yerushalayim, and even after leaving.

”ועשית מנרת זהב טהור מקשה תיעשה המנורה”
"You shall make a *menorah* of pure gold, hammered out shall the *menorah* be made." (25:31)

QUESTION: Rashi writes that Moshe had difficulty understanding the making of the *menorah*. What couldn't Moshe comprehend about the *menorah*?

ANSWER: One of the esoteric interpretations of the *menorah* is that it symbolized *klal yisroel*. (See *Likkutei Torah, Beha'alotcha*.)

The *menorah* was kindled with pure olive oil. According to the *Gemara (Menachot* 85b) olive oil is associated with knowledge.

Throughout the long exile, the Jewish people were scattered to all corners of the world. Wherever they sojourned the country benefited immensely from their wisdom, intellect, and creativity. Nevertheless anti-semitism prevailed and the Jewish people, who enhanced the country, were beaten and persecuted.

This strange phenomenon puzzled Moshe to no end. The Jewish people who have contributed so much to humanity through their intellect and wisdom should be cherished and appreciated by all, and in fact they are being hammered!?

(מצאתי בכתבי אבי הרב שמואל פסח ז"ל באגאמילסקי)

**"וששה קנים יצאים מצדיה שלשה קני מנרה מצדה האחד ושלשה
קני מנרה מצדה השני"**

**"And six branches going out of its sides; three branches of
the *menorah* out of its one side, and three branches of the
menorah out of its other side." (25:32)**

QUESTION: In what position were the branches and cups?

ANSWER: The Rambam wrote a commentary on *mishnayot*
in Arabic which was recently newly translated to Hebrew in the
Kapach Edition. This newer, more precise translation includes the
Rambam's own drawing of the *menorah (Menachot* 3:7).
Evidently, the branches *(kanim)* of the *menorah* were not curved
like semi-circles, but instead they were straight and extended
diagonally upwards. (Rashi too is of this opinion.) The cups
(gevi'im) were on the branches for beauty and were inverted with
the wide end downward.

* * *

The popular image of the *menorah* with curved branches
stems from the *menorah* which is engraved on the Arch of Titus in
Rome. Titus was the Roman general who conquered *Yerushalayim*
and destroyed the second *Beit Hamikdash.* It was customary in
those days to build a special gate through which the victorious
soldiers would enter upon returning to their homeland.

On the Arch are engraved various scenes to commemorate the
victory, and included is the *menorah* which he defiled. The
craftsmen made the *menorah* according to a general idea of how it
looked. However, according to the Rambam the *menorah* on the
Arch is an inaccurate replica of the one in the *Beit Hamikdash.*

(לקוטי שיחות חכ"א)

* * *

Some sources state that the cups were put with the wide end
upwards to catch any dripping oil.

(חזקוני)

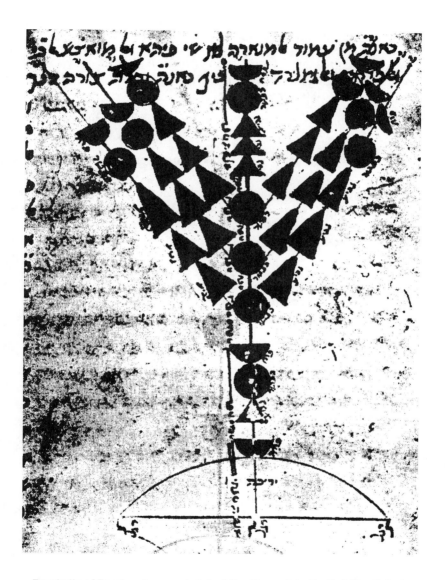

Facsimile of Rambam's own sketch of the *Menorah* in the *Beit Hamikdash*

"ועשית את הקרשים למשכן"

"And you shall make the boards for the *Mishkan.*" (26:15)

QUESTION: The boards for the *Mishkan* were of acacia wood from trees which Yaakov planted in Egypt and instructed his children to take with them upon leaving (Rashi).

These boards were over 200 years old. Why didn't the Jews send messengers to a nearby country to get fresh wood?

ANSWER: In each and every generation it is the goal of young people to construct their own homes. Often the younger generation has become acclimated to modern ideas and ideals. To demonstrate their progress, they bring their modernity into their homes and unfortunately detach themselves from the proper way of Torah life.

By mentioning the antique boards prepared by Yaakov, the Torah teaches us that a true Jewish home should conform to the "styles" and be in accordance with the tradition and heritage of our forefathers. Such a home is a miniature sanctuary in which Hashem desires to dwell.

"והבריח התיכן בתוך הקרשים מברח מן הקצה אל הקצה"

"And the middle bar in the midst of the boards, which shall pass through from end to end." (26:28)

QUESTION: How did the Jewish people get wood for the middle bar?

ANSWER: The middle bar was 70 *amot* (approximately 110 feet) long and encircled the three walls of the *Mishkan (Gemara Shabbat* 98b). When the Jews passed through the Red Sea, angels cut down the tree Avraham planted many years ago in Be'er Sheva. They cast it into the waters and it floated on the surface of the sea. The angels proclaimed, "This is the tree planted by Avraham in Be'er Sheva, and there he called in the name of G-d" *(Bereishit* 21:33). The Jewish people took it and used it for the middle bar.

(תרגום יונתן בן עוזיאל)

* * *

According to another opinion, it was Yaakov's staff with which he crossed the Jordan *(Bereishit* 32:11).

(דעת זקנים מבעלי התוס׳ ר״פ תרומה)

* * *

A miracle occurred, and when the *Mishkan* was constructed, the bar would encircle the *Mishkan* like a resilient snake. When the *Mishkan* was dismantled, the bar would revert back to its original form.

(תרגום יונתן בן עוזיאל - ועי׳ מס׳ שבת צ״ח ע״ב)

"כל עמודי החצר סביב מחשקים כסף וויהם כסף ואדניהם נחשת"

"All pillars of the court all around shall be filleted with silver and their hooks of silver, and their sockets of copper." (27:17)

QUESTION: In the *Mishkan* the pillars were covered with gold and the sockets were of silver. Why in the courtyard were they covered with silver with the sockets of copper?

ANSWER: The *Gemara (Chagigah* 9b) says: "Poverty is a beautiful thing for the Jewish people, just as a red ribbon is to a white horse." Commentaries explain that this seemingly strange statement intends to imply an important lesson. A horse is dressed up *only* when it is taken out to a fair for show, but not when it is in the stable. Likewise, in our homes we may have riches, but to the eyes of the world, the Jewish people should manifest poverty and appear very modest. Demonstrating it on the exterior would arouse the jealousy and eventual hatred of the Gentile world against us.

Inside the *Mishkan,* everything was lavishly beautiful and extremely expensive. But on the outside, the top was covered with goatskin, the pillars were filleted with silver, and the sockets were of copper. There was no show of extravagance, only modest simplicity.

(לקוטי בתר לקוטי מהדו״ת)

ଔ ଓ

TETZAVEH • תצוה

"And you shall command the Children of Israel." (27:20)

QUESTION: Why is the name of Moshe *Rabbeinu* not mentioned in *Parshat Tetzaveh?*

ANSWER: Moshe died on the seventh day of *Adar,* which usually falls during the week when *Parshat Tetzaveh* is read. Since his passing took place during the week of *Tetazveh,* his name is not mentioned. Even in a leap year, the *Magen Avraham* (580:8) says that those who fast on the seventh of *Adar* should fast in the first *Adar* because there are opinions that the year Moshe *Rabbeinu* died was a leap year and that he died in the first *Adar.*

(מאור עינים)

According to Rabbi Chanina Bar Papa, Moshe was born in a leap year in the first *Adar (Sotah* 13b). Thus, since his birth and death occurred on exactly the same day, we can conclude that he died in the first month of *Adar.*

(שאילת יעב"ץ - ועי' לקוטי שיחות חט"ז ע'324)

* * *

Alternatively, when Hashem considered annihilating the Jewish people for sinning with the golden calf, Moshe interceded and said, *"Mecheini na misifrecha asher katavta"* — "Erase me now from your book that You have written" (32:32). Hashem replied, "You have not sinned against me, and thus there is no reason for you to be erased." Nevertheless, a *tzaddik* must be extremely cautious with every word he utters (see *Berachot* 56a). Since when Moshe mentioned the concept of being erased from Hashem's book he used the extra word, **"asher katavta"** *(shekatavta* would be sufficient), his name was erased from *Parshat Tetzaveh* because the words *"asher"* (אשר) and *"Tetzave"* (תצוה) each have the same numerical value of 501.

(משכנותיך ישראל)

* * *

Alternatively, when the Jews sinned with the *eigel* (golden calf), Hashem contemplated no longer accompanying the *B'nei Yisrael* and said to Moshe: *"Hinei malachi yeileich lefanecha"* — "My angel will go before you" (32:34). Hashem wanted the angel Michael to lead the Jewish people together with Moshe. (The word "מלאכי" — "My angel" — can be rearranged to read "מיכאל".) Moshe refused to accept the angel *Michael* and insisted that Hashem Himself accompany the Jewish people (Rashi 33:15).

In *Parshat Tetzaveh,* there are 101 *pesukim* and the *siman* (mnemonic) to remember this is the word "מיכאל," which has the numerical value of 101. The *Parshah* in which there is a *remez* (hint) for מיכאל does not mention the name of Moshe because Moshe refused to go together with Michael.

(חנוכת התורה)

"ואתה תצוה"
"Now you shall command." (27:20)

QUESTION: Why does Hashem use the word *"tetzaveh"* in preference to the more commonly used words *"tomar"* and *"tedaber"*?

ANSWER: The word *"tetzaveh"* is related to the word *"tzava'ah"* — "will." It is common for a parent to leave a will and testament for his children and Hashem is telling Moshe "Since there will be a time when you will not be with *B'nei Yisrael,* leave them the following instruction for future generations":

"Veyikchu eilecha shemen zayit zach" — "They shall take for you pure olive oil." Olive oil does not mix with any other liquid, but rather separates and rises to the top. This reminds the Jews that they are unique, and should not mix and assimilate with others.

"Katit lema'or" — "Pressed for illumination." The *"ma'or"* represents the light of Torah: as stated in Proverbs (6:23), "Torah is *or* — light." In order to truly succeed in Torah study, one needs to "press" oneself, as our Sages tell us, *Yagati umatzati ta'amin"* — "If someone says 'I have toiled and I have succeeded' believe him" *(Megillah* 6b).

"Leha'alot neir tamid" — "to kindle the lamp continually." The "lamp" represents the soul of the Jew — *"Neir Hashem nishmat adam"* — "The 'lamp' of Hashem is the soul of the person" (Proverbs 20:27). The purpose of the Jew in this world is *"leha'alot neir tamid"* — to elevate his soul continually.

(משכנותיך ישראל)

"ואתה תצוה...להעלת נר תמיד"
"And you shall command ... to kindle the lamp continually." (27:20)

QUESTION: It should have said *"ve'ata tzaveih"* (צוה). Why does it say *"tetzaveh"*?

ANSWER: Our *parshah* instructs about the kindling of the *menorah* in the *Mishkan* and later in the *Beit Hamikdash.* When Hashem told Moshe to teach the construction of the *Mishkan,* He said: "Make for Me a sanctuary *veshachanti betocham"* — "that I may dwell among them." Grammatically, it should have said *"veshachanti betocho"* — "I will dwell in it." Hashem was hinting that He wants each and every Jew to make himself and his home a sanctuary for Him.

Our tables are compared in many ways to the altar, and the *Shabbat* candles to the *menorah.* It is customary in all Jewish homes for mothers and daughters to light *Shabbat* candles. A *"remez"* (hint) for this in Torah is the word *"tetzaveh"* (תצוה). The extra "ת"י has the numerical value of 400 — which is the same numerical value as the word *"nashim"* (נשים) — "women." Thus, the word "תצוה" can be read as two words (צוה, נשים = ת), and the message is "ואתה" — "and you" — "נשים צוה" — "the women command" — that they should light candles in their homes in honor of *Shabbat*.

(בעל הטורים)

"ויקחו אליך שמן זית זך"
"They shall take for you pure olive oil." (27:20)

QUESTION: Why does the Torah use the word *"zayit"* (olive) in the singular, rather than *"zeitim"* (plural)?

ANSWER: When food the size of an egg or more becomes *tamei* (defiled), it can transmit defilement to other liquids. In smaller amounts, it can become *tamei,* but cannot transmit its *tumah* (defilement).

The oil in the olive is considered as though it is enclosed in a casing within the olive. Consequently, even when an olive becomes *tamei,* the oil in it retains its purity.

Though the oil is considered a *separate entity* within the olive, it is measured together with the olive for purposes of transmitting *tumah*. Thus, if the size of the *tamei* olive is bigger than an egg, the first drop of oil pressed becomes *tamei* as soon as it touches the outside skin (see *Pesachim* 33b).

When Moshe instructed the Jews to contribute olives in order to make pure oil for the *menorah,* a problem arose. The olives in their possession were brought with them from Egypt. They were unsure about their purity and in doubt whether they could be used for the *Mishkan.*

Moshe therefore advised them to use average-sized olives, normally equal to half an egg. He also told them *not* to squeeze more than one olive at a time. Consequently, even if the olive was defiled, it would not be large enough to transmit *tumah* to the oil that came out.

(פנים יפות)

"שמן זית זך כתית למאור"

"Pure olive oil, beaten for the light." (27:20)

QUESTION: Rashi explains that the first drop of oil pressed is the finest and was used to kindle the *menorah*. The remaining oil of the olive (which was not as pure) was used for *menachot* (meal offerings).

Normally, one uses the best oil for baking and cheaper oil for burning or lighting. Why in the *Beit Hamikdash* was it the reverse?

ANSWER: The *menorah* is the prototype of spirituality. It represents Torah and *mitzvot*, as King Solomon states, *"Neir mitzvah vetorah or"* — "A candle is a *mitzvah* and Torah is light" (Proverbs 6:23). A *Karban Minchah* is eaten and represents the material and physical needs of a person.

Unfortunately, there are people who plead poverty when they have to spend money for Torah and *mitzvot*, but have plenty of money when it comes to personal pleasures. From the way things were done in the *Mishkan*, we can learn true priorities. For Torah and *mitzvot* one should spend money and use the best and purest. For personal pleasure, a Jew should practice restraint and learn to suffice with less.

(כלי יקר)

"ויקחו אליך שמן זית זך כתית למאור להעלת נר תמיד"

"They should take for you pure olive oil, beaten for the light, to kindle the lamp continually." (27:20)

QUESTION: It would have been sufficient to just say "They should take for you pure olive oil for the light," why the words *"katit"* and *"leha'alot ner tamid"*?

ANSWER: The first *Beit Hamikdash* lasted 410 years, and the second lasted 420 years. During the entire 830 years the *menorah* was kindled every day. We all hope to merit speedily the third *Beit Hamikdash*, which will last forever. The elaboration in the *pasuk* is a *remez* — hint — to this.

The word *"katit"* (כתית) — "beaten" — has in it the letters
"כ"ת"and "ת"י, which equal 420, and the letters "י"י and "ת"י, which
equal 410. The oil should be "כתית" — for 830 years of lighting
the *menorah*. Afterwards, will be *"leha'alot neir tamid"* — the
third *Beit Hamikdash* — in which the candles will be lit forever.

(בעל הטורים - תולדות יצחק)

"להעלת נר תמיד"
"To kindle [bring up] the lamp continually." (27:20)

QUESTION: Rashi explains the word *"leha'alot"* to mean to
kindle until the flame rises up by itself. In the beginning of
parshat Beha'alotcha, Rashi writes that the word *"beha'alotcha"*
teaches that there were steps in front of the *menorah* upon which
the *Kohen* would stand and prepare the candles. Why doesn't
Rashi in our *parshah* say that the word *"leha'alot"* teaches that
there was a step?

ANSWER: In our *parshah,* Hashem instructs Moshe that the
Jews should bring *him* oil in order to kindle the *menorah*. When
the *Mishkan* was erected, for the first seven days Moshe served as
the *Kohen Gadol* and performed the service in the *Mishkan*. The
Gemara (Berachot 54b) says that Moshe was ten *amot* tall
(approximately 16 feet). Thus, when he kindled the *menorah* he
did not need any step to stand on, for he was much taller than the
menorah. Therefore, Rashi explains that the word *"leha'alot"*
teaches us a rule about how to kindle the *menorah* itself.

However, *Parshat Beha'alotcha* discusses the kindling of the
menorah by Aharon and his descendants throughout the
generations. Since many *Kohanim* were not very tall and it is
forbidden for a *Kohen Gadol* to raise his hands above the *tzitz*
(forehead plate), Rashi writes that the *Kohen* would stand on a step
while kindling the *menorah*.

(פון אונזער אלטען אוצר)

"ועשו את האפד"

"They shall make the *efod*." (28:6)

QUESTION: Rashi writes: "Though I did not hear or find any place a description of the *efod*, my heart tells me that it is similar to the apron worn by princesses when they go horseback riding" (28:4).

How did Rashi get this idea?

ANSWER: Rashi was a great *tzaddik* and carefully observed Torah in all details. It is immodest for women to go horseback riding and a *tzaddik* would definitely not want to see women doing something improper.

One day, while Rashi was walking in the street, a princess rode past him on a horse and Rashi noticed her clothes. He began to contemplate why Hashem caused him to witness such a scene. When he was writing his commentary and came to the *efod*, he was unable to find a way to describe it. Suddenly, he reminded himself of the princess that he had seen ride past him and said: "My heart now tells me that Hashem showed me the princess horseback riding to suggest a way to describe the *efod*."

(אוצר החסידות - ר' יחיאל מאיר מגוסטינין זצ"ל)

"ועשית חשן משפט"

"You shall make a breastplate of judgment." (28:15)

QUESTION: Why was the descriptive word "judgment" added to the name *"choshen"* — "breastplate"?

ANSWER: Jewry eagerly awaits the ultimate redemption through *Mashiach*.

The prophet Isaiah says in the name of Hashem: "Keep justice and do righteousness, for soon my deliverance will come" (56:1). *Midrash Rabbah (Devarim* 5:7) states: "G-d says, 'if you will observe these two (Charity and Justice), immediately I will redeem you a full redemption.'" The word *choshen* (חשן) has the

numerical value of 358, which is also the numerical value of
Mashiach (משיח).

Thus the words *choshen mishpat* allude that the way to merit
Mashiach (חשן) is through *mishpat* — true and honest judgment.

(בית יעקב - חיד"א)

"והטור הרביעי תרשיש ושהם וישפה"

"The fourth row of stones [in the breastplate] was chrysolite, onyx, and jasper." (28:20)

The *Talmud Yerushalmi (Pei'ah* 1:1) says we can learn a
lesson in *kibud av* — honoring one's father — from a non-Jew by
the name of Dama Ben Netina.

Once, the *yashpeh* (jasper) stone of the breastplate got lost,
and he happened to have one. When the Jews came to him, he
refused to sell it, even at a very large profit, because the key to his
safe was under the pillow upon which his father was sleeping.

QUESTION: Why was a lesson in *kibud av* — honoring one's
father conveyed particularly through the stone *yashpeh?*

ANSWER: On each of the 12 stones of the breastplate was
written the name of one of the 12 tribes. The stone *yashpeh* had on
it the name "Binyamin." The numerical value of *"yashpeh"*
(ישפה), counting the word itself as one, is 396, which is the same
numerical value as בנימין בן יעקב.

The brothers, by plotting against Yosef and selling him,
caused much agony to Yaakov. Thus, their performance of the
mitzvah of *kibud av* was lacking. Binyamin was the only one who
had absolutely no part in his brothers' thoughts or activities
against Yosef. Consequently, he surpassed his brothers in the
observance of the *mitzvah* of *kibud av,* and it is therefore most
appropriate that a lesson in *kibud av* should be learned from the
stone which bore his name.

(מעינה של תורה)

"ולא יזח החשן מעל האפוד"

"And the breastplate will not be loosened from upon the *efod*." (28:28)

QUESTION: What is so terrible if the choshen becomes loosened from the *efod?*

ANSWER: Aharon wore the breastplate *"al libo"* — "on his heart" (28:29) The word *"efod"* (אפד) has the numerical value of 85, which is the same as the numerical value of *"peh"* (פה) — "mouth." Torah is alluding that the mouth and the heart should be in unison. Being *"echad bepeh ve'echad beleiv"* — saying things that we do not really mean — is wicked and contrary to Torah.

(דגל מחנה אפרים)

"ונתת אל חשן המשפט את האורים ואת התמים"

"And you shall place in the breastplate the *Urim* and the *Tumim*." (28:30)

QUESTION: What were the *Urim* and the *Tumim*, and how did they operate?

ANSWER: The *Urim* and the *Tumim* were two inscriptions of the Divine Name. When Moshe was in heaven studying the Torah, Hashem revealed to him the secret of how he should make the *Urim* and the *Tumim*. Only Moshe, to whom the secret was revealed, was able to make them, and he placed them into the fold of the breastplate. Therefore, it is not written anywhere that anyone should contribute to the making of the *Urim* and the *Tumim* or any instruction to the workers about how to make it.

* * *

On the 12 stones of the breastplate were written the names of the twelve tribes, the names of the patriarchs, Avraham, Yitzchak and Yaakov, and also the words "שבטי ישרון" (*Yoma* 73b). On each stone were six letters, including the name of the tribe, and thus there were 72 letters in total.

When a question was brought before the *Kohen Gadol*, he would meditate on His Holy name of the *Urim*. This would cause the letters on the stones of the breastplate to light up or protrude. These letters spelled the answer to the question. However, since they were not in any special order, again the *Kohen Gadol* would have to meditate on the Holy name of the *Tumim* and, thus, he would be given *Ruach Hakodesh* — Divine inspiration — a level of prophecy lower than the one called *"nevuah,"* to arrange the letters properly and convey the correct answer.

(רש"י ורמב"ן)

* * *

In the second *Beit Hamikdash,* though they had the breastplate, they did not seek instructions from it, either because the power of *Ruach Hakodesh* was lacking or because they lacked the *Urim veTumim.* During this period they relied on a *bat kol,* a voice which emanated from heaven, a level of prophecy lower than *Ruach Hakodesh.*

(עי' רמב"ם בית הבחירה פ"ד הל"א וספר קול צופים)

* * *

Chana, the mother of the prophet Shmuel, came to the *Beit Hamikdash* every year to pray to Hashem for a child. The *Kohen Gadol* at that time was Eli. Seeing the woman's lips moving and not being able to hear her voice, *"Vayachsheveha Eli leshikorah"* — "Eli thought that she was intoxicated" (I Samuel 1:13).

Eli knew Chana for many years as a righteous woman who yearned bitterly for a child. Why did he suddenly suspect her?

Eli was suspicious because he saw the letters *"shikora"* (שכרה) — intoxicated — begin to light up on the breastplate. Chana told him that obviously he lacked the *Ruach Hakodesh* which is given to the *Kohen* to interpret and decipher the message (see *Berachot* 31b). The letters which lit up should be read to spell the word *"kasheirah"* (כשרה), which means a good respectable Jewish woman. "No, my master, I am a deeply grieved woman, I have drunk no wine or strong drink, but I have poured out my soul before Hashem," exclaimed Chana (I Samuel 1:15).

(קול אליהו - עי' רמב"ן שמות כ"ח ל')

"פעמן זהב ורמון...על שולי המעיל סביב: ונשמע קולו בבאו אל
הקדש לפני ד' ובצאתו ולא ימות"

**"A golden bell and a pomegranate...upon the hem of the robe
round about. And his sound shall be heard when he enters the
holy place before Hashem and when he goes out so that he
not die." (28:34-35)**

QUESTION: Why was it necessary to sound bells when the
Kohen Gadol went into the sanctuary to do the service?

ANSWER: There is a popular misconception that this applies
to the service of the *Kohen Gadol* on *Yom Kippur* in the *Kodesh
Hakadashim* — inner sanctuary. This is incorrect: in the inner
sanctuary he only wore four white linen garments, and the robe
was not among them.

In *Chumash Vayikra,* chapter 16, there is a detailed description
of the services the *Kohen Gadol* performed on *Yom Kippur.* The
Torah writes, *"Vechol adam lo yihyeh be'ohel mo'eid bevo'o
lechapeir bakodesh ad tzeito"* — "No man shall be in the *Ohel
Moed* — communion tent — for the entire time that he enters the
inner sanctuary until he leaves" (16:17). According to Talmud
Yerushalmi *(Yoma* 1:5), even angels were prohibited from being
there.

Likewise, when the incense was offered by the *Kohen* on the
golden altar in the *Ohel Moed,* no one was permitted to be present,
including angels (Rambam, *Temidim U'musafim* 3:3).

On *Yom Kippur,* the *entire* service of the day was done by the
Kohen Gadol himself. Thus, even the incense offering of the
morning, which was done daily in the *Ohel Moed,* was done by the
Kohen Gadol.

When the *Kohen Gadol* would enter the *Ohel Moed* on *Yom
Kippur* morning, or if he wished to offer the incense on any other
morning, the bells would announce his entry. This was a signal for
every person and also the angels to leave. Should he enter
suddenly without warning the angels, there would be a possibility
that they would kill him. When he concluded the offering and was

walking out, the sounding of the bells was a signal to the angels that they could return to the *Ohel Moed.*

The law of 'no one being present' is the same if the *Kohen Gadol* or an ordinary *Kohen* offers the incense. However, due to the eminence of the *Kohen Gadol*, he is always subject to intense scrutiny, and as a precautionary measure, a special announcement is made when he enters.

* * *

Alternatively, the bells served as a request for permission to enter. When one wants to enter a King's palace, it is proper to knock on the door and ask permission to enter. For sudden entry without permission, one may be put to death. (As Queen Esther told Mordechai regarding Achashveirosh — Esther 4:11).

(רמב״ן כ״ח, מ״ג, הדרש והעיון)

"ופתחת עליו פתוחי חתם קדש לד'"

"And engrave upon it the engravings of a signet, 'Holiness to Hashem.'" (28:36)

QUESTION: The words *"pituchei chotam"* — "the engravings of a signet" — are superfluous. What do they come to teach us?

ANSWER: The *Gemara (Ta'anit* 2a) states that Hashem entrusts the keys to all treasures into the hands of the *tzaddikim.* He appoints them as his messengers and gives them the power to use them as they see fit. An exception to this are the keys to three treasures: 1) The power enabling birth (חיה), 2) The power to resurrect (תחית המתים), and 3) The power to make rain (מטר). The keys to these treasures are reserved and controlled only by Him.

The word *"pituchei"* (פתוחי) can be interpreted to mean "opening" (its root is the same as that of the word *"maftei'ach"* — key). The word *"chotam"* (חתם) is an acronym for תחית ,חיה המתים ,מטר. Thus, the Torah is implying that the keys to "חתם" are *"kodesh laHashem"* — uniquely reserved and sanctified, to be used only by G-d Himself.

(קול אליהו)

"ועשית ציץ זהב טהור ופתחת עליו פתוחי חתם קדש לד'"

"You shall make a head-plate of pure gold, and you shall engrave upon it, engraved like a signet ring, 'Holy to G-d.'" (28:36)

QUESTION: Why were the words "Holy to G-d" engraved on the head-plate?

ANSWER: The *Gemara (Zevachim* 88b) states that the garments of the *Kohen Gadol* were a source of forgiveness for various iniquities and transgressions committed by the Jewish people. The head-plate forgave the sin of *azut panim* — shamelessness or boldness. On the other hand, Yehudah Ben Teima says, "הוי עז כנמר לעשות רצון אביך שבשמים" — "Be bold *(az)* as a leopard when fulfilling the will of your Father in heaven" *(Pirkei Avot* 5:20).

The words "Holy to G-d" engraved on the head-plate indicated that *azut panim* should be *consecrated* — used only for the purpose of serving Hashem.

(כתב סופר)

"וזה אשר תעשה על המזבח כבשים בני שנה שנים ליום תמיד"

"This is what you should offer upon the altar, two sheep within their first year, every day, continually." (29:38)

QUESTION: The word *"tamid"* — "continually" — seems superfluous?

ANSWER: The *Shulchan Aruch Orach Chaim* discusses the proper daily behavior of a Jew, and begins by quoting the *pasuk "Shiviti Hashem lenegdi tamid"* — "I place G-d before me continually" (Psalms 16:8). At the end of the *Shulchan Aruch Orach Chaim,* there is a discussion about eating a festive meal on *Purim Katan* (14th day, *Adar* I), concluding with the *pasuk "Vetov leiv mishteh tamid"* — "And to the goodhearted, life is a continuous feast" (Proverbs 15:15).

The Torah is alluding that on a daily basis, a person should constantly observe the two *"tamid"*s — fear G-d and worship Him with joy. (In a leap year, *Purim Katan* takes place in the week of *Parshat Tetzaveh,* and the above may be a *remez* — hint — to *Purim Katan* in the *parshah.*)

(לקוטי בתר לקוטי מהדו״ת)

"את הכבש האחד תעשה בבוקר ואת הכבש השני תעשה בין הערבים"

"You shall offer one lamb in the morning and the second lamb at dusk." (29:39)

QUESTION: According to *Yalkut Shimoni (Bereishit* 99), when Avraham bound Yitzchak for a sacrifice, Hashem instituted the offering of two lambs daily, one in the morning and one in the afternoon. What is the connection between the *Karban Tamid* and the *Akeidah?*

ANSWER: When man is young, he is full of zest, and pursues his aspirations of wealth and success. Parallel to the day, this stage of life is the *"shacharit"* — the morning period. Many times, unfortunately, he claims that this preoccupation does not allow time for Torah study and service of Hashem.

When man passes the mid-years of his life, which is parallel to *"bein ha'arbayim"* — twilight — he claims that he lacks the strength to study Torah due to physical weakening.

At the *Akeidah,* Avraham was an old man of 137 years and Yitzchak was a young man of 37. Regardless of their respective ages, the two of them dedicated themselves entirely to the service of Hashem. At that time, Hashem instituted the two daily sacrifices, to teach man that, regardless of his age, he must serve Hashem everyday.

(הדרש והעיון)

"ושכנתי בתוך בני ישראל והייתי להם לאלקים"

"And I will dwell amidst the children of Israel, and I will be their G-d." (29:45)

QUESTION: It should have said *"veshachanti betocham,"* — "I will dwell among them"; what special meaning is conveyed by the words *"betoch"* — "amidst" — *B'nei Yisrael?*

ANSWER: Hashem's holy name, the Tetragrammaton, consists of four letters and was only pronounced in the *Beit Hamikdash.* In our times, it is common practice, in lieu of the four letters to print two *"Yudden"* (י-י).

An explanation for this practice may be this *pasuk,* in which Hashem says, "I will dwell *in the midst* of *B'nei Yisrael."* The letters in the middle of the words "בני ישראל" are two *"Yudden."*

(נחלת חמשה)

* * *

Hashem's name is written with two *"Yudden" alongside* each other and not one above the other. The reason is that Hashem desires to see His beloved children united and coexisting. When one *Yid* wants to be on "top" of the other, the vowel of *sh'va* (:) is formed, which is the equivalent of naught. Hashem distances himself from the Jew who suffers from *arrogance* and perceives himself to be "above" another Jew. When one *Yid* stands alongside another *Yid* and helps him, He is delighted to be among them.

(ר' נפתלי מראפשיץ זצ"ל)

"ועשית מזבח מקטר קטרת"

"You should make an altar on which to burn incense." (30:1)

QUESTION: Why isn't the golden altar discussed in *Parshat Terumah,* together with all the other vessels of the *Mishkan?*

ANSWER: Without an altar, it would be impossible to bring sacrifices. Without the Ark, there would be no place to store the *tablets.* Without a *menorah,* it would be impossible to kindle candles on a daily basis.

The golden altar was used *only* to burn the daily offering of incense. Even without an altar, incense could be offered on the *place* where the altar stood *(Zevachim* 59a). Therefore, this altar is not recorded together with all the other items, since the *Mishkan* could function without it.

(קרבן מנחה)

     Cઙ ଚ૦

KI TISSA • כי תשא

"כי תשא את ראש...ונתנו איש כפר נפשו לד'...זה יתנו...מחצית
השקל"

"When you take a census...every man shall give G-d an atonement for his soul...This they shall give...a half-*shekel.*"
(30:12-13)

QUESTION: Rashi writes that Moshe had difficulty understanding what Hashem was telling him; therefore, He showed him a fiery coin which weighed a half-*shekel*.

Why was it so difficult for Moshe to comprehend?

ANSWER: When Hashem spoke about the half-*shekel,* He called it *"kofer nafsho"* — "atonement for the soul" — for Torah violations. Moshe could not comprehend how money can accomplish forgiveness for the soul. Therefore, Hashem said to Moshe, *"Zeh yitnu"* — They should give just *such* a coin (a fiery coin). The giving of a coin in itself cannot atone for a grave sin such as worshipping the golden calf. However, if one gives with warmth and enthusiasm that stems from the fiery core of the Jewish soul, then a half-*shekel* can truly become the cause of forgiveness, even for sins that affect the essence of the Jewish soul.

(לקוטי שיחות ח"ג)

"זה יתנו כל העבר על הפקדים מחצית השקל...."

"This shall they give — everyone who passes through the census — a half *shekel*...." (30:13)

QUESTION: Rashi says, "He showed him a kind of coin of fire, the weight of which was a half-*shekel,* and He said to him, 'Thus shall they give.'" What is the reason for a half-*shekel?*

ANSWER: Hashem told the prophet Hosea, "Ephraim is united in idol-worship, [joined to idols, lit.] let him alone" (Hosea 4:17). From this our Sages *(Bereishit Rabbah* 38:6) derive that the power of peace and unity is so great that even when the Jewish people, G-d forbid, sin, if unity prevails among them, G-d does not rebuke or punish them.

The construction of the *Mishkan* was a means to attain forgiveness for the worshipping of the golden calf. The half-*shekel* teaches that no Jew should consider himself a complete entity; he needs to be united with the collective Jewish people. When there is peace and unity among the Jewish people, Hashem says, as it were, 'I have no dominion over them.'

"זה יתנו כל העבר על הפקדים מחצית השקל...."

"This shall they give — everyone who passes through the census — a half *shekel*...." (30:13)

QUESTION: Rashi says, "He showed him a kind of coin of fire, the weight of which was a half *shekel,* and He said to him, 'Thus shall they give.'" Why a *fiery* coin?

ANSWER: Hashem demonstrated a fiery coin, to illustrate the positive and negative qualities of money. Fire has both beneficial and destructive effects. On the one hand, it can destroy, but through the smelting of metals, it can also unite and join together. Similarly, money can destroy a relationship or family, or unite and help build a beautiful family. The fiery coin was Hashem's way to caution the Jewish people to use money properly and reap the marvelous benefits it can produce.

(נועם אלימלך)

"ולא יהיה בהם נגף בפקד אתם זה יתנו כל העובר על הפקודים מחצית השקל"

"So that there will not be a plague among them when counting them." (30:12-13)

QUESTION: Why does the Torah call the half-*shekel* that averts a plague *"machatzit"* (מחצית) and not *"chatzi"* (חצי)?

ANSWER: The word *"machatzit"* (מחצית) — "a half" — has five letters, and the middle letter is a "צ", the first letter of the word *"tzedakah."* Flanking the "צ" there is a "ח" and a "י", which spell the word "חיי" — "life." The exterior letters of the word are "מ" and "ת", which mean death. Thus, the Torah is alluding that "צ" — *tzedakah* — is the power which stands for the Jew and which can represent the difference between life and death. *Tzedakah* can distance death and bring life to those who practice it.

(פרדס יוסף)

*   *   *

The "צ" in the word "מחצית" can be a reference to a *tzaddik* (righteous person). Being in the surroundings of a *tzaddik* and closely attached to him, one can benefit from his holiness — *"chai"* (חי) — profound spiritual life. Detaching oneself from the *tzaddik* is the equivalent to the opposite of life, heaven forbid.

(עיטורי תורה)

"מחצית השקל תרומה לי-ה-ו-ה"

"A half *shekel*, an offering to Hashem." (30:13)

QUESTION: What is the connection between the half-*shekel* and Hashem's holy four lettered name?

ANSWER: The giving of *tzedakah* is connected to the four-lettered name of Hashem (the Tetragrammaton). The "י" represents the coin. The "ה" is for the hand (five fingers) of the giver. The "ו" is the stretching out of the giver's arm, to the other "ה", the hand of the receiver.

Hashem has placed His hand upon His throne and has sworn that His name and throne are incomplete as long as the Jewish people are in exile (Rashi 17:16). When the Jewish people will be redeemed from exile, the last two letters will be restored, thus causing His name and throne to be complete and glorious.

The prophet explains that *tzedakah* is the medium through which we will be taken out of exile (Isaiah 1:27).

By stating that the half-*shekel* is an offering to Hashem, the *pasuk* alludes that through the giving of a half-*shekel* for *tzedakah* we will merit the coming of *Mashiach* and the ultimate redemption. Thus, the missing half of G-d's name will be restored.

"אך את שבתתי תשמרו"

"However, My Sabbaths you must observe." (31:13)

QUESTION: Why is *Shabbat* expressed in plural?

ANSWER: According to the *Gemara (Shabbat* 119b), two angels accompany a Jew on his way home from *shul* Friday night: one is good and the other is evil. When they enter the house and find a nice atmosphere prevailing and a table bedecked with *Shabbat* candles, the good angel blesses the family that they should merit the same spiritual atmosphere the next *Shabbat*. Reluctantly, the evil angel answers, *"Amen."*

Thus, proper observance of *one Shabbat* is a source of Angelic blessing to observe another *Shabbat*.

(מלא העומר)

"ושמרו בני ישראל את השבת לעשות את השבת לדרתם ברית עולם"

"The Israelites shall keep *Shabbat,* to make the *Shabbat* an eternal covenant for their generations." (31:16)

QUESTION: Why is the word *"ledorotam"* (לדרתם) — "for their generations" — written without a "ו"?

ANSWER: A person arrives home Friday night accompanied by the above-mentioned angels, who bless the family.

The word *"ledorotam"* (לדרתם) without the ״יו״ can be read *"ledirotam,"* meaning, "their dwelling places." The Torah is teaching that *"la'asot et haShabbat"* — the Jewish people should strive to make the *Shabbat* beautiful and majestic, *"ledirotam"* — in their dwelling places. In this way they will receive blessings from angels.

(עיטורי תורה)

״ויקהל העם על אהרן ויאמרו אליו קום עשה לנו אלהים״
"The people gathered around Aharon and said to him, 'Get up and make us a god.'" (32:1)

QUESTION: *Avodah zarah* — idol worship — is one of the three transgressions for which there is a rule, *"Yeihareig ve'al ya'avor"* — "Be killed instead of transgressing." Why didn't Aharon let himself be killed and not make the golden calf?

ANSWER: A person is required to let himself be killed only if someone wants to force *him* to bow to an idol. In this case they demanded Aharon to make "for us" a god. As far as Aharon was concerned, on his part it was only a question of *"Lifnei iveir lo titein michshol"* — "Do not place an obstacle in front of the blind" — which includes helping someone violate Torah law. There is no requirement to let yourself be killed in order not to cause one to transgress Torah law.

(אמרי שפר)

״ויקרא אהרן ויאמר חג לד׳ מחר״
"Aharon announced, 'Tomorrow there will be a festival to G-d.'" (32:5)

QUESTION: How was it possible that a *tzaddik* like Aharon should make such a declaration?

ANSWER: The golden calf was made on the sixteenth day of *Tammuz,* and on the seventeenth day of *Tammuz* Moshe came down from heaven. Upon seeing the golden calf and the celebration, he broke the *tablets.*

Many years later, on the seventeenth day of *Tammuz,* our enemies penetrated the wall which surrounded Jerusalem and went on to destroy the *Beit Hamikdash.* Therefore, the seventeenth day of *Tammuz* has become a day of fasting. The prophet conveys, however, in the name of Hashem that "the fasting which takes place in the fourth month (17 days in *Tammuz*) will in the times of *Mashiach,* be converted to a day of joy and festivity" (Zechariah 8:19).

Indeed, Aharon was heart-broken over what was taking place and realized that this would bring trouble to the Jewish people. However — he hinted that eventually, "tomorrow" — the 17th day of *Tammuz* — will become *"chag laHashem"* — "festival to G-d."

(מעינה של תורה)

"לֵךְ רֵד כִּי שִׁחֵת עַמֶּךָ"
"Descend — for your people have become corrupt." (32:7)

QUESTION: On the words *"Leich, reid"* — "Descend" — Rashi comments, *"migedulatcha"* — "from your high position."

Why was Moshe demoted because of the sin of the Jewish people?

ANSWER: Later in our *parshah,* it states "כִּי לֹא תִשְׁתַּחֲוֶה לְאֵל אַחֵר" — "You shall not bow to another god" (34:14). The letter "ר" can easily be exchanged with a "ד". Therefore, to prevent the possibility, G-d forbid, of reading "אֶחָד" which would mean "You shall not bow down to the one and only G-d," the "ר" is enlarged.

In the *Shema Yisrael (Devarim* 6:4), the word אֶחָד is written with a large "ד" to emphasize that G-d is *one,* and should not be mistakenly read as *"acher"* (אַחֵר) — "G-d is another."

Rashi is alluding that in *addition* to telling Moshe to physically descend from heaven to earth, Hashem demoted the enlarged holy letters of the Torah "ר'" and "ד'" saying "I made you bigger for the benefit of the Jewish people. I wanted to help them avoid making a mistake in reading. Since they have committed idolatry, obviously this was to no avail. Consequently, *Reid migedulatcha* — the letters ר' and ד' should temporarily descend from their heights."

(מרגניתא דרב)

"ויחל משה את פני ד' אלקיו"
"Moshe pleaded before G-d, his G-d." (32:11)

QUESTION: Why the emphasis on *his* G-d?

ANSWER: The Ten Commandments start with the words, *"Anochi Hashem Elokecha..."* — "I am G-d, *your* G-d...." *"Lo yihyeh lecha"* — "You shall not have..." (20:2-3). Since Hashem was speaking to *all* the Jews, He should have expressed Himself in the plural — *"Anochi Hashem Elokeichem...Lo yihyeh lachem."* Rashi writes that this was in order to enable Moshe to speak in defense of *B'nei Yisrael* after the sin of the golden calf: "Your command 'You shall not have other gods,' was directed to *me* alone" *("Elokecha...lecha"* is in the singular).

Thus, the *pasuk* reads *"Elokav"* — *his* G-d, in the singular — indicating that Moshe now said, "Lord, why are you angry with Your people?" The command of faith in G-d was directed to me and not the entire Jewish people. They never violated any command!"

(פרדס יוסף)

"זכר לאברהם ליצחק ולישראל עבדיך"
"Remember Avraham, Yitzchak and Yisrael Your servants." (32:13)

QUESTION: Why did Moshe mention our forefathers when he entreated Hashem on behalf of the Jewish people?

ANSWER: In the year 1801 (תקס"א) the first Lubavitcher Rebbe, Rabbi Shneur Zalman of Liadi, known as the *Alter* Rebbe, was imprisoned the second time for his activities on behalf of the Chassidic movement, and he was released on the fifth day of *Chanukah.*

A prominent Jew, Reb Nota Notkin, offered to use his influence in the government to gain the release of the *Alter* Rebbe if he would agree to meet with three very prominent Rabbis of the *"misnagdishe"* (non-Chassidic) community. The *Alter* Rebbe agreed, and the first whom he visited was the venerable sage renowned for his Torah knowledge, *Hagaon*, Reb Moshe Chayfitz. Without formally greeting the *Alter* Rebbe, he immediately started asking him questions, which the *Alter* Rebbe answered successfully. The *Gaon* then said, "I will now ask you a question that I asked many scholars and no one was able to answer it. If you can answer it, I will greatly respect you."

The *Midrash Rabbah* (44:7) says that when Moshe began to pray for the Jewish people, Hashem said, "When Avraham prayed for Sodom, I was ready to spare them if he came up with ten *tzaddikim;* I will do the same now." Moshe replied, "You have me, Aharon, Elazar, Itamar, Pinchas, Yehoshua, and Kaleiv." Hashem said, "I see only seven." Moshe was in a quandary and asked, "Are the righteous deceased alive [in the world to come]"? Hashem responded in the affirmative. "If so," responded Moshe, *"Zechor le'Avraham, le'Yitzchak, ule'Yisrael avadecha"* — "Remember Avraham, Yitzchak and Yisrael Your servants, and together with them there are ten."

Another *Midrash* on this subject *(Devarim* 3:15) says that Moshe offered to come up with 80 *tzaddikim.* He mentioned the 70 elders and the seven *tzaddikim,* as mentioned in the previous *Midrash.* When Hashem said, "That was only 77," Moshe replied, "Remember Avraham, Yitzchak, and Yisrael, Your servants." How do we explain the contradiction between the two *Midrashim?*

The *Alter* Rebbe explained: There is an argument in the *Gemara (Horayot* 5b) whether each tribe is considered a *"kahal"* (community) or if, when the Torah uses the word *"kahal,"* it refers to the entire community of Israel.

The *Midrash* in our *parshah* follows the opinion that the entire people are considered one *"kahal."* Thus, to gain forgiveness for *Klal Yisrael,* it was sufficient to have ten *tzaddikim.*

The other *Midrash* follows the opinion that each tribe is called a *"kahal."* Since in the making of the golden calf, the tribe of Levi did not participate, only eleven tribes were in need of forgiveness. Each tribe had to find seven *tzaddikim* and could use our forefathers, the fathers of *Klal Yisrael,* as the other three. Therefore, Moshe mentioned 77, which is seven for each tribe and said, "Remember Avraham, Yitzchak, and Yisrael, Your servants. Add to each tribe our three ancestors and now they each have the merit of ten *tzaddikim* and deserve to remain alive."

The *Gaon* Reb Moshe Chayfitz was greatly impressed with the *Alter* Rebbe and showed him honor and respect. He personally gave him a chair to sit on and instructed his wife to prepare a nice repast for their honored guest.

(סיפורי חסידים)

"וירד משה מן ההר ושני לחת העדת בידו"

"Moshe descended from the mountain with the two tablets of Testimony in his hand." (32:15)

QUESTION: In what form were the *tablets* made?

ANSWER: The generally accepted illustration of the tablets, square on the bottom with rounded semi-circular tops, is inaccurate.

The *Gemara (Bava Batra* 14a) states that each of the *tablets* was six *tefachim* (hand breadths) in length, six *tefachim* in breadth, and three *tefachim* in depth.

From this alone, we see that the tablets were square at both ends (6×6 *tefachim)* and not rounded at one end.

Furthermore, the *Gemara* accounts for all the space in the Ark
— how it was filled up — either by the tablets and the *sefer Torah*
or the tablets and silver pillars (called *"amudim"*) alongside them.
There were no spaces unaccounted for, as there would have been if
the tablets had been rounded at one end.

(כ״ק אדמו״ר)

"לחת כתובים משני עבריהם מזה ומזה הם כתבים"
"They were tablets written on both sides, with the writing visible from either side." (32:15)

QUESTION: Rashi says that it was *"ma'aseh nisim"* —
"miraculous work." What was so miraculous about the writing on
the *tablets?*

ANSWER: The letters on the *tablets* were chiseled out. When
a *samach* (ס) or a final *mem* (ם) is chiseled through a stone, there is
nothing to prevent the center piece from falling out. The miracle
of the *tablets* was that the center piece of the *samach* and final
mem hung suspended in the air. Though they were not attached,
they never fell out.

In addition, there was also a miracle in regard to the words:
The letters were chiseled straight through the stone, yet it was
possible to read the writing from either side from right to left,
though normally all the words on the opposite side should have
been backwards.

(מס׳ שבת ק״ד ע״א, ועי׳ ילקוט מעם לועז)

* * *

There are also various opinions as to how the commandments
were written on the tablets. According to Rabbi Chaninah there
were only five on the front of each tablet. Others say that all the
ten were written on the front of *each* tablet. According to Rabbi
Shimon Bar Yochai on each tablet there were ten on the front and
ten on the back, a total of forty on the two tablets. Rabbi Sima'i
holds that there were four sets of the ten commandments on *each*

tablet, one on front and one on back and also on the width of each side.

(ירושלמי שקלים פ"ו הל"א)

"מזה ומזה הם כתבים"
"They were inscribed on one side and the other." (32:15)

QUESTION: When a "מ" and a "ס" are engraved through a stone, the center piece will fall out. Miraculously, in the Tablets the center piece hung in the air *(Shabbat* 104a). What is the significance of this miracle?

ANSWER: The letters "מ" and "ס" spell the word *"mas"* — "tax." When a person earns money, he "taxes" his income by setting aside part of the money for pleasure, and a portion of the money for necessities.

The Jewish people are known as "the people of the book," and have always established *yeshivot,* without which the continuity of our people would be in jeopardy. Unfortunately, many people are reluctant to "tax" their income for this noblest charity — supporting Torah institutions, and one often wonders, how will the *yeshivot* continue to exist? How will they meet their budgets? Hashem demonstrated to Moshe that the "מ" and the "ס" of the Tablets — the "tax" that is necessary to support Torah — will miraculously always be there.

(הרב מאיר ז"ל שאפירא מלובלין)

"ויחר אף משה וישלך מידו את הלחת וישבר אתם תחת ההר"
"Moshe's anger flared up. He threw down the Tablets from his hands and shattered them at the foot of the mountain." (32:19)

QUESTION: When Moshe saw the golden calf, he immediately wanted to break the Tablets. The elders grabbed onto them and did not let him throw them down, until he finally overpowered them and shattered the Tablets. *(Avot DeRabbi Natan* 2). What was the basis of the dispute between Moshe and the elders?

ANSWER: There are people who excel in inter-human relationships, but who are lacking in their relationship with G-d. They generously help a person in need but are lax in the performance of purely spiritual *mitzvot*. On the other hand, there are people who are meticulous in their relationship with Hashem, but much is to be desired in their dealings between man and man. The Tablets consisted of the Ten Commandments, five on each stone. The first five belong to the category of *mitzvot* between man and G-d, while the other five are *mitzvot* between man and man.

The elders argued, "It is true that the Jewish people violated what is written in the first group of Commandment, but they are all from the category of *mitzvot* between man and G-d. Let them at least remain with the second group of Commandments, which belong to the category of *mitzvot* between man and man."

Moshe insisted, "Although they were written on separate stones, the two stones were united to accentuate their inseparability. The rationale for obeying the ethical principles of the Torah in dealing with fellow human beings is not because they are self evident and logical, but because these principles were given at Sinai and are also the word of G-d."

(פרדס יוסף)

"וַיַּעֲשׂוּ בְנֵי לֵוִי כִּדְבַר מֹשֶׁה וַיִּפֹּל מִן הָעָם בַּיּוֹם הַהוּא כִּשְׁלֹשֶׁת אַלְפֵי אִישׁ"

"The Levites did as Moshe had ordered, and approximately 3,000 people were killed that day." (32:28)

QUESTION: Why were 3,000 people killed?

ANSWER: Concerning this *pasuk* there is a wondrous *Midrash* which quotes the *pasuk*, "One who steals an ox and sells it or slaughters it — *'Chamishah bakar yeshaleim tachat hashor'* must pay back five oxen for the ox" (21:37). What is the connection between this *pasuk* and our subject?

This *Midrash* can be explained as follows. King Shlomo says, *"Echad mei'elef matzati ve'ishah bechol eileh lo matzati"* — "One man in a thousand I have found, but one woman among them

I have not found" (Ecclesiastes 7:28). The *Midrash* on Ecclesiastes explains that the first part of the *pasuk* refers to the sin of the golden calf (a young ox — see Rashi 32:4). It is telling that one of every 1,000 men committed the sin of worshipping it. The latter part of the *pasuk* refers to the fact that though the men proclaimed, *"Eileh elohecha, Yisrael"* — "This is your god, O Israel" (32:8), not one Jewish woman participated in any way.

The census of the Jewish community was 600,000. Thus, if one of every thousand sinned, then there were 600 sinners. The wondrous *midrash* is teaching that to atone for this grave iniquity, five people died for every single sinner. Consequently, the Levites killed a total of 3,000 people.

(קול אליהו)

* * *

There still remains a question: Why does the Torah say *"approximately* 3,000"? Perhaps the reason is that the actual amount of males between twenty and sixty years of age was 603,550 (Bamidbar 2:32). Accordingly, 303 people actually sinned and when punishing five for each one, the total would be 3,015. The Torah says "approximately 3,000 people" in order to round it off to the closest round number.

"אנא חטא העם הזה חטאה גדלה ויעשו להם אלהי זהב: ועתה אם תשא חטאתם ואם אין מחני נא מספרך אשר כתבת: ויאמר ד' אל משה מי אשר חטא לי אמחנו מספרי"

"'I implore, this people has committed a grievous sin and made themselves a god of gold. And now if You would forgive their sin — but if not, erase me now from this book that you have written.' G-d said to Moshe, 'Whoever has sinned against Me I shall erase from My book.'" (32:31-33)

QUESTION: 1) Why did Moshe have to identify for Hashem the sin of the Jewish people? 2) Moshe should have said, "If you forgive their sin, *good!* But if not, erase me now from this book that you have written"? (See Rashi.) 3) In Hashem's response, the word *"li"* — "against Me" — is superfluous?

ANSWER: Moshe said to Hashem, "By worshipping the golden calf the Jewish people has committed *two* sins: 1) 'This people has committed a grievous sin' — against *You,* G-d, for You had commanded them, 'You shall not recognize the gods of others in My presence' (20:3) 2) 'and made themselves a god of gold' — the making of the *golden calf* as a replacement for me, their leader, was a blatant insult to *me."*

Thus, Moshe said further to Hashem, "And now" — *"im tisa chatatam ve'im ayin"* — "whether *you* forgive them or not" — *"mecheini na misifrecha asher katavta"* — "erase what they did against *me* from this book that you have written, because I am forgiving them wholeheartedly."

Hashem responded, "If you, a mortal being, are prepared to forgive them for the sin that they committed against *you,* then 'whoever has sinned against *Me* I shall erase from My book' — I, too, will forgive them for the sin that they committed against *Me."*

(ילקוט הדרוש - שמות)

"ויאמר ד' אל משה מי אשר חטא לי אמחנו מספרי"
"G-d said to Moshe, 'Whoever who has sinned against Me I shall erase from My book.'" (32:33)

QUESTION: Why was it necessary for Hashem to tell Moshe that He would erase those who sinned. He should have simply said, "I do not accept your proposal to be erased"?

ANSWER: When the Jews sinned with the golden calf, Moshe requested to be erased from Hashem's book in the event He did not forgive them. Hashem's response to Moshe was a rhetorical question and not a statement, thus revealing His great mercies. Hashem said, "Do you think that 'the one who sinned against Me I will erase from My book?'" This means to say the Jews are an eternal people: all of them have a place in My book and are inscribed forever. None of them will be erased from my book, so much more *you,* who has never sinned! Therefore, your concept of being erased cannot be applied."

(פרדס יוסף)

"וביום פקדי ופקדתי עליהם חטאתם"

"When I will have to punish them for something else, I will take their sin into account." (32:34)

QUESTION: Hashem is always interested in the good and welfare of the Jewish people; why does He not want to forget entirely about the sin of the golden calf?

ANSWER: Hashem's statement can be interpreted as an act of loving kindness between Him and the Jewish people. Hashem is saying *"Uveyom pakdi"* — "Should there come a time when the Jews will, G-d forbid, sin again and I will have to consider what to do, at that time" — *"ufakadeti aleihem chatatam"* — "I will take into account the terrible transgression they committed with the calf. I will rationalize the following: Just as when they worshipped the calf, which was indeed a grave iniquity, I forgave them; likewise, even if they sin in the future, I will forgive the Jewish people and not destroy them, G-d forbid!"

(ר' יעקב דוד מאמשינוב זצ"ל)

"ויגף ד' את העם על אשר עשו את העגל אשר עשה אהרן"

"And G-d plagued the people for their making the calf which Aharon made." (32:35)

QUESTION: Aharon made the calf and not the people. Why were *they* struck with *"mitah bidei shamayim"* — "A heavenly death"?

ANSWER: According to *halacha* if one appoints a messenger to violate a Torah law in his behalf, the messenger is liable, because one must listen to the teacher — Hashem — and not to the pupil. Nevertheless, the sender is absolved only *"bedinei adam"* — "in our courts" — but *"bedinei shamayim"* — "in the heavenly court" — the sender is also held responsible.

Therefore, *they* were struck with a heavenly punishment for Aharon's making of the calf, because he did it upon *their* request and the heavenly court considers *them* liable for the doings of their emissary.

(פנים יפות)

"וַיֹּאמֶר ד' אֶל מֹשֶׁה גַּם אֶת הַדָּבָר הַזֶּה אֲשֶׁר דִּבַּרְתָּ אֶעֱשֶׂה כִּי מָצָאתָ
חֵן בְּעֵינָי"

**"G-d said to Moshe, 'Also this thing which you have spoken I
will do, for you have found grace in My eyes.'" (33:17)**

QUESTION: What was Hashem referring to with the words
"this thing"?

ANSWER: Moshe was the greatest prophet of the Jewish
people. Only to him did Hashem speak "face to face." All others
received their prophecies in an indirect way. Therefore, when
Moshe conveyed a prophecy he would use the term *"zeh,"*
indicating *"this* is the thing that Hashem has spoken — I saw it
directly."* All other prophets would say *"koh"* — *"thus* said
Hashem."

When the Jews sinned with the Golden Calf, Hashem removed
Himself from the Jewish people and also demoted Moshe. No
longer did He speak to him "face to face." Therefore, now when
Moshe had to convey Hashem's instructions to the Levites he said
"Koh amar Hashem" — "thus said Hashem" (32:27).

Moshe was greatly perturbed about his demotion and
Hashem's changed relationship with the Jewish people, and he
beseeched Hashem to return everything to its original status.
Hashem accepted his plea and told him that He would personally
continue to lead the Jewish people.

Hashem said, "Regarding *hadavar **hazeh** asher dibarta* —
This thing which you have spoken — your request to continue
speaking with the term *'zeh,'* as you have done previously — I
will grant your request, because you have found favor in My
eyes."

(אמרי צדיקים בשם בעל מנחת חינוך)

"וראית את אחרי ופני לא יראו"

"You will see My back; however, My face will not be seen." (33:23)

QUESTION: Rashi explains that Hashem showed Moshe *"kesher shel tefillin"* — the knot of the *tefillin shel rosh* — head *tefillin*. Moshe asked Hashem to show him His glory, how did seeing the *tefillin* satisfy him?

ANSWER: The *Gemara (Berachot* 6a) says that the A-mighty dons *tefillin* in which it is written, "Who is like Your people, Israel, one nation on earth (1 Chronicles 17:21).

When the Jewish people sinned by worshipping the Golden Calf, Moshe was very concerned about G-d's future relationship with them. Upon seeing that G-d was still wearing His *Tefillin,* Moshe was very happy because it demonstrated that Hashem still loved His people and praised them highly.

(שו"ת תירוש ויצהר סי' קס"ו)

"וראית את אחרי ופני לא יראו"

"You will see My back, however, My face will not be seen." (33:23)

QUESTION: Rashi explains that Hashem showed Moshe the *"kesher shel tefillin"* — the knot of the *tefillin*. There are different customs concerning how to make the knot of the *tefillin* worn on the head. (See *Magen Avraham, Shulchan Aruch, Orach Chaim* 32:52.) What kind of knot was on Hashem's *tefillin?*

ANSWER: The *tefillin* consist of two parts. One is placed on the hand and the other, on the head. The hand represents inter-human relationships *(bein adam lechaveiro).* With our hands we extend aid and assistance to our friends. The head is the seat of the human intellect by which we perform *mitzvot* between man and Hashem *(bein adam leMakom).*

There are people who excel in their inter-human relationships but who are lacking in their connection with Hashem. On the other hand, there are people who study Torah diligently and consider themselves close to Hashem, but unfortunately, their behavior leaves much to be desired in their inter-human relationships. The proper thing for a Jew is to excel in both.

Moshe asked Hashem to show him His glory so that he would have a better understanding of what Hashem wants of the Jewish people. The showing of the *"kesher shel tefillin"* was an allegory. The message was that it is a Divine wish that each Jew *bind together* the significance of the *two tefillin*. A person should do his utmost for a fellow Jew and be exemplary in his Torah and devotion to Hashem.

(הדרש והעיון)

"נצר חסד לאלפים נשא עון ופשע וחטאה ונקה לא ינקה"

"Preserver of kindness for two thousand generations, Forgiver of iniquity, willful transgression and sin, and He cleanses — but He will by no means clear the guilty." (34:7)

QUESTION: This *pasuk* concludes the passage known as the "Thirteen Attributes of Mercy." How does "He will by no means clear the guilty" fit in?

ANSWER: Rabbi Meir says, *"Al tistakeil bekankan elah bemah sheyesh bo"* — "Do not look at the vessel, but rather at what it contains" *(Pirkei Avot* 4:20). The word *"kankan"* (קנקן) — "vessel" — is composed of the middle letters of the words *venakeih yenakeh"* (ונקה ינקה).

Possibly, Rabbi Meir is alluding that when we look at the words *"venakeih lo yenakeh"* (ונקה לא ינקה) — superficially, they do not appear to fit among the Thirteen Attributes of Mercy. However, when we take out the "נק" from "ונקה" and the "נק" from "ינקה", then each word spells half of Hashem's name (ו-ה, י, ה). Thus, by not looking at the letters "קנקן," the words "ונקה לא ינקה" fit very well among the Thirteen Attributes of Mercy.

(חיד"א על פרקי אבות)

"אלהי מסכה לא תעשה לך. את חג המצות תשמר שבעת ימים תאכל מצות"

"Do not make any idols...Keep the festival of *matzot;* eat *matzot* for seven days." (34:17-18)

QUESTION: What is the connection between idol worship and eating *matzot?*

ANSWER: Haman's plan to destroy the Jewish people was a punishment for worshipping idols in the days of Achashveirosh *(Gemara Megillah* 12a). Before Esther went before Achashveirosh to plead for the Jewish people, she told Mordechai to declare a three-day period of fasting. Since the fast day took place on *Pesach,* the Jews were unable to properly observe *Pesach* that year by eating *matzah* for seven days. The Torah is hinting to this event by telling us *"Elohei maseichah lo ta'aseh"* — "Do not worship any idols" and consequently you will be able to eat *matzah* seven days during *Pesach.*

(ילקוט האורים)

"כי קרן עור פניו"

"The skin of his face sent forth beams-of light."(34:29)

QUESTION: The *Midrash Rabbah* (47:6) states thát Moshe was given a sufficient amount of ink to write the entire Torah, however a small measure of ink remained in Moshe's quill, and he rubbed it on his head, causing the radiance.

Why was there leftover ink, and why is it alluded to in this *parshah?*

ANSWER: Originally it was intended that Moshe's name be mentioned in every *parshah* from the beginning of *Chumash Shemot* until the end of the Torah. When Moshe pleaded "Erase me from your book," G-d responded by omitting his name from *Parshat Tetzaveh.* Thus, a small measure of ink remained.

It is particularly appropriate in *Parshat Ki Tissa,* in which Moshe demonstrates *mesirat nefesh* — willingness to give his life for *Klal Yisrael* — to tell us the reward he received.

(חנוכת התורה)

ଔ ଛ

VAYAKHEIL • ויקהל

"ויקהל משה את כל עדת בני ישראל"

"And Moshe assembled the entire Israelite community." (35:1)

QUESTION: What message does *Parshat Vayakheil* impart to each and every Jew?

ANSWER: Generally, the *parshiyot Vayakheil* and *Pekudei* are read together. *Vayakheil,* "And you shall gather," points to the unification of all the entities in this diverse world, uniting them within the domain of holiness. *Pekudei,* by contrast, means "counting," and highlights how every entity possesses its own unique importance. For every creation was given a unique nature with which it can serve G-d.

Although the sequence of the two *parshiyot* indicates that *Vayakheil* prepares one for *Pekudei, Vayakheil* represents an independent service in its own right. This concept receives greater emphasis when *Vayakheil* is read and studied as a separate *parshah.*

In particular, the message of *Vayakheil* applies to the Jewish people and alludes to their being gathered together to form a single collective entity in the spirit of the *mitzvah* "Love your fellow man as yourself." This is possible, because all Jews share a single essence; all are "truly a part of G-d from above." (See Tanya, chapter 32.)

The importance of this service is emphasized by the fact that the *Alter* Rebbe, Rabbi Shneur Zalman, the founder of Chabad Chassidism, placed in the *Nusach Ari Siddur* the declaration "Behold I accept upon myself the fulfillment of the *mitzvah* 'Love

VEDIBARTA BAM—AND YOU SHALL SPEAK OF THEM

your fellowman as yourself'" at the very beginning of the prayer service, making it the foundation of one's daily activities.

This is the message of *Parshat Vayakheil,* that one seek to unite with every member of the Jewish people. This approach, the thrust to unite with one's fellow Jews, will lead to the ultimate fulfillment of *Vayakheil,* the ingathering of the Jewish people to *Eretz Yisrael.*

A significant lesson results from the fact that *Vayakheil* and *Pekudei* are read as separate *parshiyot.* There is no need to wait for *Pekudei,* the census of the Jewish people, for the beginning of *Vayakheil,* the ingathering of the exiles. On the contrary, the Jews will first gather together in *Eretz Yisrael,* and afterwards there will be a census.

(מהתוועדות אחרונה של כ"ק אדמו"ר, כ"ה אדר א', תשנ"ב)

"ויקהל משה את כל עדת בני ישראל"
"And Moshe assembled the entire Israelite community." (35:1)

QUESTION: Rashi writes that the gathering took place on the day after *Yom Kippur.* Why is it necessary to know when the assembly took place?

ANSWER: Moshe *Rabbeinu* is known as the most humble person who ever lived *(Bamidbar* 12:23). One might ask, did not *Shmuel HaNavi* personally visit different communities and sit in judgment, in order not to trouble the people (I Samuel 7:17), while Moshe *Rabbeinu* caused the people to come to him?

Possibly, Rashi wants to answer this as follows: Moshe, as King of the Jewish people, was entitled to the highest respect and forbidden to relinquish any due honor.

When the Jewish people sinned with the golden calf, Hashem demoted Moshe. On *Yom Kippur* he was forgiven and reinstated as King. Moshe was indeed the most humble person who ever lived, but since he was speaking to the Jews after *Yom Kippur* — at which time he was already reinstated as the King — it would have been a lowering of his dignity to go around personally to visit the

Jewish people. Consequently, it was proper to gather the people together via messenger.

(פרח לבנון)

"ויקהל משה את כל עדת בני ישראל"

"And Moshe assembled the entire Israelite community." (35:1)

QUESTION: This gathering took place on the day after *Yom Kippur* (Rashi). When Yitro visited Moshe the Torah relates, "ויהי ממחרת וישב משה לשפט את העם" — The following morning Moshe sat in judgment." There too, Rashi writes that it was the day after *Yom Kippur" (Shemot* 18:13). Why did these two events take place on the very same day?

ANSWER: At the gathering Moshe instructed them about donating for the construction of the *Mishkan.* Giving charity is a very great *mitzvah,* and it is vital that the money not be illegally acquired. Moshe knew that the Jews would contribute generously towards the *Mishkan,* but he wanted to make sure that the money was absolutely "kosher." Therefore, on the day that he proclaimed the *Mishkan* appeal, he also sat in judgment to settle all cases and determine the rightful ownership of any disputed moneys.

(מפניני התורה)

"ויקהל משה את כל עדת בני ישראל ויאמר אלהם אלה הדברים אשר צוה ד' לעשת אתם"

"Moshe assembled the entire assembly of the Children of Israel and said to them: 'These are the things that G-d commanded, to do them.'" (35:1)

QUESTION: The words "to do them" appear superfluous?

ANSWER: *"Vayakheil"* indicates that Moshe made a "convention" of *B'nei Yisrael.* It is normal for a convention to consist of speeches, thoughts, and resolutions which do not lead to concrete results. Hashem commanded Moshe to ensure that the thoughts and resolutions shared at this "convention" are *"la'asot otam"* — brought down to actual practical results.

(לקוטי בתר לקוטי)

"ששת ימים תעשה מלאכה וביום השביעי יהיה קדש שבת שבתון
לד'"

"Six days work shall be done and the seventh day shall be holy, a Sabbath of rest to G-d." (35:2)

QUESTION: Man was created to labor (Job 5:7). Why does the Torah talk about work in a "passive" form "תֵּעָשֶׂה מלאכה" — "work shall be done" — instead of using an active form "תַּעֲשֶׂה מלאכה" — "You shall do work"?

ANSWER: A *chasid* of the *Mitteler* Rebbe, Rabbi Dov Ber Schneersohn (the second Lubavitcher Rebbe), went into the business of producing overshoes. It was soon apparent that his mind was more preoccupied with business matters than the observance of Torah and *mitzvot*. Once, when he visited Lubavitch, the Rebbe said to him, "Feet enveloped in overshoes are commonplace, but imagine a 'head' sunk in overshoes!"

The Torah is in favor of people working, but is against the entire person (head, mind, heart, and soul) being completely preoccupied and immersed in the work. Therefore, even during the six week days "work shall be done" (as if it is done on its own), but one's primary preoccupation and major concern should be Torah and *mitzvot*.

(לקוטי שיחות ח"א)

* * *

Alternatively, in the merit of observing *Shabbat* properly, Hashem sends His *berachah* into the work done during the week, and the success experienced is much more than anticipated and disproportionate to the efforts.

The Torah alludes to this fact by telling us that during the six days "תֵּעָשֶׂה מלאכה" — work will be *done for us* if the seventh day *(Shabbat)* is observed properly as a Holy day of rest.

(עיטורי תורה)

"ביום השביעי יהיה לכם קדש שבת שבתון לד'"

**"The seventh day shall be holy, a Sabbath of rest to G-d."
(35:2)**

QUESTION: It would be sufficient to say, "קדש שבתון לד'" — holy, a day of rest to G-d." The word *"Shabbat"* seems extra?

ANSWER: The word *"Shabbat"* is an acronym for "שנה בשבת תענוג", which can be read in two ways.

1) שָׁנָה בְּשַׁבָּת תַּעֲנוּג — "Studying Torah on *Shabbat* is a delight" (as in the word "ושננתם" = You shall teach).

2) שֵׁנָה בְּשַׁבָּת תַּעֲנוּג — "Sleeping on *Shabbat* is a delight."

Workers and business people who do not have much time to study Torah during the week should intensify their study of Torah on *Shabbat*. However, Torah scholars who study Torah the entire week, in order to fulfill the *mitzvah* of *Oneg Shabbat*, should indulge a bit in eating and drinking since they experience the delight of Torah study throughout the week *(Shulchan Aruch, Orach Chaim* 290).

Thus, the acronyms of the word *"Shabbat"* are a directive to all of *Klal Yisrael,* teaching each respective group the way to conduct itself on the holy day of *Shabbat*.

(מיוסד על פנינים יקרים)

"לא תבערו אש בכל משבתיכם ביום השבת"

"You shall not kindle fire in any of your dwellings on the Sabbath day." (35:3)

QUESTION: Why does the Torah single out this prohibition and not any of the other 39 major forbidden activities?

ANSWER: Heated fights and arguments are like fire: Unfortunately, they destroy many homes, partnerships and relationships. When people are busy, they do not have time to argue and fight.

Because *Shabbat* is a day of rest, the Torah warns, "Beware not to kindle the 'fire of dispute' on the *Shabbat* day. Keep yourself busy with Torah study and *davening,* and avoid idleness."

(של"ה)

* * *

It is interesting to note that the last letters of the words "תבערו אש בכל משבתיכם" spell the word "שלום" — peace. This hints that, especially on *Shabbat,* we should exert all effort to keep the peace.

(בית יעקב)

* * *

In the Ten Commandments *(Shemot* 20:1-14), Hashem commanded the Jews to observe *Shabbat,* because in six days heaven and earth and everything in it were created, and on the seventh day He rested. Adam was created on Friday and there was light the entire Friday night and *Shabbat.* Saturday night, seeing darkness for the first time, Adam rubbed two stones together and produced fire *(Midrash Rabbah, Bereishit* 11:2). Because of this, we recite the *berachah "Borei me'orei haeish"* during *Havdalah* on Saturday night *(Pesachim* 54a).

Some people may think that since fire was not created during the first six days, Hashem did not rest from it on *Shabbat,* and thus one is permitted to make a fire on *Shabbat.* Therefore, Moshe had to stress that it is forbidden to ignite any fire on *Shabbat.*

(פרדס יוסף)

"לא תבערו אש בכל משבתיכם ביום השבת"

"You shall not kindle fire in any of your dwellings on the Sabbath day." (35:3)

QUESTION: Why is it customary to eat *cholent* on *Shabbat?*

ANSWER: In the times of the Sages of the *Gemara* there was a group of people known as the *"Tzedokim"* (Sadducees). They accepted only the Written Torah and refused to follow the explanations and interpretations rendered in the Oral Torah. Their philosophy was that Torah should be translated literally. According to them, the *pasuk* "Do not kindle fire in any of your dwellings on *Shabbat*" forbids one to have any fire burning during *Shabbat,* even when kindled before *Shabbat.* Thus, on *Shabbat* they would sit in the dark and eat only cold food.

To demonstrate that we have no affiliation with the *Tzedokim* and their erroneous theories, we intentionally let food cook on the fire during *Shabbat* and eat it for the afternoon meal.

The importance of eating hot food on *Shabbat* is mentioned in the *Shulchan Aruch, Orach Chaim* (257:8), which states that one who does not observe this custom should be investigated for heresy.

"ויאמר משה אל כל עדת בני ישראל לאמר זה הדבר אשר צוה ד'
לאמר"

"And Moshe spoke to all of the congregation of Israel, saying, 'This is the thing which G-d commanded, saying.'" (35:4)

QUESTION: The word *"leimor"* means to convey a message to others. Since Moshe was speaking to the *entire* community, the word *"leimor"* employed twice in this *pasuk* is superfluous?

ANSWER: According to the Rambam, giving *tzedakah* to help a person in need is one of the greatest *mitzvot*. Anonymity is recommended and praised. The highest level of *tzedakah* is achieved when the giver does not know to whom his contribution goes and the receiver does not know who helps him (Rambam, *Matanot Aniyim* 10:8). However, this applies only when the *tzedakah* is given to an individual. Otherwise, the Rashba (Responsa 582) states that it is proper to publicize the names of those who give generously for a charitable endeavor. Therefore, names of donors are inscribed on *yeshivah* buildings, synagogues, etc.

Regarding donating to the construction of the *Mishkan,* Moshe spoke to the entire community and told them *"leimor,"* to publicize those who will contribute generously. He stressed that this was not merely his words and thinking, but the command and will of Hashem — *"leimor"* — to make known the donors so that others would be encouraged to generously emulate their good deeds.

(פרדס יוסף)

"ויבאו האנשים על הנשים"
"And the men came with the women." (35:22)

QUESTION: Why did the women bring their husbands with them?

ANSWER: Everybody wanted the merit of participating in building of the *Mishkan.* Men and women were eager to contribute their most valuable possessions for this holy purpose. Since many women do not work and do not have their own income, it is permitted to take only a small contribution from them. Taking a large sum is forbidden because the husbands may not agree *(Yoreh Dei'ah* 248:4). The women, wanting to donate their expensive gold jewelry for the *Mishkan,* brought their husbands with them to show that they were giving with spousal consent.

(ספורנו)

"ויבאו האנשים על הנשים"
"And the men came with the women" (35:22)

QUESTION: The word *"al"* usually means "on" or "above." Why does it not say *"im hanashim"* which would mean "together with the women?"

ANSWER: While Moshe was up in heaven receiving the Torah, men gave their gold to produce the Golden Calf and the women refused to participate. According to *Midrash Rabbah (Shemot* 51:8), the donating of gold for the *Mishkan* was a form of repentance for that sin.

The women who did not sin were *"tzidkaniot"* — "righteous women" — and did not need to repent, the men, through their generosity, became *ba'alei teshuvah.* The *Gemara (Berachot* 34b) states that a *ba'al teshuvah* stands higher than a *tzaddik.* Thus, through giving their gold for the *Mishkan,* the men *rose above* the women.

(חידושי הרי״ם)

”כל נדיב לב הביאו חח ונזם...”
"All willing hearted brought bracelets and earrings." (35:22)

QUESTION: Why are the people who brought jewelry referred to as *"nediv leiv"* — "willing hearted" people?

ANSWER: Though gold is very valuable, a person's own jewelry is cherished. Unlike gold which can easily be replaced, jewelry often has a sentimental value or uniqueness which is irreplaceable.

Donations of gold are indeed generous, but not as generous as donations of personal items to which one has become attached. Such benevolence demonstrates that the person is *"nediv leiv"* — "willing hearted."

”וכל אשה חכמת לב בידיה טוו ויביאו מטוה את התכלת...”
"Every wise-hearted woman spun with her hand, and they brought the spun yarn of sky-blue wool." (35:25)

QUESTION: According to *halacha,* the work a woman produces belongs to her husband. How was the *Mishkan* permitted to accept donations from women?

ANSWER: According to the *Gemara (Ketubot* 59a) the Rabbis instituted that a woman must give what she produces to her husband because he is obligated to provide her sustenance. In the wilderness Hashem fed the Jewish people with manna from heaven. Since no husband personally provided food for his wife, the above mentioned *halacha* did not apply. The *wise-hearted* women reasoned this and donated their dexterity for the benefit of the *Mishkan.*

(פרדס יוסף)

"וכל הנשים אשר נשא לבן אתנה בחכמה טוו את העזים"

"All the women whose hearts stirred them up in wisdom spun the goat's hair." (35:26)

QUESTION: Rashi says, "This was a special skill, for they spun the goat's hair upon the backs of the goats."

Hashem's instructions for the *Mishkan* do not require that the goat's hair be spun on the back of the goats. Why does the Torah convey to us the way the women spun the goats' hair?

ANSWER: The Torah is teaching a very important lesson: When people possess special talents it is important for them to remember that it is Hashem who blessed them with these talents and that they should be used to make this world a holy dwelling place for Hashem.

Therefore, since there were women who were blessed with the unique skill of spinning hair still on the backs of the goat, they utilized this skill for the holy purpose of making a *Mishkan,* in which Hashem would dwell.

(כ"ק אדמו"ר)

"וכל הנשים אשר נשא לבן אתנה בחכמה טוו את העזים: והנשאם הביאו את אבני השהם ואת אבני המלאים"

"All the women whose hearts inspired them with wisdom spun the goat hair. The leaders brought the *shoham* stones and the stones for the settings." (35:26-27)

QUESTION: What is the connection between the women spinning the goat hair and the *nesi'im* bringing their contributions?

ANSWER: Rashi cites Rabbi Natan *(Bamidbar Rabbah* 12:16) that the word *"nesi'im"* (נשאם) is spelled without a "יו" because the leaders were somewhat lax in bringing contributions for the *Mishkan*. Originally they waited to see what would be lacking, intending to give everything still needed. Seeing that the people gave in abundant measure, they immediately brought their generous offering of *shoham* stones and stones for the settings.

The Torah emphasizes that unlike the *nesi'im,* the women acted with *zerizut* — zeal and alacrity for the building of the *Mishkan.* They hastened to do the spinning while the hair was still on the goats because they were too impatient to wait for the hair to be shorn off and delivered.

(עיטורי תורה - גבורי ישראל)

"והנשאם הביאו את אבני השהם"
"The *nesi'im* brought the stones of *shoham.*" (35:27)

QUESTION: The word *"nesi'im"* is written without a *"yud"* because in the beginning they did not contribute to the *Mishkan.* They thought, "Let the other Jews first give what they can, and whatever is lacking we shall complete." Due to their failure of alacrity, the letter *"yud"* was omitted from their title (Rashi).

Why the letter *"yud"* and not any other letter?

ANSWER: In Hebrew, one way to change a word from singular to plural is to add a *"yud."* For example the word<div dir="rtl">"פתיל"</div> means "a thread" and the word <div dir="rtl">"פתילי"</div> means "threads." <div dir="rtl">"נשיא"</div> means "a Prince" and <div dir="rtl">"נשיאי"</div> means "many Princes."

Originally all the *nesi'im* decided to be a separate entity and not to participate together with the entire *Klal Yisrael* in the *Mishkan* construction. Therefore, while everybody was contributing generously to the construction, they stood idly on the side. Hence, the letter *"yud,"* which indicates plurality, was omitted from their name.

(אבני אזל)

"ראו קרא ד' בשם בצלאל בן אורי בן חור למטה יהודה"
"See, G-d has called by name Betzalel son of Uri son of Chur, of the tribe of Yehudah." (35:30)

QUESTION: Why is it necessary to list Betzalel's genealogy?

ANSWER: The Jewish people anticipated Moshe's return from heaven at a specific time. When, according to their calculations, he did not return, they approached Aharon requesting a new leader. His nephew Chur opposed them vehemently and was ultimately killed by the violent crowd (see Rashi 32:5).

As a means of atonement for the sin of worshipping the golden calf, Hashem ordered the construction of the *Mishkan,* for which much gold was to be used. Due to the link between the *Mishkan* and the golden calf, Chur, who died *"al kiddush Hashem"* — sanctifying Hashem — merited that Hashem select his grandson as the architect of the *Mishkan.*

(משך חכמה)

"וימלא אתו רוח אלקים בחכמה בתבונה ובדעת ובכל מלאכה ולחשב מחשבות לעשת בזהב ובכסף ובנחשת"

"And He had imbued him with a G-dly spirit, with wisdom, in understanding, and in knowledge, and in all workmanship. And to devise skillful works in gold and silver." (35:31-32)

QUESTION: The words *"velachshov machashavot"* — "to devise skillful works" — seem redundant. Since he was "imbued with a G-dly spirit in all workmanship," obviously he could do the most skillful work.

ANSWER: People generously contributed gold, silver, and copper for the construction of the *Mishkan.* Undoubtedly every donor would want *his* valuable metals to be used in the construction of the *most* prestigious and holy artifact.

In Hebrew the word *"machashavot"* means "thoughts." Betzalel was imbued with a G-dly spirit to be a *chosheiv machashavot* — a mind reader. He was able to hold a piece of metal in his hand and know the thoughts and intentions of the donor. Those which were given with holy and pure thoughts were used for the more exalted items.

(פרדס יוסף)

"ולהורת נתן בלבו הוא ואהליאב בן אחיסמך למטה דן"

"And He has put it into his heart that he may teach, both he and Oholiav son of Achisamach of the tribe of Dan." (35:34)

QUESTION: Why is it necessary to mention Betzalel's teaching ability?

ANSWER: In the times of the *Beit Hamikdash* there were a few families and individuals that had uniquely talented in preparing things for the *Beit Hamikdash.* The Gormu family were experts in the baking of the *lechem hapanim,* the Avtinus family were very talented in preparing the *ketoret,* etc. *(Yoma* 38a). The Sages were very upset with them for refusing to convey their dexterity to others.

Betzalel and Oholiav were blessed with exceptional architectural talent. They did not consider this a personal asset, but rather something to pass on to others.

When Hashem blesses a person, it is incumbent upon him to share and convey to others his divine blessings and talents. Therefore, the Torah praises Betzalel for sharing his knowledge with others.

(אור החיים)

"ועשה בצלאל ואהליאב וכל איש חכם לב אשר נתן ד' חכמה ותבונה בהמה לדעת לעשת את כל מלאכת עבדת הקדש לכל אשר צוה ד'"

"Betzalel shall carry out — with Ahaliav and every wise-hearted man within whom G-d had endowed wisdom and insight to know and to do all the work for the labor of the Sanctuary — everything that G-d had commanded." (36:1)

QUESTION: In lieu of *"baheimah"* — "in them" — it should have said *"bahem."* From this the *Midrash Rabbah* (48:3) derives that Hashem had endowed wisdom and insight also in the *beheimah* — animal. Why was it necessary that there should be wisdom in the animal?

ANSWER: The women spun the goat hair while it was on the goat (Rashi 35:26). It was requisite that the animal be granted wisdom so that it would cooperate when used for this kind of difficult spinning.

(כתב סופר)

"והם הביאו אליו עוד נדבה בבקר בבקר"
"They brought additional donations each morning." (36:3)

QUESTION: What donations did the workers bring each morning?

ANSWER: According to *halacha* the working day starts at sunrise and ends at night when the stars appear. At sunrise the worker leaves his home for the job, and the travel time and time to eat breakfast is at the employer's expense.

For the building of the *Mishkan,* — *"veheim"* — the workers — gave a special donation of *"boker"* — "morning." They woke up especially early and started working at *alot hashachar* — rising of the morning star, so they would have more time to work during the day.

(פנינים יקרים ועי' בבא מציעא דף פ"ג ע"ב תוס')

"ויבאו כל החכמים...איש איש ממלאכתו אשר המה עשים"
"And all the wise people came ... every man from his work that they were doing." (36:4)

QUESTION: The *Gemara (Sanhedrin* 69b) learns from the word *"Ish"* that Betzalel the chief architect was only 13 years old. There were undoubtedly many older people with much more experience; why was such a young person selected as chief architect?

ANSWER: Regarding the *Mishkan* it is said, "And they shall make for me a sanctuary — *'veshachanti betocham'* — and I will dwell among them." Grammatically it should have said *"veshachanti betocho"* — "and I will dwell in it." From this it is deduced *(Shelah)* that Hashem's intent was to dwell in each individual — that every Jew make himself a dwelling place for G-dliness.

The selection of Betzalel at the young age of 13 implies that as soon as a Jewish boy becomes obligated in the performance of *mitzvot,* he is required to make *himself* a Holy sanctuary in which G-d will want to dwell.

"איש ואשה אל יעשו עוד מלאכה לתרומת הקדש ויכלא העם מהביא"

" 'Man and woman shall not do more work toward the gift for the Sanctuary.' And the people were restrained from bringing." (36:6)

QUESTION: Why was it necessary for a complete cessation of donations? It could have been proclaimed that the people continue bringing, and the additional contribution would be kept in reserve for future charitable needs.

ANSWER: Moshe notified the Jews that there was no longer a necessity for further donations for the construction of the *Mishkan;* but if they wanted to contribute, the materials would be kept for future charitable purposes. The Jewish people are great performers of *gemilut chasadim* — deeds of kindness — and they indeed continued to donate generously, relying on Moshe's discretion.

The term *"am"* refers to *"Eirev Rav"* — the mixed multitude of people who joined with the Jews when they left Egypt. It was they who stopped giving because they were only interested in donating for the building of the *Mishkan,* something for Hashem, but not in benefiting another person.

(פניני התורה בשם ר' שלמה ז"ל קלוגער)

* * *

In the *Beit Hamikdash,* Gentiles too were able to bring offerings. However, they would only bring a *Korban Olah,* a burnt-offering which went entirely for Hashem. Jews could also bring a *Karban Shelamim* — peace offering — from which not only Hashem received a part, but which the *Kohen* also enjoyed.

"ויכלא העם מהביא"

"And the people stopped bringing." (36:6)

QUESTION: The *Ba'al Haturim* notes that the word *"Vayikalei"* — and they stopped" — is found twice in the Torah. Once here and also in *Bereishit* (8:2): *"vayikalei hageshem min hashamayim"* — "and the rain from the heaven stopped."

What is the connection between the two?

ANSWER: Rain produces material abundance: Plentiful rain brings affluence, and drought leads to famine and deprivation.

Many people give charity generously when Hashem showers them with heavenly blessings. As soon as *"vayikalei hageshem min hashamayim"* — they experience restraint in their income — immediately *"vayikalei ha'am meihavi"* — the first thing they curtail is the giving of *tzedakah*. Unfortunately, little do they realize that their wealth will not be minimized by the giving of *tzedakah*.

(לקוטי בתר לקוטי ח"א)

* * *

The Prophet states, "So says Hashem *'Ani Rishon veAni Acharon'* — 'I am the First and I am the Last'" (Isaiah 44:6). According to a homiletic interpretation, Hashem is bemoaning the fact that when a person has to limit his spending, instead of reducing personal pleasures, he cuts *first* his expenditures for Torah and *mitzvot*.

On the other hand, when one is blessed with financial success, after satisfying himself with all the amenities of life, *lastly* he thinks of Hashem and begins to spend for His causes.

"והמלאכה היתה דים לכל המלאכה לעשות אתה והותר"

"But the materials were sufficient for all the work that had to be done and more than enough." (36:7)

QUESTION: The words *"dayam"* and *"vehoteir"* are contradictory. *"Dayam"* means sufficient and *"vehoteir"* means "more than enough."

ANSWER: When Moshe announced the need for contributions to construct the *Mishkan*, the response was enthusiastic. People from all over brought gold, silver, copper, etc., and much more was donated than actually needed.

If it had happened that some of the donations had gone unused, people would have been disappointed, attributing the non-use to their personal unworthiness. In order to not disappoint anyone, Hashem made a miracle that everything donated be utilized for the construction.

The Torah alludes to this by observing that though it was *"vehoteir"* — more than enough — yet *"dayam lechal hamelachah"* — miraculously the work that had to be done was enough to utilize everything that was donated.

(אור החיים)

"ויעש בצלאל את הארן עצי שטים"

"And Betzalel made the Ark of cedar wood." (37:1)

QUESTION: Why is the name of Betzalel mentioned in connection with the Ark and not in relation to other vessels of the *Mishkan?*

ANSWER: Moshe broke the first set of *tablets* on the 17th day of *Tammuz*. Forty days later Hashem said to him, "Carve out two tablets of stone like the first and come up to Me on the mount, and make for yourself an Ark of wood." This Ark was not the Ark built by Betzalel, because the construction of the *Mishkan* first began after *Yom Kippur*. Consequently, there was an Ark made by Moshe and another one by Betzalel. The Ark made by Moshe traveled with the Jewish people when they went to war, and the one made by Betzalel always remained in the *Mishkan* except in the days of Eli, the High Priest (see *Devarim* 10:1,3, Rashi).

Therefore, though Betzalel was involved in the making of all of the vessels of the *Mishkan,* his name is mentioned specifically only in the making of the Ark. This is to emphasize that he made the Ark which was in the *Mishkan,* in addition to the one previously made by Moshe.

(פרדס יוסף)

"ויעש בצלאל את הארן.. ויעש לו זר זהב סביב...ויעש את
השלחן..ויעש לו זר זהב סביב..ויעש את מזבח הקטרת..ויעש לו זר
זהב סביב"

"And Betzalel made the Ark ... and he made for it a crown of gold round about ... and he made the table ... and he made for it a crown of gold round about ... and he made the altar of incense ... and he made for it a crown of gold round about" (37:1-2, 10, 11, 25-26)

QUESTION: The crown around the Ark represents the crown of Torah. The crown around the table represents the crown of *malchut* — kingship —and the one around the altar represents crown of *Kehuna* — the crown of Priesthood.

In *Pirkei Avot* (4:13) when Rabbi Shimon speaks of these three crowns, he concludes that *"Vecheter shem tov oleh al gabeihen"* — "A crown of a good name surpasses them all." Why wasn't there another crown in the *Mishkan* to represent *Keter Shem Tov?*

ANSWER: A crown is a symbol of grandeur which brings magnificence and splendor to its bearer. Sometimes, one who has earned the crown of Torah, Priesthood, or Kingship may still lack a good reputation due to his poor personality. Rabbi Shimon teaches that in reality there are *only* three crowns. The crown of a good name is not an additional one, but rather the integral part of each of the three others. The three crowns add glory to the one who wears them *only* if he possesses a good name and reputation.

(מדרש שמואל - הר"מ אלשקאר ז"ל)

**"ויעש את הכיור נחשת ואת כנו נחשת במראת הצבאת אשר צבאו
פתח אהל מועד"**

"He made a laver of copper and its base of copper, from the mirrors of the legions who massed at the entrance of the Tent of Meeting." (38:8)

QUESTION: According to Rashi, the "legions" were the women. They had mirrors for adorning themselves; and even these objects of personal pride they did not refrain from bringing as a contribution for the *Mishkan*. However, Moshe saw these as objects of vanity and personal pride and was hesitant to take these mirrors for use of the *Mishkan*. Therefore, Hashem told them, "Take them, because these are the most beloved to me."

1) Why the emphasis that the women gathered; didn't all the people gather? 2) Why were these most beloved to Hashem? 3) Why was the laver made specifically from copper of the mirrors of the women?

ANSWER: 1) All the other people brought their donations and left immediately. However, since Moshe was apprehensive about the gift the women brought, a crowd of women gathered and waited for Moshe to receive Divine guidance.

2) A woman's beauty is confirmed with mirrors. Thus, while all others gave contributions from their various resources, the women gave from their most personal quality: their beauty. Therefore, because of this profound emotional sacrifice, the mirrors were most beloved to Hashem.

3) Water from the laver was used to test wives suspected of being unfaithful. If the allegations against them were found to be untrue, they merited heavenly blessings. The mirrors were donated by righteous women to create the laver, through which the unfaithful were excluded and the righteous rewarded accordingly.

೮೩ ಐಲ

PEKUDEI • פקודי

"אלה פקודי המשכן"

"These are the accounts of the Mishkan..." (38:21)

QUESTION: The Torah is careful not to repeat a word or write an extra letter; why are the *parshiot* of *Vayakheil* and *Pekudei* a complete redundancy of *Terumah* and *Tetzaveh*?

ANSWER: The Torah discusses at great length the episodes that took place when Eliezer goes to find a suitable wife for Yitzchak. When he meets with her family, the entire story is repeated. Rashi explains, "The ordinary conversation of the servants of the Patriarchs is more pleasing before Hashem than the Torah of the sons. Therefore, the section of Eliezer is repeated in the Torah, whereas many important principles of the law were given only by hinting." (See *Bereishit* 24:42, Rashi)

The gravest sin ever committed by the Jewish people was the making and worshipping of the Golden Calf. It incited the wrath of Hashem to the extent that He considered, G-d forbid, annihilating the entire people. The *Mishkan* is referred to as the *Mishkan* of Testimony (משכן העדות) because it serves as a testimony that G-d forgave the sin of the Golden Calf (see *Vayikra* 9:23, Rashi). Consequently, since the *Mishkan* accomplished forgiveness for His beloved people, he enjoys talking about it in great detail.

(לקוטי שיחות חט״ז)

"אלה פקודי המשכן משכן העדת"

"These are the accounts of the tabernacle, [the] tabernacle of testimony." (38:21)

QUESTION: Rashi says in the name of the *Midrash* that the word *"Mishkan"* is repeated twice as a hint to the *Beit Hamikdash*, which was taken as a pledge *("mashkon")* at the two destructions for the sins of the Jewish people."

How does the word *"Mishkan"* — "Tabernacle" — hint for the *Beit Hamikdash?*

ANSWER: The first *Beit Hamikdash* stood a total of 410 years and the second *Beit Hamikdash* lasted 420 years. The word "משכן" has the numerical value of 410 and the word "המשכן" has the numerical value of 415. If we add to the numerical value the five letters of the word, we will then have 420.

(רבינו בחיי)

* * *

The *Gemara (Yoma 21b)* relates that in the second *Beit Hamikdash* there were five things missing which were in the first *Beit Hamikdash*. Therefore, the Torah's allusion to the second *Beit Hamikdash* (המשכן) has the numerical value of only 415.

(חתם סופר)

"אלה פקודי המשכן משכן העדת"

"These are the accounts of the Mishkan...." (38:21)

QUESTION: In the beginning of *Parshat Mishpatim*, Rashi gives a rule that the word *"eileh"* dismisses, and the word *"ve'eileh"* adds. What does the word *"eileh"* in our *pasuk* dismiss?

ANSWER: In the nineteenth century there lived in England the famous Jewish philanthropist Sir Moses Montefiore. Queen Victoria once asked him, "What is the extent of your wealth? How much do you own?" Sir Moses told her it would take him a few days to do some accounting, afterwards he would be able to reply.

When Sir Moses told her the amount of his wealth, she became upset, saying, "You are insulting me. Everyone knows that you have much more." Sir Moses explained that he considered as *his* wealth whatever money he gave away to *tzedakah.* Anything else that he had was only temporary and subject to confiscation or loss.

The usage of the word ״אלה״ — *"these are"* — suggests homiletically that the only meaningful holdings one possesses are the resources that are devoted to building G-d's sanctuaries or otherwise used for the sake of heaven. Only such investments are eternal; all others are transitory.

* * *

According to the *Midrash Rabbah (Bamidbar* 22:8), the Hebrew names for money and resources indicate that they are temporary, i.e. the word *"mamon"*— ״ממון״ is an acronym for ״מה אתה מונה״ — "What are you counting? It is nothing!"

(אור החיים)

״משכן העדת״

"The tabernacle of testimony." (38:21)

QUESTION: Why is the *Mishkan* called *"Mishkan Ha'eidut"* (Tabernacle of Testimony)?

ANSWER: From the time the *Mishkan* was built in the dessert till the construction of the first *Beit Hamikdash* by King Shlomo there elapsed a period of 479 years. The word *"Ha'eidut"* (העדת) has the numerical equivalent of 479. This alludes to the fact that for 479 years the *Mishkan* served as a testimony to Hashem's dwelling among the Jewish people.

(רבינו בחיי)

"אשר פקד על פי משה"

"Which was counted according to the commandment of Moshe." (38:21)

QUESTION: Shouldn't it say "the commandment of Hashem"?

ANSWER: In the times of *Mashiach* we will have the third *Beit Hamikdash.* The words *"al pi"* (על פי) — "according to" — have the numerical value of 190, which spells the word "קץ"— *"keitz"* — the word used to describe the end of *galut.* Consequently, in the same *pasuk* where there is a hint to the two *Batei Mikdash* which were destroyed (see Rashi), there are mentioned the words *"al pi Moshe"* — to allude that through studying the Torah which was given through Moshe, we will merit the *keitz* — end of *galut* — and the coming of *Mashiach,* and ultimately the building of the third *Beit Hamikdash.*

"ובצלאל בן אורי בן חור למטה יהודה עשה את כל אשר צוה ד' את משה"

"And Betzalel the son of Uri, the son of Chur, of the tribe of Yehudah, made all that G-d commanded Moshe." (38:22)

QUESTION: Rashi explains that it says Betzalel did all that G-d commanded Moshe and not that he did as Moshe commanded him because Moshe told Betzalel to make the vessels first and the *mishkan* afterwards. Betzalel objected and made the *Mishkan* first and then the vessels. His reasoning was that it is logical for one first to buy a house and afterwards the furnishings.

Moshe agreed with Betzalel and said to him, "The name 'Betzalel' which means 'in the shadow of G-d'" is most appropriate for you because you display prophetic knowledge. This is exactly what Hashem told me: to first make the *Mishkan* and later the vessels."

If Hashem had told Moshe to make first the *Mishkan* and then the vessels, why did he reverse the order when instructing Betzalel?

ANSWER: When Moshe had instructed Betzalel to be in charge of the construction of the *Mishkan*, he feared being accused of nepotism. People might have complained, "Why did you choose your young nephew for such a lofty position and not seek someone more qualified?" Moshe wanted to prove that though Betzalel was related to him and only thirteen years old, it was indeed Hashem who had designated him.

Therefore, Moshe reversed the order he received from Hashem and publicly instructed to first make the vessels, certain that Betzalel possessed *Ruach Hakodesh* and that he would act in the way Hashem *actually* instructed. Based on Betzalel's response, Moshe declared to the people, "See that Hashem selected Betzalel, the son of Uri, the son of Chur (35:30). It was not I who chose him; he was appointed by Hashem and he knew G-d's exact command."

(שער בת רבים)

* * *

Alternatively, when Hashem conveyed the command of constructing the *Mishkan*, He said to Moshe, "Like everything that I show you, the form of the *Mishkan* and the form of all its vessels; *"Vechein ta'asu"* — "And so shall you do" (25:9).

The *"vav"* in the word *"vechein"* seems to indicate that there were *two* messages given to Moshe. 1) To make everything according to how he was shown by G-d. 2) *"Vechein ta'asu"* — "and so shall you do." Rashi explains that the second command referred to the future, should there be a need to replace any vessels of the Tabernacles. However, it can also be interpreted to refer to the chronological order according to which the vessels of the Tabernacle should be made.

Moshe originally explained it as Rashi does, and thus he had no directive from Hashem for the order in which to make the vessels. Consequently, he considered making the vessels before the *Mishkan*. When Betzalel disagreed and argued that it is customary to build the house before the furniture, Moshe agreed saying, "You are correct and are in the shadow of G-d. Indeed, when G-d commanded me to make the *Mishkan* and said '*Vechein ta'asu,*' He must have been referring to the order of priority, and thus I agree with you that the *Mishkan* should be made before the vessels."

(שו"ת תירוש ויצהר סי' קל"ד)

"ויעשו את בגדי הקדש אשר לאהרן כאשר צוה ד' את משה"

"And they made the holy garments for Aharon, as G-d had commanded Moshe." (39:1)

QUESTION: Why was it necessary to stress "as G-d had commanded Moshe"?

ANSWER: The words "as G-d had commanded Moshe" are repeated 18 times in this *parshah*. Eighteen is equal to *"chai"* (חי) — "life." The Torah conveys that throughout his entire life, Moshe continuously strived to do as G-d commanded him.

(עי' בעל הטורים)

"ויעשו את ציץ...ויכתבו עליו פתוחי חותם קדש לד'"

"They made the head-plate...and they wrote in the same manner as a signet ring's engraving, *'Kodesh LaHashem'* (Holiness to G-d)." (39:30)

QUESTION: Why does it say, *"vayichtevu"* — "They wrote" —in plural?

ANSWER: The *Gemara (Yoma* 38a) tells of Ben Kamtzar, who was able to hold four pens in his hand and write the four letters of Hashem's name at the same time. The Rabbis were upset with him because he refused to teach this skill to anyone else. The Rabbis wanted him to teach others because the first two letters of Hashem's name (י-ה) form one of his names. The next letter, "ו", changes it to a regular word, and this raises the question of *mechikah* (erasing) Hashem's name *(Minchat Chinuch* 437). Ben Kamtzar avoided this question by writing all four letters at one time.

Consequently, when they made the head-plate, in order to avoid any halachic problems connected with erasing Hashem's name, *they* wrote — four people together — each writing one letter of Hashem's name on the head-plate at the same time.

"ותכל כל עבדת משכן אהל מועד ויעשו בני ישראל ככל אשר צוה ד' את משה"

"All the work of the *Mishkan* was completed and the Jewish people did according to all that G-d commanded Moshe." (39:32)

QUESTION: Why is it necessary to emphasize that the Jews did "according to all" that Hashem commanded Moshe? Who would dare do otherwise?

ANSWER: According to *halacha,* when one is involved in performing a *mitzvah,* he is exempt from doing other *mitzvot (Ha'oseik bemitzvah patur min hamitzva").* When the Jews were preoccupied in the building of the *Mishkan,* there were many *mitzvot* that they let pass by and did not fulfill. The *pasuk* tells us that once the work on the *Mishkan* was completed, the *B'nei Yisrael* resumed performing *all* the *mitzvot* of the Torah, which Hashem had commanded through Moshe.

(אמרי שפר)

"וירא משה את כל המלאכה...ויברך אתם משה"

"Moshe saw all the work...And Moshe blessed them." (39:43)

QUESTION: His blessing was "יהי רצון שתשרה שכינה במעשה ידיכם" — "May His divine presence abide in the work of your hands" (Rashi). Why didn't Moshe say, "May the *Shechinah* rest in the *Mishkan"?*

ANSWER: When the Jews were involved in building the *Mishkan,* Hashem was delighted with His chosen people because they were in a lofty and exalted spirit. After the *Mishkan* was completed, they returned to their regular daily mundane activities.

Undoubtedly, Moshe prayed that the *Shechinah* should be pleased with *Klal Yisrael* and dwell in the *Mishkan*. However, in addition, he also blessed the Jews that when they are involved in *"ma'aseh yedeichem"* — their regular daily activities and preoccupations — even then they should conduct themselves in such a way to merit that the *Shechina* should feel comfortable to be among them.

(פרדס יוסף)

"ויקם משה את המשכן ויתן את אדניו וישם את קרשיו ויתן את בריחיו ויקם את עמודיו"

"And Moshe erected the *Mishkan* and he put down its sockets, and set up its boards, and inserted its bars and erected its pillars." (40:18)

QUESTION: Since the *pasuk* enumerates "its sockets," "its boards," "its bars," "its pillars," it would appear that the words *"vayakem Moshe et haMishkan"* are superfluous.

ANSWER: A number of coverings were placed upon the *Mishkan*. Actually, the lower covering created a closed entity which in itself is the true *Mishkan*. Thus, the passage "And Moshe set up the *Mishkan*" specifically means the hanging of the bottom covering.

Though the workers first made the boards and sockets and afterwards the covering, when Moshe erected the *Mishkan*, he put up the covering *first* and caused it to be suspended miraculously. Consequently, only later did he place the additional components of the "sockets," "boards," "bars," and "pillars" to the miraculously suspended *Mishkan*.

(ספורנו)

* * *

QUESTION: Obviously, it would have been much easier to first raise up the boards and then place the coverings over them. Why did Moshe do it in this complex way, relying on a miracle to suspend the curtains in mid-air?

ANSWER: The *Midrash (Tanchuma, Pekudei* 11) states that the *Mishkan* paralleled the creation of heaven and earth. There is an opinion in the *Gemara (Chagiga 12a)* that the heavens were created first, and the earth afterwards. Therefore, Moshe, corresponding to Hashem's actions, first placed the curtains, which are equal to the heavens, before putting up the sockets and the boards, which are comparable to the earth.

(דברי ירמיהו)

"ויקם משה את המשכן"

"And Moshe erected the *Mishkan.*" (40:18)

QUESTION: According to *Midrash Rabbah (Bamidbar* 12:10), during the first seven days of dedication Moshe would erect and dismantle the *Mishkan* daily.

In a seven day period there must be a *Shabbat.* How was Moshe allowed to do this work on *Shabbat?*

ANSWER: The completed *Mishkan* was extremely heavy and the people were not able to stand it up. They confronted Moshe with their dilemma, and he, too, was unable. He turned to Hashem saying, "How is it possible to erect it by means of man?" Hashem told him, "Put your hand to it." It appeared as though Moshe erected it, but actually it stood up by itself (Rashi 39:33). Since in reality everything was a miracle of Hashem and Moshe did not do any physical labor, there was no question of desecrating *Shabbat.*

(הדרש והעיון)

"ויקח ויתן את העדות אל הארן"

"He took and he put the tablets into the Ark." (40:20)

QUESTION: The word *"Vayikach"* — "he took" — seems extra, it is not used for any other thing in the *Mishkan?*

ANSWER: When Moshe received the tablets the *Mishkan* was not built yet. Moshe made an Ark of wood in which he placed the tablets and stored it in his tent *(Devarim* 10:1). When the *Mishkan* was constructed, Betzalel made an Ark of gold to house the tablets. Therefore, the Torah tells us that *"vayikach"* — Moshe took out the tablets from the temporary wooden Ark and *"Vayitein"* — he put them into the permanent Ark of gold.

(רמב״ן)

״וישם את הבדים על הארן״
"And he inserted the staves on the Ark." (40:20)

QUESTION: The staves were on the *side* of the Ark; why is it written *"on* the Ark"?

ANSWER: The Ark represents the Torah scholars, and the staves represent those who support them. Not only should they be alongside and offer help when they are needed, but they should also be "on top" of the Torah scholars. It is incumbent on the supporters of Torah to project the needs of the scholars and assure that they be able to study Torah in peace and tranquillity.

(באר משה)

״אלה פקודי...בכל מסעיהם״
"These are the accounts...Throughout all their journeys" (38:21, 40:38)

QUESTION: At the end of every *parshah* of the Torah is written the number of *pesukim* and a word which adds up to that amount. The word is supposed to serve as a *siman* (סימן) — a symbol to remember the amount of *pesukim*. Why is this omitted at the end of *Parshat Pekudei*?

ANSWER: The reason *may be* because in *Parshat Pekudei* there are 92 pesukim. The words "בלי כל" have the numerical value of 92. Possibly, in a early prints of the *Chumash,* a typesetter who was a mediocre scholar noticed that it was written at the end of the *parshah* ״צ״יב, בלי כל סימן״. Erroneously, he understood it to mean "92, without any *siman,"* and therefore he omitted it.

(ספר תומכי תמימים בשם כ״ק אדמו״ר)

"כי ענן ד' על המשכן יומם ואש תהיה לילה בו...בכל מסעיהם"

"A cloud of G-d was on the *Mishkan* by day and fire used to be over it by night...throughout their journeys." (40:38)

QUESTION: This is the concluding *pasuk* of *Chumash Shemot*. Torah is never ending. What parallel can be drawn between the closing and opening passages of *Chumash Shemot*?

ANSWER: "Day" represents the good times and happy periods the Jewish people experience. "Night" is an allusion to gloomy and difficult times that may, G-d forbid, confront us. The Torah assures us that throughout all our travels, regardless if things are shining for us or G-d forbid the reverse, clouds of Hashem and heavenly fire protect us to guarantee our safety and survival.

Chumash Shemot begins with the journey of the Jewish people down to Egypt, which was one of the darker periods in our history. Knowing that Hashem's watchful eye is with the Jewish people throughout "all their journeys" helped them survive the ordeal of slavery.

* * *

Another way to link together the end and beginning of *Chumash Shemot* may be the following:

In the beginning of *Chumash Shemot* the Torah relates how the daughter of Pharaoh saved Moshe when he was placed in a little box on the waters. On the *Pasuk "vatishlach et amatah"* — "she stretched out her arm" (2:5) — Rashi says, Hashem miraculously elongated it and it was able to reach the box.

In the concluding *parshah* of *Chumash Shemot* we learn that when the *Mishkan* was completed, no one was able to stand it up due to the weight of the boards. It was brought to Moshe and he, too, was puzzled: how could he possibly pick it up? Hashem told him, "Put your hand to it and then it will stand up by itself" (Rashi 39:33).

The lesson which we are taught in the beginning and end of this *Chumash* is that when something has to be accomplished, we should not become disillusioned and frightened because it seems difficult or impossible. If we will make an honest effort to do the utmost, Hashem will bless us with success and the impossible will become a reality.

PURIM • פורים

13th of *Adar* — Fast of Esther

QUESTION: Why is the fast on the day before *Purim* called *Ta'anit Esther* — the Fast of Esther? (The three-day fast which Mordechai proclaimed upon the request of Esther took place during *Pesach*.)

ANSWER: Though Achashveirosh originally agreed to Haman's plan to kill *all* the Jews on the 13th of *Adar,* he later instructed the Jews to defend themselves against the Persian armies. According to *halacha,* people defending themselves against enemies are forbidden to fast, so as not to weaken their strength. *(Shulchan Aruch, Orach Chaim* 571:3) Consequently, on the 13th of *Adar* it was forbidden for any Jew to fast. Esther lived in the King's palace, and thus did not fear the armies. Hence, she was the *only* person able to fast while the Jewish people defended themselves against the Persians. Therefore, the day is known as *Ta'anit Esther*.

(לקוטי שיחות ח״ו, הוספות)

"שאלו תלמידיו את רשב״י מפני מה נתחייבו שונאיהן של ישראל שבאותו הדור כליה אמר להם אמרו אתם אמרו לו מפני שנהנו מסעודתו של אותו רשע"

"The students asked Rabbi Shimon Bar Yochai, 'Why were the Jews destined to be annihilated in the days of Achashveirosh?' He said to them, 'What is your opinion?' They replied, 'Because they derived pleasure (ate) from the meal of the wicked person.'" *(Gemara, Megillah* **12a)**

QUESTION: According to Biblical Law, death is not the punishment for eating non-kosher?

ANSWER: The prophet Yirmeyahu prophesied that seventy years after the destruction of the first *Beit Hamikdash,* Hashem would bring back the Jewish people from exile. According to Achashveirosh's calculation, the seventy year period had already passed, and since there was no redemption, Hashem had obviously, G-d forbid, forsaken His people. To celebrate his victory, he used the vessels of the *Beit Hamikdash* and arranged lavish festivities to which he invited everyone, including the Jewish people *(Gemara, Megillah* 11b).

The food and drink served to the Jews was strictly kosher, even according to the most stringent standards. However, instead of attending the festivities reluctantly, with a sense of grief, *"nehenu"* — they had a sense of "pleasure" because they were accepted to Persian high society. Such behavior angered Hashem, to the extent that He considered annihilating the Jewish people, G-d forbid. Had the *Gemara* meant that their iniquity was the eating of the food, it would have written *"she'achlu"* — "Because they ate from his meal."

(עי' רשימות כ"ק אדמו"ר ח"ו)

קרעפכין

Krepchen

QUESTION: Why do we eat *"krepchen"* (meat covered with dough) on *Purim?*

ANSWER: On *Yom Tov* it is forbidden to do any work (except food preparation) and it is a *mitzvah* to experience the utmost joy. Thus it is customary to eat meat during *Yom Tov,* because it brings one into a joyous state of mind.

On *Purim,* one must be joyous and refrain from doing work, but the prohibition is not the same as on other *yamim tovim.* Therefore, we eat meat in order to bring us into a joyous mood, but because it is not a complete *Yom Tov* and it is permissible to work if needed, we cover the meat with dough. (This also explains why *krepchen* are eaten on *Erev Yom Kippur* and *Hosha'ana Rabbah.*)

(אוצר כל מנהגי ישרון ע' 186)

CB 80

MEGILLAT ESTHER • מגילת אסתר

"הקורא את המגילה למפרע לא יצא"

"If one reads the *Megillah* backwards, he has not fulfilled his obligation." *(Gemara, Megillah 17a)*

QUESTION: Why would one do such a strange thing?

ANSWER: The purpose of reading the *Megillah* is to bring to our attention that in all generations there are Hamans who plot our destruction. Miraculously, Hashem comes to our salvation thanks to our adherence to Torah and *mitzvot*.

"Reading the *Megillah* backwards," means thinking that the *Purim* narrative is a historical event with no contemporary relevance. One who takes such an attitude is missing the entire significance of Purim and the *Megillah.*

(כתר שם טוב הוספות סי' ע"ח)

"אם על המלך טוב יצא דבר מלכות מלפניו... להיות כל איש שר בביתו"

"If it pleases the King, let there go a forth a royal edict from him... that every man should rule in his own home." (1:19-22)

QUESTION: The King asked Haman only what to do with Vashti; why did Haman offer additional advice?

ANSWER: It was the custom in Persia that the King not decide any issue on his own; instead he would gather his advisers and seek their opinion (see Esther 1:13). Haman decided that this should be changed. Therefore, in addition to telling the King to kill Vashti, he suggested that from then on Achashveirosh should make all decisions on his own, without leaving room for appeal.

Additionally, from then on every man should be the ruler of his home.

Everything recorded in the *Megillah* is connected to the Miracle of *Purim*. Were it not for these two recommendations made by Haman, Esther would not have become queen, and Haman would not have been hung.

After Vashti was killed, a search began for a new Queen. Had it not been the rule of the land that each man be the ruler of his home, when agents would have arrived at the home of Mordechai searching for Esther, he would have told them, "I don't know where Esther is. She left without my permission and did not say when she would be back." Thanks to Haman's advice, Mordechai was unable to hide Esther and thus she was forced to come to Achashveirosh and eventually become the queen.

When Achashveirosh heard from Charvonah that Haman had prepared gallows upon which to hang Mordechai, the King angrily said, "Hang him on it!" (7:9) Haman began to demand, "Before you hang me there must be a trial with a jury deciding if I am guilty." Achashveirosh told Haman, "Sorry! It was you who gave the advice some time ago that *'yeitzei devar malchut milfanav'* — the King should make decisions on his own and no one can appeal them." Thus, Haman was hung immediately.

(חתם סופר)

"איש יהודי היה בשושן הבירה ושמו מרדכי"

"A Jew by the name of Mordechai lived in the Capitol city of Shushan." (2:5)

QUESTION: When the *Megillah* is read in public, it is a custom for everyone to say this *pasuk* aloud. What is special about this *pasuk*?

ANSWER: In the *Megillah* we find the expression *Shushan Habirah (Shushan* the Capitol) ten times, and nine times *Ha'ir Shushan* — "The City of *Shushan"* or just plain *"Shushan."* Obviously this is intentional. Why the distinction?

Shushan Habirah was the capitol of Achashveirosh's kingdom. Near it was a suburb known also as *"Shushan."* It was forbidden for Jews to live in the capitol city, but they were permitted to live in the city of *Shushan*. Therefore, when the *Megillah* talks about Achashveirosh or the issuing of decrees, *Shushan Habirah* is mentioned. Whenever the *Megillah* talks about the Jewish people, *Ha'ir Shushan* is mentioned.

By Divine Providence, Mordechai was the *only* Jew who happened to be living in the capitol. Thanks to this, he had access to the King's palace and was able to overhear the conversation of Bigtan and Teresh, which eventually brought about the downfall of Haman and the miracle of *Purim*.

(שפתי חכמים בהקדמה על מס׳ מגילה)

* * *

According to Rabbi Yehudah *(Gemara Megillah* 19a), the reading of the *Megillah* in public should begin with this *pasuk* because it portrays the strength and prominence of Mordechai. The above-mentioned explanation offers an insight into Rabbi Yehudah's opinion.

"ושמו מרדכי"

"And his name was Mordechai." (2:5)

QUESTION: According to the *Gemara (Menachot* 65a), Mordechai's real name was Petachya (פתחיה). There is a מדרש פליאה (wondrous *Midrash*) that says that this can be understood through the *pasuk "* והיה ראשיתך מצער ואחריתך ישגה מאד" — "Your beginning will be small, yet your latter end will greatly increase" (Job 8:7).

How through this *pasuk* is there a connection between מרדכי and פתחיה?

ANSWER: The first letter in the name פתחיה is a "פ", which equals 80. If you divide that in half, you have 40, which corresponds to "מ". The second letter is a "ת", which equals 400, and when it is divided in half you have 200, which corresponds to "ר". The third letter is a "ח", equaling 8, which divided in half equals 4, corresponding to "ד". The fourth letter, "י", equals 10 and when doubled equals 20, corresponding to "כ". The last letter is a ה"ה — 5, which when doubled equals 10 — יו"י. Thus, when the beginning (first three letters of פתחיה) is made smaller, and the end (last two letters) is made bigger, פתחיה equals מרדכי.

(ר' שמשון זצ"ל מאסטראפאלי)

"ובמות אביה ואמה לקחה מרדכי לו לבת"
"And when her father and mother had died, Mordechai adopted her as his daughter." (2:7)

QUESTION: The *Gemara (Megillah* 13a) says, "read not *'lebat'* — 'a daughter' but *'lebayit'* — 'a wife,'" [lit. "a home"]. Instead of alluding, why doesn't it say *"bayit"* explicitly?

ANSWER: The *Gemara (Ketubot* 59b) says that the purpose and desire of a women is in three things. 1) *"Bonim"* (בנים) — children. 2) *"Yofi"* (יופי) — beauty. 3) *"Tachshitim"* (תכשיטים) — jewelry. The acronym of these three is the word *"Bayit"* (בית).

The *Gemara (Megillah* 13a) says Esther was of greenish complexion (like a myrtle). However, G-d endowed her with a touch of grace — kindness. This made her appear beautiful in the eyes of the people and Achashveirosh (Rashi).

Consequently, of the three characteristics which make up the uniqueness of the women she was lacking the *"yud"* which stands for *"yofi"* beauty. Hence, in consideration of the two feminine qualities the *Megillah* refers to her relationship with Mordechai as *"Bat"* — "a daughter," but our sages tell us that she was really *"Bayit"* — a full fledged wife.

(בחירת אברהם)

"קצף בגתן ותרש... ויבקשו לשלח יד במלך אחשורש: ויודע הדבר למרדכי ויגד לאסתר המלכה ותאמר אסתר למלך בשם מרדכי... אחר הדברים האלה גדל המלך אחשורוש את המן"
"Bigtan and Teresh became angry... and sought to lay hand on King Achashveirosh: The plot became known to Mordechai, who told it to Queen Esther; and Esther informed the King in Mordechai's name... After these things King Achashveirosh promoted Haman." (2:21-22, 3:1)

QUESTION: Why was Haman promoted and not Mordechai, who provided the information?

ANSWER: Achashveirosh figured that if Mordechai was in fact concerned about his well-being, rather than telling Esther about the plotted assassination, he should have come directly to him. Therefore, he was in doubt as to Mordechai's true intentions. However, Esther, who revealed the secret plot to him, was indeed loyal and deserving of a reward. Since Esther as Queen had the maximum any woman could desire, Achashveirosh was in dilemma: what more could he give her?

Achashveirosh concluded that Esther esteemed Haman very highly, because upon his advice Vashti was killed, thus making it possible for her to become Queen. Assuming Haman to be Esthers trusted ally, Achashveirosh rewarded Esther by promoting him.

(שו״ת תירוש ויצהר סי׳ ק״ה)

"ויגידו להמן לראות היעמדו דברי מרדכי כי הגיד להם אשר הוא יהודי"

"They told Haman, to see whether Mordechai's words would avail; for he had told them that he was a Jew." (3:4)

QUESTION: What words of Mordechai did they convey to Haman?

ANSWER: Achashveirosh was once at war with another country. He selected two armies and placed one under the command of Mordechai and the other under the command of Haman. He gave each army a supply of food which was to last for the duration of the war. When Haman mismanaged his allotment and quickly ran out of food, his soldiers became very angry and planned a mutiny against him. Helpless, he ran to Mordechai and begged for food for his troops. Mordechai agreed to give him food on the condition that Haman become his slave.

According to *halacha,* when a Jew acquires a Gentile as a slave, he is required to put him through a ritual in which he is converted to be a quasi-Jew, and he becomes required to fulfill some *mitzvot.*

When the people questioned Mordechai's violation of the King's edict to bow down to Haman, he answered, *"Asher hu Yehudi"* — that Haman, by becoming his slave, was really a Jew.

As his master, he could not be expected to bow down to him. The people were surprised to hear this and conveyed these words to Haman to see whether Mordechai's words would avail. Haman, knowing this to be true, was embarrassed and filled with rage.

(תורת משה)

"ויבז בעיניו לשלח יד במרדכי לבדו כי הגידו לו את עם מרדכי ויבקש המן להשמיד את כל היהודים"

"It seemed contemptible to him to lay hands on Mordechai alone, for they had made known to him the people of Mordechai. So Haman sought to destroy all the Jews." (3:6)

QUESTION: What did Haman hear about Mordechai's people that made him decide to kill the entire nation and not just Mordechai alone?

ANSWER: Mordechai's refusal to bow upset Haman immensely. He considered this a great *chutzpah* and wanted to kill him. When he discussed it with his advisors, they told him, "You do not know who and what the Jewish people are. It is important for you to realize that Mordechai is not unique. The Jewish people are *'Am Mordechai'*— a nation consisting of many Mordechais. Killing Mordechai will not accomplish anything because immediately a new leader with the same ideals as Mordechai will take over. He therefore decided to get rid of the entire people and, thus, there would no longer, G-d forbid, be any Mordechais to contend with.

(כ"ק אדמו"ר)

"המן בן המדתא האגגי צרר היהודים"

"Haman the son of Hamdata the Jews enemy." (3:10)

QUESTION: Haman is described with many adjectives, how did he acquire the title *"Tzoreir haYehudim"*?

ANSWER: When Haman maligned the Jewish people, he told the King, *"Yeshno am echad mefuzar umeforad"* — "There is one nation, scattered and separated" (3:8). Commentators explain this to mean that they were in total disharmony. To counteract this, Esther felt that unity was the call of the hour and therefore instructed Mordechai, *"Leich kenos et kal haYehudim"* — "Go gather together *all* the Jews" (4:16).

In Hebrew, the word *"tzoreir"* means to bind and tie together. Haman, through vicious plots against the Jewish people, united and bound them together.

(עיטורי תורה - הרב י. מיכאלזאהן ז"ל מווארשא)

"ויאמר המלך להמן הכסף נתון לך והעם לעשות בו כטוב בעיניך"

"And the King said to Haman: The silver is given to you, the people also, to do with it as it seems good in your eyes." (3:11)

QUESTION: The *Gemara (Megillah* 14a) portrays the feelings of Haman and Achashveirosh towards the Jewish people with the following parable: There were once two farmers; one had a mountain of earth in his field while the other had a deep pit. The owner of the earth thought, "I would happily pay this man to permit me to dump my earth in his pit." On the other hand, the owner of the pit thought to himself, "I would unhesitatingly pay this man to fill my pit with his earth." Meeting personally, the owner of the pit offered to pay for the earth, and the owner of the earth responded immediately, "It is all yours, take it without cost and fill up your pit."

A parable is necessary to explain something difficult to understand; why was a parable needed to describe their hatred?

ANSWER: Undoubtedly, Achashveirosh and Haman both hated the Jewish people with a passion. However, they differed as to what was the best way to destroy them. The intent of the parable is to reveal the profound ideological differences between Achashveirosh and Haman as to how to destroy the Jewish people. Achashveirosh took the "mountain" philosophy. He elevated the Jews to important government positions and invited them to festive non-kosher meals. Surely they would assimilate and relinquish their Jewish identity.

Haman pursued the "pit philosophy": The Jews should be broken physically, degraded, oppressed, and killed. Thus, they would cease to exist. To bring his plan to fruition, he offered the

King money to physically kill every member of the Jewish people. Achashveirosh told him, "They are yours 'for free'; do with them as you wish."

(הרב מאיר ז"ל שאפירא מלובלין)

"ומרדכי ידע"

"And Mordechai knew...." (4:1)

QUESTION: The *Midrash Rabbah* (7:16) relates that after Haman had the evil decrees written and signed, Mordechai met three children returning home from *yeshivah* and asked them, "What did you learn today?" The first child quoted the *pasuk,* אל" תירא מפחד פתאם" — "Do not fear sudden terror." The second one mentioned the *pasuk* "עצו עצה ותפר דברו דבר ולא יקום כי עמנו א-ל" — "They will make plans, but it will be foiled, they will discuss thoughts, but it will not materialize, for G-d is with us." The third child quoted the *pasuk* "ועד זקנה אני הוא ועד שיבה אני אסבל...ואמלט" — "Until old age I am with you, to your aged years I will sustain you ... and deliver you." Upon hearing this Mordechai was very happy. What good tidings did Mordechai see in the words of the children?

ANSWER: The Jewish people were confronted by Amalek three times: 1)Upon leaving Egypt, they were *suddenly* attacked by Amalek *(Devarim* 25:18, Rashi). 2) Years later Amalek appeared, talking like a Canaanite, and attempted to wage war against the Jewish people *(Bamidbar* 21:1, Rashi). 3) Haman was a descendant of Amalek, and viciously planned the annihilation of the Jewish people.

Mordechai understood the words of the first child, "Do not fear *sudden* terror..." as an allusion to Amalek's first attack. The second child's message, *"dabru davar velo yakum"* — "they will speak, but it will not materialize" — was that regardless of Amalek's attempts to disguise himself and change his dialect, it would be to no avail because Hashem was with the Jewish people.

When Haman discussed his evil plans for the Jews with his advisors, they told him, "Don't be a fool, whenever someone sought to harm these people, their G-d came to their salvation and destroyed the enemy. Stay away from them or you will suffer the consequences." Haman presumptuously told them, "There is nothing to fear, now their G-d is old and weak and unable to help them." Mordechai understood the words of the third child as Hashem saying, "Regardless of Haman thinking I am old, I have not changed; I will carry, sustain, and save the Jewish people now and at all times."

(קול אליהו)

"ותצוהו על מרדכי לדעת מה זה... ואת פתשגן כתב הדת... נתן לו
להראות את אסתר... לבא אל המלך... ולבקש מלפניו על עמה"

**"And she ordered him to go to Mordechai, to know what it
was... And he gave him the copy of the writing of the decree...
to show Esther... that she should go in to the king... and to
make request before him for her people." (4:5,8)**

QUESTION: How was it possible that Esther should not know anything about the decree against the Jewish people?

ANSWER: Haman and Achashveirosh were both great anti-semites. They hated the Jews with a passion and would have been happy to see them annihilated. Since the Jews resided in the country and paid taxes, it would have been undiplomatic to publicize their feelings about the Jewish people. Therefore, they spoke of them as "a people" and did not specify which nation. Haman said, "There is a people...." Achashveirosh told him, "You may keep the money, and regarding 'the people,' do as you please."

Haman sent a confidential letter to the head of each province, informing them of the planned extermination of the Jewish people. The letter was sealed (3:12) and was not to be opened before the 13th of *Adar*. Another letter was sent to the residents of each province, which only notified them be ready for that day (3:14) without any particulars. This way, until the last moment no one would detect their vicious plans, and the Jews would lack an opportunity to plead before the King.

Fortunately, Mordechai "learned of *all* that had been done" (4:1) and thus he knew of Haman's vicious plan to destroy the Jewish people. He therefore sent Esther a copy of the text which was distributed to the public, telling them to be "ready for that day," and told her what the intention was. He instructed her to tell the King her nationality and beseech him to save her people.

(מלבי"ם)

"כי אם החרש תחרישי בעת הזאת...ואת ובית אביך תאבדו"
"If you persist in keeping silent at a time like this...you and your father's house will perish." (4:14)

QUESTION: Why would Esther's "silence" and non-intervention on behalf of the Jewish people cause her *father's* house to perish?

ANSWER: King Shaul was instructed to destroy the entire people of Amalek. Out of compassion for their leader Agog, he spared his life. The next morning the prophet Shmuel killed Agog and admonished Shaul for not following instructions. The preceding night, Agog had married a maid who later gave birth to the ancestor of Haman.

Mordechai reminded Esther that she was a descendant of King Shaul and that her rise to glory was by Divine Providence. By bringing about the downfall of Haman she would remove the blemish on King Shaul, which was caused by his oversight. Should the salvation of the Jewish people come about through other means, her father's house would perish due to King Shaul's unforgiven iniquity.

(אלשיך)

"וצומו עלי ואל תאכלו ואל תשתו שלשת ימים"
"And fast for me; do not eat or drink for three days." (4:16)

QUESTION: Why did Esther tell Mordechai that the Jews should fast *three* days and nights?

ANSWER: To celebrate the success of his kingdom, Achashveirosh made a seven-day feast for the residents of *Shushan HaBirah*. Unfortunately, the Jews attended and partook in the non-kosher festivities. The seventh and final day was *Shabbat*. In view of the fact that the celebrations were held in a garden, the Jews refrained from coming, out of fear that they might violate the

Shabbat by pouring liquids on the ground *(Gemara, Megillah 12a)*.

The Jew's eating of non-kosher food for six days caused the rise of Haman. To counteract this, Esther told Mordechai to have the Jews fast for three days and three nights, which would atone for the six days of eating non-kosher.

(יערות דבש ח"א, י"ז)

"ויהי כראות המלך את אסתר המלכה עמדת בחצר נשאה חן בעיניו"

"When the King saw Esther standing in the courtyard, she found favor in his eyes." (5:2)

QUESTION: Why was the King so gracious to Esther?

ANSWER: After Achashveirosh married Esther he was struck with blindness *(Yalkut Shimoni* 1056:5). As soon as Esther walked in, an angel turned his head in her direction and suddenly he regained his vision and was able to see her. Achashveirosh understood that this miracle happened to him in her merit, and therefore, she found favor in his eyes.

(אורה ושמחה)

"ויאמר המלך לאסתר במשתה היין מה שאלתך וינתן לך ומה בקשתך עד חצי המלכות ותעש"

"And the King said to Esther at the banquet of wine, 'What is your petition? and it shall be granted you: and what is your request? even to the half of the kingdom it shall be performed.'" (5:6)

QUESTION: It has been mentioned twice previously that he was invited to the *"mishteh"* — "banquet" — and that he came to the *"mishteh"*; why are the words *"mishteh hayayin"* repeated here?

ANSWER: Although the name of Hashem is not explicitly mentioned in the *Megillah,* according to *Midrashim* the term *"Hamelech"* the King, refers also to the King of the world — Hashem. and *Lamelech Achashveirosh* is an abbreviation for the

King, שאחרית וראשית שלו — who is in command of past and future. The name "Esther" refers to *Klal Yisrael*.

While it is customary to use prayer as a way to beseech Almighty G-d, the *Megillah* is hinting that the King told Esther (a metaphor for Hashem telling *Klal Yisrael*) that when people *unite* in a "wine feast," He is very proud of them and asks, "What is your desire?" and he is prepared to fulfill it.

(ר' מנחם מענדל מקוצק זצ"ל, ועי' מחיר יין א:י"ב)

* * *

The previous Lubavitcher Rebbe, Rabbi Yosef Yitzchak Schneerson, related, that the *Alter* Rebbe, Rabbi Shneur Zalman of Liadi, once said that when *chassidim* get together in *farbrengen* and in *simchah,* they can accomplish even more than the angel Michael can.

(קובץ מכתבים על תהלים)

"וכל זה איננו שוה לי בכל עת אשר אני ראה את מרדכי"
"Yet all this is not worth anything to me so long as I see Mordechai." (5:13)

QUESTION: The word *"zeh"* — "this" — seems superfluous; it could have just said *"eineno shoveh li"* — "It is not worth anything to me"?

ANSWER: Haman told his wife Zeresh and his advisors about the royal treatment the King had afforded him. In the course of the conversation, he also expressed his fear of Mordechai and Esther, saying that together their names had the numerical value of 26 (in single numerals), which is the numerical value of Hashem's four-lettered name, indicating that He was with them.

Zeresh comforted Haman that he had nothing to worry about, because their names, Haman (המן) and Zeresh (זרש), also add up to 26 (in singular numerals). Haman responded, "Mordechai *alone* adds up to 13 as does Esther *alone*. This is also the numerical value of the word *"echad"* (אחד), indicating that the *one and only* — Hashem — is with each of them, and there is unity among them. In unity there is strength. However, I alone add up to 14 and am short 12. Thus, the *"zeh"* (זה), which has the numerical value of 12, which you, Zeresh, contribute is worthless because Hashem is not with us and there is also no unity among us."

(בית יעקב, לקוטים מפרדס)

"ותאמר לו זרש אשתו וכל אהביו יעשו עץ גבה חמשים אמה ובבקר
אמר למלך ויתלו את מרדכי עליו"

"Zeresh his wife and all his friends said to him, 'Let a gallows be made of fifty cubits high, and tomorrow speak to the King and have them hang Mordechai on it.'" (5:14)

QUESTION: Why doesn't it say what they advised Haman to tell the King?

If their advice was that he should ask the King that they should hang Mordechai on it, grammatically, the expression should have been *"sheyitlu"* — "they should hang him" — not *"veyitlu"* — "and they will hang him."

ANSWER: Haman complained to his family about Mordechai. Their advice was that he should tell the King that Mordechai so distressed him that he felt like committing suicide, and that he, therefore, built a gallows 50 cubits high. Achashveirosh, they said, loved Haman and would undoubtedly say, "I cannot afford to lose you," and order Mordechai's death on the gallows.

Incidentally, later on it is stated, "Haman had just come into the outer court of the palace to speak to the King about hanging Mordechai on the gallows — *"asher heichin lo"* — that he had prepared for him" (6:4). On this, the *Gemara (Megillah* 16a) says that *"lo"* means "for *himself"* — "Haman."

(שו"ת תידוש ויצהר סי' ק"ה)

"וימצא כתוב אשר הגיד מרדכי על בגתנא ותרש"

"It was found written what Mordechai reported about Bigtana and Teresh." (6:2)

QUESTION: In the beginning of the *Megillah* (2:21), it is stated that the servants who plotted to kill the King were Bigtan and Teresh. Why in the records was the name spelled "Bigtana" (בגתנא)?

ANSWER: The secretaries who recorded the event were sons of Haman. They felt that some day historians would read the King's book of records and conclude that credit was due to a Jewish person for saving the King's life. Therefore, they falsified the records and wrote that Mordechai reported about Bigtan *or* Teresh. This would mean that Mordechai was not really sure if it was Bigtan or Teresh who plotted to kill the King. Since both were put to death, an innocent person was possibly killed through Mordechai, and he did not deserve any reward.

A miracle happened and the word "או" which means "or" separated itself and the "א" moved close to בגתן and the "ו" close to תרש. Thus, it read that Mordechai told about Bigtana *and* Teresh (בגתנא ותרש), that the *two* of them plotted to kill the King, and that thanks to Mordechai's alertness the King's life was saved, rightfully entitling Mordechai to a great reward.

(מדרש תלפיות)

"מהר קח את הלבוש ואת הסוס כאשר דברת ועשה כן למרדכי היהודי"

"Hurry, take the robes and horse as you said, and do this for Mordechai the Jew." (6:10)

QUESTION: Why did Achashveirosh insist that Mordechai receive his acknowledgment *speedily?*

ANSWER: When Esther invited Achashveirosh to a banquet the day before she did not reveal an agenda. That night Achashveirosh could not sleep and ordered his servants to bring him the book of records. As it was read to him, he realized that he had been remiss in rewarding Mordechai for saving his life. Achashveirosh thought, "Possibly, Esther invited me to the banquet and will perhaps request that proper recognition be given to Mordechai." Consequently, he told Haman, "Give Mordechai his honors and do it expeditiously. Thus, should Esther ask at the banquet why we did not honor Mordechai, I will be able to tell her that it was already taken care of earlier in the day."

(אלשיך)

וִיסַפֵּר הָמָן..אֶת כָּל אֲשֶׁר קָרָהוּ וַיֹּאמְרוּ לוֹ חֲכָמָיו..אִם מִזֶּרַע הַיְּהוּדִים
מָרְדֳּכַי אֲשֶׁר הַחִלּוֹתָ לִנְפֹּל לְפָנָיו לֹא תוּכַל לוֹ כִּי נָפוֹל תִּפּוֹל לְפָנָיו"

**"Haman told them all that happened to him... and his wise men said to him... 'If Mordechai is of Jewish descent you will not prevail against him, but will undoubtedly fall before him.'"
(6:13)**

QUESTION: What sage counsel did his "wise men" give him?

ANSWER: Haman came home and conveyed to his family and friends the humiliation he had experienced. He had no faith in Divine Providence and arrogantly told them that this was *"karahu"* — "a *haphazard* occurrence." "Moreover," he said, "now that Mordechai received his reward, I will return to my glorious position and no longer suffer from him."

His *wise* men told him that he was mistaken: "Mordechai is a descendant of the Jewish people and his G-d is not allowing you to prevail against him. Your only salvation may be *'ki nafol tipol lefanav'* — 'Bow to him and beg him to forgive you.' The Jewish people are merciful people. King Shaul had compassion and spared our grandfather Agog; likewise Mordechai will pardon you if you beg his forgiveness."

Out of desperation, Haman considered following their advice. However, before he had a chance to speak to Mordechai, the King's chamberlains arrived and hurried him off to the banquet which Esther had arranged.

Later Haman, realizing the King's intention to execute him, tried to follow his wise men's advice and fell on Esther's couch. The King, however, entered the room and became enraged. Before anything else could happen, they covered Haman's face (7:8).

(אלשיך)

כִּי נִמְכַּרְנוּ אֲנִי וְעַמִּי לְהַשְׁמִיד לַהֲרוֹג וּלְאַבֵּד וְאִלּוּ לַעֲבָדִים וְלִשְׁפָחוֹת
נִמְכַּרְנוּ הֶחֱרַשְׁתִּי...וַיֹּאמֶר הַמֶּלֶךְ אֲחַשְׁוֵרוֹשׁ... מִי הוּא זֶה וְאֵי־זֶה הוּא
אֲשֶׁר מְלָאוֹ לִבּוֹ לַעֲשׂוֹת כֵּן"

"'For we have been sold, I and my people, to be annihilated, and had we been sold as slaves I would have been silent...

'King Achashveirosh exclaimed... 'Who is this and where is he who had the audacity to do this?'" (7:4-5)

QUESTION: 1) Why would she be silent if the Jews were sold for slaves? 2) Haman operated with Achashveirosh's consent. Why did he naively ask who was responsible?

ANSWER: Haman hated the Jewish people and greatly wanted to wipe them out, but he doubted that Achashveirosh would agree. Therefore, he fooled Achashveirosh into issuing a decree to destroy the Jewish people.

When they consulted earlier Haman said to Achashveirosh, *"im al haMelech tov yikateiv le'avdam* (3:9) — "If the King agrees, letters should be sent out to make *slaves* (לעבדם) out of the Jewish people." Achashveirosh consented and gave Haman authority to send the letters. However, in the letters, Haman did not write לעבדם (slavery) but "לאבדם" *(le'abdam)* "complete annihilation."

Therefore, Esther said to Achashveirosh, "If we had been sold for slavery as you and Haman originally planned, I would reluctantly be quiet because you are the King and this is your wish, but the scoundrel falsified and sent letters to annihilate the Jewish people."

Achashveirosh became very upset when he heard that he was fooled and bellowed, "Who is this with the audacity to do such a thing?"

(אוהב ישראל)

"ויאמר לאסתר המלכה מי הוא זה ואי־זה הוא...ותאמר אסתר איש צר ואויב המן הרע הזה"

"And he said to Esther the Queen, 'Who is he, and where is he...?' And Esther said, 'The adversary and enemy is this wicked Haman.'" (7:5-6)

QUESTION: Achashveirosh and Haman together planned the destruction of the Jewish people. Why did Achashveirosh suddenly ask Esther, "Who..."? Moreover, when Esther responded she should have said only one word, "Haman"?

ANSWER: In Hebrew grammar the word *"hu"* is used for third person, and the Hebrew grammatical term for the third person is *"nistar"* — literally "hidden." The word *"zeh"* is used in second person and applies to a subject matter which is present and therefore revealed.

Esther told Achashveirosh that the Jewish people were suffering from two enemies: "One of our enemies openly displays his hatred, while the other hates us deep down in his heart, though he does not say so openly." Achashveirosh asked Esther, "Since you talk of *two* enemies, please tell me *mi hu* — who do you refer to as — *'zeh'* — 'the open enemy' — and *ve'ei-zeh* — who is it that you consider — *'hu'* — 'the hidden enemy'"?

Esther responded *"Haman hara* — the wicked Haman — is *'hazeh'* — our open and revealed enemy" and she left it to Achashveirosh's imagination to figure out who was — *"hu"* — the "concealed" enemy.

(הרב מאיר ז"ל שאפירא מלובלין)

"ויאמר חרבונה.... גם הנה העץ אשר עשה המן למרדכי אשר דבר טוב על המלך עמד בבית המן גבה חמשים אמה"

"Charvona said, 'Furthermore the 50 cubit high gallows which Haman made for Mordechai who spoke good for the King, is standing in Haman's house.'" (7:9)

QUESTION: When did Mordechai ever "speak good" for King Achashveirosh?

ANSWER: Haman's advisors told him to make a gallows and get the King's consent to hang Mordechai. Immediately he hired one of the best carpenters in *Shushan Habirah* and instructed him to build a 50-cubit-high pole. The carpenter was not aware of its purpose, but, knowing Haman's wealth, he made it of the most expensive wood and adorned it with gold.

Upon completion, he handed Haman a hefty bill. Somewhat surprised, he said to the carpenter, "Who ever heard of paying such a huge amount for a 50-cubit pole?" The carpenter replied, "Why don't you look at what I did and then you will agree that my fee is reasonable." When Haman saw the pole, he became enraged and shouted, "I wanted this to serve as a gallows for Mordechai; the one you made is good for the King!"

Upon hearing from Charvonah that *Haman said* the gallows "is good for the King," Achashveirosh immediately bellowed, "hang *him* on it!"

(שמעתי מהרב שמואל צבי שי' פוקס)

"ביום ההוא נתן המלך אחשורוש לאסתר המלכה את בית המן ותשם אסתר את מרדכי על בית המן"

"On that day, King Achashveirosh gave Queen Esther the house of Haman. Esther placed Mordechai over Haman's house." (8:1-2)

QUESTION: Why did Esther convey to Mordechai the gift she received from Achashveirosh?

ANSWER: In the famous incident in which Mordechai and Haman were both in command of armies (see 3:4), Haman had to sell himself as a slave to Mordechai for food.

According to *halacha,* *"mah shekanah eved kanah rabo"* — "Whatever a slave acquires becomes the property of his master." Consequently, in keeping within the realm of *halacha,* Esther conveyed the house to Mordechai, who in reality was the rightful owner.

(הרב אברהם מרדכי זצ"ל מגור)

"ואתם כתבו על היהודים כטוב בעיניכם בשם המלך וחתמו בטבעת המלך כי כתב אשר נכתב בשם המלך ונחתום בטבעת המלך אין להשיב"

"Write for the Jews in the name of the King as you please, and seal it with the King's ring, for something written in the King's name and sealed with the King's ring cannot be retracted." (8:8)

QUESTION: 1) Achashveirosh seems to be contradicting himself. If an edict issued by the King cannot be retracted, what will be accomplished by a second letter? 2) He should have said *"kitvu laYehudim"* — "write *to* the Jews," — in lieu of *"kitvu al haYehudim"* — "Write *about* the Jews"?

ANSWER: To save face, Achashveirosh told Esther that he was a sincere friend of the Jewish people and furious at Haman.

He told Esther, "We agreed to write *'lehashmid laharog ule'abeid et kal haYehudim'* — 'to destroy, to slay, and to exterminate all Jews' (3:13). However, I had instructed him to *put* a comma before the word *'haYehudim'* because my intent was that all the *goyim* should be wiped out, and it should be accomplished through *'haYehudim'* — 'the Jews.' Haman left out a comma between the words *'kal'* — 'all' — and *'haYehudim.'* Thus, it can be interpreted to mean 'to annihilate the Jewish people.'

Therefore, I advise you to write a letter explaining *'al haYehudim'* — the *reference* to *'Yehudim'* in the previous letter — in a way which is favorable and beneficial to you. Consequently, your second letter will merely clarify and support my intention in the first letter: that all the *goyim* should be killed *through* the Jews. Such a letter of clarification is in accordance with accepted decorum."

(אלשיך)

"לעשות אותם ימי משתה ושמחה ומשלח מנות איש לרעהו ומתנות לאביונים"

"That they should make them days of feasting and joy, and of sending portions one to another, and gifts to the poor." (9:22)

QUESTION: The Rambam in *Hilchot Megillah* (2:17) writes: "It is better to increase in gifts to the poor than in sending portions to one another." If so, why in the *pasuk* is sending portions to one another mentioned *before* gifts to the poor?

ANSWER: When giving *tzedakah* to the poor, it is very important that one should be extremely careful not to embarrass the recipient. (See Rambam, *Matanot Aniyim* 10.)

When Mordechai instituted *Purim* as a day of giving gifts to the poor, he was greatly concerned lest it become known as the *poor's* day to receive handouts. Therefore, he also instituted the exchanging of portions among friends so that an observer would be unable to distinguish gifts to the poor from gifts to friends. To conceal the gifts to the poor, the *Megillah* preceded it with sending portions to one another.

(אפריון ועי' שו"ת תירוש ויצהר סי' קע"ב)

* * *

With the above-mentioned we can understand why no *berachah* is made over the *mitzvah* of *mishlo'ach manot* — sending portions to one another.

The Rashba (responsa 18) writes that when one performs the *mitzvah* of *tzedakah*, he does not make a *berachah* — because possibly the person will refuse to accept. According to Ramah *(Orach Chaim* 615:4), when one sends portions on *Purim*, he fulfills the *mitzvah* of *mishlo'ach monot* even if the recipient refuses them.

Consequently, if a *berachah* would be made over *mishlo'ach manot* and not *matanot le'evyonim*, it would be obvious what is *mishlo'ach manot* and what is *matanot le'evyonim*, thus defeating the entire purpose of instituting *mishlo'ach manot*.

(שו״ת תירוש ויצהר סי׳ קע״ב)

״לעשות אותם ימי משתה ושמחה ומשלח מנות איש לרעהו ומתנות לאביונים״

"They should make them days of feasting and joy, and of sending portions one to another, and gifts to the poor." (9:22)

QUESTION: Why did Mordechai institute this as a way to celebrate the miracle of Purim?

ANSWER: Haman complained to Achashveirosh about the Jewish people that though they were only *one* nation among many nations, they were *"mefuzar umeforad bein ha'amim"* — in total disharmony among themselves. They lacked love and compassion for their fellow Jews. To counteract this claim, Esther said to Mordechai, "Go gather together *all* the Jews" (4:16), and stress to them the importance of unity and *Ahavat Yisrael.*

Since the decree was caused by Haman's allegation that there was disunity among the Jewish people, Mordechai instituted that on Purim we exchange edibles with friends and give gifts to the poor to demonstrate our love for one another.

(מנות הלוי)

"על כן קראו לימים האלה פורים על שם הפור"

"Therefore they called these days 'Purim' because of the *Pur* (the Lot)." (9:26)

QUESTION: *"Purim"* is the plural for *pur*. Why isn't the *yom tov* called *"Pur"*?

ANSWER: In order to be sure that the day determined by the 'lot' was indeed correct, Haman made *two* lots. In one box he placed 13 pieces of paper, each containing one of the Hebrew months of the year (the miracle of Purim took place in a leap year, see *Talmud Yerushalmi Megillah* 1:5, *P'nei Moshe*). In the other box he put 385 pieces of paper, each containing a number from 1 to 385, for all the days of the year. Haman thought as follows: If from the first box he pulled the month of *Sivan* (the third month) and from the second box he pulled the number 200, then something would be wrong, since the 200th day of the year cannot occur in the third month.

Haman was satisfied when he pulled *Adar Sheini* (the thirteenth month) from the first box, and 368 from the second, because this came out to be the 13th day of *Adar Sheini,* and obviously the two lots supported each other. Hence, the *yom tov* is known as *"Purim,"* because of the *two* lots.

(יערות דבש דרוש ג' ועי' שו"ת חת"ס סי' קס"ג ולקו"ש חט"ז ע' 349)

ഗ ഇ

PURIM TORAH • פורים תורה

"This wicked Haman" (7:6)

QUESTION: There is no doubt that Haman was a *rasha*. In the *Haggadah* of *Pesach* we are told that the way to deal with a *rasha* is to knock out his teeth. Why didn't Mordechai knock out Haman's teeth?

ANSWER: According to the *Midrash,* Achashveirosh once sent two divisions of his army to battle. One was headed by Haman and the other by Mordechai. He gave each one an equal supply of food. Haman was careless and let his soldiers finish the food in a short period of time. He ran out of food and came begging Mordechai to give him some of his food, but Mordechai refused. Haman, fearing that his soldiers would revolt against him, sold himself to Mordechai as a slave and, thus, Mordechai supplied him with food.

When a Jewish master knocks out the tooth of his non-Jewish servant he becomes free. Not wanting to lose such a slave as Haman, Mordechai refrained from knocking out Haman's teeth.

"And Vaizata" (9:9)

QUESTION: Why is the name "Vaizata" (ויזתא) written with a long *"vav"*?

ANSWER: According to *Halacha,* when a person has ten cows *(beheimot),* he is to bring them into a room and let them come out through a door. The tenth cow to pass through the door is considered *ma'aser beheimah,* and is given to the *Kohen.* If the tenth cow jumps through the roof, the farmer is not obligated to give it away to the *Kohen* as *ma'aser beheimah.*

The *Kohanim* in *Shushan Habirah* considered Haman's ten sons as ten animals. Haman also thought very little of his children, and agreed with the *Kohanim* that they were like *beheimot.* A *Kohen* came to Haman and told him that since his children were like animals, he was supposed to give one of them away as *ma'aser beheimah.* Haman agreed with the *Kohen* and told him that he would take them into a room and let them walk out one by one. After nine of Haman's children walked out and Vaizata was about to come through, Haman grabbed him, and attempted to pull him by his head through the roof. The *Kohen,* wanting to get him, tried to pull him by his feet. Thus Vaizata was stretched, and the big *"vav"* symbolizes this.

"ביום שלשה עשר לחדש אדר ונוח..."

"On the thirteenth day of the month *Adar* and *Noach*..." (9:17)

QUESTION: What is Noach's connection with the *Megillah?*

ANSWER: Haman was very upset with Mordechai and did not know how to deal with the problem. His wife Zeresh suggested that he make gallows 50 *amot* (cubits) high upon which they would hang Mordechai. Haman ran all around town, searching for a massive piece of wood. Suddenly, he remembered that many years ago Noach had built a *Teivah* which was 50 *amot* wide, so he must have very large pieces of lumber. Haman ran all over until he finally found Noach and said to him, "Do me a favor, please lend me a 50 *amot* piece of lumber."

Old Noach asked wicked Haman, "Could you tell me what you need this for?" Haman replied, "I want to hang Mordechai." Old Noach began to yell, "Are you crazy? Do you think I am going to permit you to hang Mordechai the *Tzaddik* on my lumber?" Haman began to fight with old Noach, trying to get a piece of lumber away from him. Noach held on to it with all his might, but unfortunately Haman, being much younger, dragged the piece of wood together with Noach all the way into the *Megillah.*

"ומשלוח מנות איש לרעהו"

"Sending of portions a man to his friend" (9:19)

QUESTION: The word *"ish"* is superfluous?

ANSWER: An *Apikores* who disliked the town Rabbi, who vehemently ridiculed and denounced him, decided that Purim would be an opportune time to get even with him. To fulfill the *mitzvah* of *mishlo'ach manot,* he bought a few pounds of chopped liver which he molded into the form of a pig, put it on a platter, and sent it to the Rabbi. When the Rabbi received it, he took a portrait of himself, put it on a platter, and sent it to "his friend" with the following explanation:

"For a long time I have been bothered with an extra word in the *Megillah.* When *mishlo'ach manot* is mentioned in *Megillah,* we are told *"mishlo'ach manot **ish** lerei'eihu"* — sending of portions, a man to his friend. I always wondered, it would have been sufficient to say *"mishlo'ach manot lerei'eihu"* — sending portions to a friend, without the extra word *"ish"*?

After receiving your thoughtful package, my question was answered. The *Megillah* is saying, the portions being sent should consist of *"ish"* — the type of person you are. Obviously, you fulfilled the *mitzvah* accurately and sent me a description of yourself. To reciprocate, enclosed is my picture so you may have a vivid description of me."

"להיות עשים את יום ארבעה עשר לחדש אדר...בכל שנה ושנה"

"To observe annually the fourteenth day of *Adar*" (9:21)

QUESTION: Moshe *Rabbeinu* was born seven days in the month of Adar, thus his *brit* took place on the 14th day of *Adar,* which is *Purim.* Was the *brit* performed before the reading of the *Megillah* or after?

ANSWER: Moshe was a great *tzaddik* and he died on the same day he was born. Since Moshe passed away on *Shabbat* he was also born on *Shabbat.* Thus, his *brit* took place eight days later on *Shabbat* — 14 days in the month of *Adar.* Being that it was

Shabbat, the reading of the *Megillah* took place on Thursday the 12th of *Adar.*

”לעשות אותם ימי משתה ושמחה”
"Observe them as days of feasting and gladness" (9:22)

QUESTION: Is a festive meal on *Purim* and drinking till intoxicated a Torah rule or only a Rabbinic ordinance?

ANSWER: From the *pasuk* in *Bereishit* 21:8, ויעש אברהם משתה גדול ביום הגמל את יצחק" — "And Avraham made a great feast on the day Yitzchok was weaned" — we can derive that eating and drinking on *Purim* is a statute of the Torah.

The Torah is telling us that Avraham made a great feast and drinking party on the day of "הגמל” — which can be arranged to spell the word "מגלה,” on *Purim* when the *Megillah* is read.

If that is the case, why does the *pasuk* conclude את יצחק? What does Yitzchak have to do with the reading of *Megillah?*

The reason is because from Yitzchok we learn an important *halacha* regarding *Purim.* The *shofar* is blown on *Rosh Hashanah* to recall of the *Akeidah* of Yitzchak. When *Rosh Hashanah* falls on *Shabbat,* our Rabbis tell us to refrain from blowing *shofar* because one may forget and carry the *shofar* four cubits in a public domain. For the same reason when *Purim* falls out on *Shabbat,* the *Megillah* is not read *(Rosh Hashanah* 29b).

Since Avraham's festivities were in honor of *Purim,* why does it say "הגמל” and not "מגלה”? This proves that during the *Purim* meal it is incumbent to become intoxicated to the extent that one does not know the difference between "מגלה” and "הגמל.”

”ודבר שלום לכל זרעו”
"Concerned for the welfare of all his posterity" (10:3)

QUESTION: Why isn't *Kaddish* said after the reading of the *Megillah?"*

ANSWER: On Purim they hung Haman and *all* his sons and, thus, there were no survivors left to say a *Kaddish."*

Cʒ ഗ

Appendix

Many of the *divrei* Torah in this *sefer* are suited to be developed into speeches on the following holidays and special occasions:

Index to *Derush* Material